THE AWAY GAME

THE
AWAY
GAME

*The Epic Search for
Soccer's Next Superstars*

Sebastian Abbot

W. W. NORTON & COMPANY
Independent Publishers Since 1923
New York London

For information about permission to reproduce selections from
this book, write to Permissions, W. W. Norton & Company, Inc.,
500 Fifth Avenue, New York, NY 10110

For information about special discounts for bulk purchases, please contact
W. W. Norton Special Sales at specialsales@wwnorton.com or 800-233-4830

Manufacturing by LSC Communications, Harrisonburg
Book design by Lovedog Studio
Production manager: Anna Oler

ISBN 978-0-393-29220-6

W. W. Norton & Company, Inc.
500 Fifth Avenue, New York, N.Y. 10110
www.wwnorton.com

W. W. Norton & Company Ltd.
15 Carlisle Street, London W1D 3BS

1 2 3 4 5 6 7 8 9 0

To my wife Liz,
the best teammate ever

And my brother Spencer,
who left us far too soon

Contents

Prologue

Josep Colomer knows soccer. He started his first training center when he was just a teenager in Spain, helped Brazil's coaching staff win the World Cup in 2002, and rose to become youth director of soccer juggernaut FC Barcelona. He also helped jump-start the career of one of the greatest players in history, Lionel Messi.

Colomer knows markedly less about Nigerian militants. For example, they hate being called militants. They much prefer the term "freedom fighters." Not surprisingly, Colomer never ran into a Nigerian militant during his years working as a scout and coach at the pinnacle of international soccer. But now he stood on a weathered dock in Nigeria's turbulent Niger Delta. A small gray Yamaha motorboat floated nearby on a carpet of green water hyacinths. One of its passengers was Clemente Konboye, a Nigerian militant with a potbelly, a missing front tooth, and an intimidating air. His eyes were fixed on Colomer.

He wasn't the only one staring. All around the ramshackle boat launch in Warri, one of the main cities in Delta State, locals working out of rusty metal shacks and battered motorboats stopped to ponder the squat, bald bulldog of a man in his late 30s. As usual, he looked like he was headed to the gym. Colomer always seemed to be dressed in a T-shirt, soccer shorts, and running shoes. Warri was no different. No attempt to blend in here.

The summer of 2007 certainly wasn't the safest time to be a foreigner standing on a dock in the Niger Delta. The militants' fight for a greater share of the impoverished region's vast oil wealth was at its peak. Armed with AK-47s and RPGs, the militants raced about in small motorboats attacking government forces and kidnapping foreign oil workers. They eluded capture by speeding off into the labyrinth of waterways and mangrove forests that dominated the area. Many of them, including Konboye, followed a colorful leader known as Tompolo, who helped found the Movement for the Emancipation of the Niger Delta. His gang started the trend of targeting foreigners for ransom in 2006 by kidnapping nine oil workers from a barge stationed near the small fishing town of Ogulagha, where Tompolo's mother lived. Colomer also happened to be headed to Ogulagha on that cloudy August afternoon in 2007. Konboye was at the dock because he and his fellow militants had been tipped off. But he wasn't there to kidnap Colomer. He was there to protect him.

Colomer wasn't interested in the Niger Delta's oil. He wasn't drawn to Africa in search of diamonds or gold, the kind of spoils that had long brought foreigners to the continent's shores and interior. He had no interest in what was underneath Africa's soil. He was hoping to find his prize on top of it. It could be next to a highway in Nigeria's teeming megacity, Lagos, or on a sparsely populated island in the Niger Delta. It could be anywhere really. That was just one of the many difficulties he faced.

Knowing exactly what to look for was also a challenge. The process was more art than science. Science can easily tell you whether you've found gold or diamonds, but the answers are much less definitive in Colomer's line of work. Experts have long relied on intuition drawn from years of experience rather than hard data, although that is slowly shifting. Either way, it can take years to reveal whether you actually found what you were looking for. But if you're successful, the accolades are global. Forget oil and diamonds, Colomer was in Africa pursuing something much rarer. He was looking for the next Messi.

The trip to Ogulagha was one of hundreds that Colomer and his team of scouts made across the African continent in 2007 as they launched what may be the biggest talent search in sports history. In that year alone, Colomer's team held tryouts for more than 400,000 boys in seven African countries looking for soccer's next superstars, and that was just the beginning. They eventually expanded the search, named "Football Dreams," to over three dozen countries in Africa, Latin America, and Southeast Asia and held tryouts for more than 5 million kids. Each year, the scouts chose a handful of the best players and trained them to become professionals at a special academy. To call these kids elite would be an understatement. The process was over a thousand times more selective than getting into Harvard.

The scouts targeted 13-year-old boys so academy coaches would have enough time to shape them into potential world beaters by the time they graduated at the age of 18. To put the figures into perspective, the average number of kids they scouted each year, roughly 500,000, was greater than the total population of 13-year-old boys in almost every country in the FIFA top 20. In some cases, it was over 10 times larger. Imagine what you would find if you scouted every 13-year-old boy in Argentina, Germany, or France, every single year. Call up images of young Messi, Pelé, Beckenbauer, or Zidane. That's the kind of talent Colomer hoped to find when he set off in 2007. But he wasn't looking in Europe or South America, at least not at first. Even when he expanded his search to a few countries in Latin America and Asia, his primary focus continued to be Africa.

The Spanish writer Manuel Vázquez Montalbán once described soccer as "a religion in search of a God." Nowhere is that more true than Africa. There might be a few countries in the east known more for their world-class runners, but soccer is worshipped almost everywhere else with unbending faith, especially by the continent's children. Their backgrounds and places of worship are almost always humble, but they still dream of becoming gods.

If you walk along the corniche in Senegal's capital of Dakar and gaze down from the rocky cliffs, you'll see dozens of barefoot men and boys on a narrow strip of beach battling in the late afternoon like it's a Champions League final. Dressed in knockoff jerseys from their favorite European teams, they fire the ball at their version of a goal, a pair of old tires half buried in the sand. It's a race against time to see how long they can play before the incoming tide washes away their pitch, although the water is by no means out of bounds. They run into the ocean and flick the ball out of ankle-deep water with consummate skill, their bodies silhouetted against the setting sun.

Scenes like this abound across the African landscape. In the continent's increasingly crowded cities, kids squeeze into whatever space they can find to grab a game. They set up bamboo goals under a busy highway overpass in Lagos. They weave around sharp-edged tombstones in a red dirt cemetery in Accra. They apologize for overturning plates of small red tomatoes and blackened fried fish in a busy Abidjan market. Kids living in Africa's vast rural areas have it a bit easier, at least when it comes to finding a patch of sand to call their own. But then there's the issue of coming up with a ball. Kids often make do with whatever they have: a wad of plastic bags tied together with string, a bundle of clothes, or an empty water bottle.

The conditions might be basic, but the touch, instinct, and athletic ability young African players develop through thousands of hours of practice can be otherworldly. In fact, researchers believe it's precisely these kinds of pickup games that help make Brazilian players so good. They train the body, but even more important, they transform the brain. The number of hours spent playing with friends in the street or on a patch of sand has proven to be a key factor in whether a player can cut it at the professional level.

It's no surprise then that Africa has produced some of Europe's biggest soccer stars in recent years, including Cameroon's Samuel Eto'o and Ivory Coast's Didier Drogba and Yaya Toure. European clubs have relied on African players since the colonial era, but the number migrating to Europe and elsewhere has ballooned over the past 20 years as money has poured into professional soccer and the sport has become increasingly globalized. Africans now make up nearly 10 percent of the players in England's Premier League and have spread to every other major league across the globe, including Major League Soccer in the United States. Clubs have paid hundreds of millions of dollars to acquire the best African players, and prices have been spiking. The Senegalese forward Sadio Mané became the most expensive African player in history in 2016 when Liverpool paid 34 million pounds to acquire him from Southampton.

Colomer believed that the African players making headlines were just the tip of a massive iceberg of talent and that much of the continent remained overlooked. By casting a wide enough net across Africa, he believed he could uncover players who could become soccer's next superstars. That's why he was standing on a dock in the Niger Delta in August 2007.

But things weren't going as planned. The trouble started as soon as Colomer pulled up to the dock and got out of his Toyota SUV with the two paramilitary police officers armed with AK-47s who were protecting him. The policemen had been arranged by Colonel Sam Ahmedu, a retired army officer who served as the Football Dreams country director in Nigeria. Colomer and the other European scouts who were part of the program had taken police with them everywhere they went in Nigeria as a precautionary measure. But their man on the ground in Warri, Austin Bekewei, knew that wasn't going to be possible in Ogulagha. The militants would never allow armed government forces into their territory. He was keenly aware of that because he was from Ogulagha and knew many of the militants personally, including Konboye, who was standing beside him when Colomer arrived at the boat launch.

Bekewei was a good decade younger than Colomer and now faced the unenviable task of telling him he couldn't bring police to guard him as he traveled to one of the most dangerous parts of the Delta. He also needed to convince Colomer that Konboye would provide protection and return him to Warri unharmed. He had spoken to Konboye and his fellow militants beforehand, who assured him they had no problem with Colomer's visit. The residents of Ogulagha wanted him to come because they saw it as the only chance for their kids to showcase their skills. They had never even had a Nigerian scout visit, much less a European one who had worked at the pinnacle of world soccer and helped nurture one of the best players in history.

Colomer wasn't the one who found Messi in Argentina and then brought him to Barcelona. The future star first arrived at the club as a shy, skinny 13-year-old in September 2000, over two years before Colomer became Barcelona's youth director. But Messi's meteoric rise was thanks in part to Colomer's guidance and confidence in the young player. Soon after arriving, Colomer promoted Messi four levels at once to put him on Barcelona's reserve squad, something that had never happened before at the club. A few months later, in November 2003, Colomer had the pleasure of telling a shaggy-haired, 16-year-old Messi that he would be getting his first chance to play with Barcelona's senior team. "He told me that I should just go and enjoy the game and the experience," Messi told the club's TV channel on the 10th anniversary of his debut.

It was an experience neither would ever forget, and the two remained close even after Colomer left Barcelona. Messi forever appreciated the support at such a critical point in his career, and

Colomer cherished the experience of nurturing one of the game's greatest players. Perhaps he would do it again with Football Dreams, but first he had to decide whether to get in a boat with a Nigerian militant.

Bekewei, Colomer, and his police guards huddled on the dock discussing the situation. Bekewei pledged that nobody would harm Colomer but was more concerned than he let on. He knew he couldn't totally control what happened during the one-hour boat ride from Warri through the creeks to Ogulagha. The militants in his hometown had given their word, but what about other groups in between? There was largely no cell phone service out on the water, so they would be on their own if something happened. It was a risk Bekewei was willing to take. He was a budding soccer agent himself and knew Colomer's visit would give local players exposure and boost his standing in the community.

The police protested that the situation was just too dangerous, prompting Colomer to make a frantic call to Ahmedu to see whether he should get in the boat. The colonel assured him he would be the safest person on the island because the locals wanted him to hold the tryout. In fact, Ahmedu told Colomer he was safer with the militants than the police. "I said, 'Coach, you have two policemen. They have arms, maybe 40 rounds of ammunition. They cannot match the youths, so already it's a risk being there. Since they're cooperating and saying they'll protect you, don't worry,'" said Ahmedu.

What the colonel didn't tell Colomer or anyone else is that he already had a Plan B in place. He normally worked with the state security service to send intelligence officers ahead of the scouts to assess an area the day before the scouts arrived. Sometimes they dressed as soccer players and headed to the field the scout would visit to see if they got wind of plans to harm him. That wasn't possible in Ogulagha because of the risk that they would be discovered. Ahmedu instead spoke with his contacts in the military who arranged for a quick-reaction force to stand by in case anything happened. The soldiers would jump into a speedboat armed with a massive submachine gun and race after Colomer if needed. He also thought about getting a pair of satellite phones so he could communicate with Colomer while he was on the water, but Bekewei advised him against it. "Those kids are smart, and when they see you with sophisticated equipment, they begin to think you are a spy," said Ahmedu.

It's fair to say most people faced with Colomer's situation would say thank you for the opportunity, get back into the Toyota SUV, and get out of there. But Colomer had been obsessed with looking for undiscovered talent ever since he was a teenager growing up in the small medieval town of Vic, north of Barcelona. He spent weekends there searching for skilled young players for his fledgling soccer school while his friends partied and chased girls. If there was anyone who was going to get in a boat with a Nigerian militant on the chance that the world's next soccer star was living in a small fishing town in the Niger Delta, it was Colomer. And that's precisely what he did. He was scared but followed Bekewei and Konboye down the dock and stepped into the motorboat that was waiting for him. As the driver pulled away, careful not to tangle the propeller in the floating water hyacinths, Colomer looked out toward the Forcados River that would take him to Ogulagha. He wondered what he would find when he arrived, and who would find him.

The boat quickly picked up speed as it left the dock, and they were soon moving so quickly that the muddy water whizzed by like a solid dirt road. Colomer sat on a small white cushion next to the outboard motor, his right arm resting on the side of the boat. The look on his face was tense. A seemingly impenetrable green wall of mangroves and palm trees dominated both sides of the river, which was only about a hundred feet wide at times. Narrow creeks occasionally branched off on either side, but mostly there was nowhere to escape if they ran into trouble. The buzz of the motor was so loud that even basic communication was difficult.

The river widened to several hundred feet as they neared Ogulagha and passed the massive Forcados oil terminal on their left. Visible in the distance were several circular white oil tanks the size of large buildings. They were a small part of a sprawling complex operated by Shell that had the capacity to export about 400,000 barrels of crude a day. It was a popular target for militants. They had attacked the terminal's loading platform on the same day in 2006 that they had kidnapped nine foreign oil workers from a barge near Ogulagha in military-style predawn raids.

Immediately after passing the terminal, the boat pulled up to Ogulagha, a jumble of mostly dilapidated wood and metal shacks perched on the sandy bank of the river. The town's poverty stood in stark contrast to the wealth represented by the Shell terminal next door. As the boat approached the riverbank, a group of teenage boys walked toward them through the shallow water. One of them was wearing a red and white striped soccer jersey.

"Good afternoon," Colomer said calmly, without revealing any apprehension he may have felt. "Are you football players? Are you ready to play?"

"Yes," they said. "We are ready."

But they weren't striding toward the boat because they were interested in soccer. They wanted something else from Colomer: a tip. The kids normally offered to carry passengers to the bank on their backs so they wouldn't get their shoes wet. In return, they hoped for a few Nigerian naira. But Colomer wasn't worried about wet feet. "He just jumped into the water with his tennis shoes on," said Bekewei. "That's to show the commitment. He was ready."

Bekewei and Konboye led Colomer from the riverbank into the

heart of town, following dirt paths that snaked through Ogulagha. A couple dozen kids trailed behind them, curious about the white man who had made such an unexpected visit. Most of the buildings they passed were rusty shacks made out of corrugated metal that reached baking temperatures during the hottest months. They crossed makeshift wooden bridges over small canals clogged with trash. The air was filled with the pungent odor of frying fish, one of the main staples in Ogulagha.

They were late, so the kids whom Colomer had come to see had been waiting for hours at the community field in the center of town for their tryout. They weren't the only ones who had showed up. When Colomer arrived, he saw spectators of all ages crowded around the pitch, a sea of green surrounded by metal shacks strung with drying laundry. The organizers had even set up a tent so old men could sit in the shade and watch.

Normally, the tryouts observed by Colomer across Africa that year included 176 players each, enough for sixteen 11-a-side teams that would play a total of eight 25-minute games. Colomer and the other scouts would pick the best 50 players from each country out of this pool and invite them to the capital for a four-day trial. The three best field players from each country, and several goalkeepers from across Africa, would then be invited to a final tryout outside the continent that lasted several weeks. The top players at this final test would then be invited to join the academy and train to become professionals.

Setting up these tryouts required nearly 6,000 local volunteers in Africa, about the same number of people needed to operate an aircraft carrier. Many of the volunteers were local coaches who ran the thousands of small, informal soccer schools that dot neighborhoods across Africa. To enlist their support, Colomer and his team distributed thousands of dollars of free Nike gear at each of the fields where they held tryouts. Volunteers were also given a free trip overseas if one of their boys was selected for the final try-out, a big perk since many had never traveled outside their countries before.

Football Dreams was like nothing the soccer world had ever seen, and not simply because of its size. Soccer has long been called the global game, but the program took globalization to an almost absurd new extreme, for Football Dreams is not simply a story of European scouts chasing future African stars. It's also a tale of rich Arab sheikhs who play soccer on their palace grounds, South American wonder kids who grow up to become legends, and small-town European fans worried about the takeover of their little local club. The combination of these disparate worlds made Football Dreams one of the most radical experiments in sports history. It was up to Colomer to find a small number of African boys who were good enough to make the experiment work. He would make soccer history if he succeeded. So would the boys he found.

In Ogulagha, Bekewei couldn't quite assemble 176 players for the tryout, even though he had paid for several dozen kids from neighboring communities to take boats to the town. The players who had showed up were a hodgepodge. Some wore proper soccer gear, complete with cleats. Others were barefoot or planned to play in their socks. The field turned out to be a great equalizer. From a distance, the grass looked a little overgrown but fairly inviting. Closer inspection revealed a swampy bog. It was the rainy season in Nigeria, and water had flooded the pitch. The goalmouths sported small ponds that ducks used to bathe when the field wasn't in action.

The players who took the field wore reversible Nike training bibs that were several sizes too large for many of the kids. They battled against each other and the conditions on the field in an attempt to impress Colomer. It wasn't easy. An encouraging dribble could be stopped dead by a pool of water, knocking the player off balance and into the mud at the same time. A key skill was being able to flick the ball out of this standing water to get the game restarted—not something you see youth players at Barcelona practicing. The conditions showed just how difficult it could be for Colomer and his team of scouts to evaluate a player's true level of skill at some of the fields across Africa. But Colomer was intent on casting his net as wide as possible. There was no way to know where the next Messi might be hiding.

PART ONE
BOYS

CHAPTER 1

The Tornado

Bernard Appiah had no idea he was about to trade one miracle for another. The pint-sized midfielder was sweeping the floor of his modest wooden church, Miracle Temple, in Ghana's crowded capital of Accra when his coach came to tell him a foreign scout was expected in the neighborhood that morning to hold a tryout. It was a fitting coincidence. The only thing that could match Bernard's passion for soccer was his faith in God. In fact, the church, a squat building with a gently sloping gable roof and fading light blue paint job, was more than just a church. It was basically Bernard's home. And his coach, Justice Oteng, a regular Bible teacher at the church, was like a second father. So when Oteng told him he should attend the tryout being held at a dusty public field in his neighborhood of Teshie, Bernard obediently grabbed his black and white Nike cleats and headed out the door.

Bernard first began turning coaches' heads as a young child in the dirt courtyard of his school in Teshie. The large open space is an oasis for kids seeking an escape from the chaotic web of humanity and commerce outside. The area where Bernard grew up is dominated by a sea of small ramshackle homes and shops made of wood, concrete, and metal. They're set along a maze of red dirt roads shared by a tangle of cars, bikes, wooden carts, pedestrians, traders, chickens, and goats. Noxious green sewage seeps down some of the town's dirt alleyways. The assault on the senses is softened only slightly by the presence of an occasional palm tree. The ocean and its cooling breeze aren't far away, but it's easy to forget amid the bustle.

From a young age, Bernard spent every minute he could at his schoolyard playing soccer, usually with his younger brother, Eric. They tried to play in the patch of dirt in front of their cramped two-room home, but the landlord always yelled at them. They would sprint off in the direction of the school, carrying the small plastic ball their parents bought for them. Bernard constantly seemed to lose his, earning a scolding from his parents. They didn't have much money for such things.

Like millions of Africans in recent decades, Bernard's parents, Noah Appiah and Elizabeth Ansare, moved to the city from the country looking for a better life. They came from Ghana's Central Region, where their parents had been uneducated cocoa farmers. But life in Teshie proved harder than they anticipated. Bernard's father, who suffers from a persistent stutter, soon found work opportunities hard to come by in his newfound home. He and his wife had more education than their parents, but neither had finished high school. Noah worked at a clothing factory when Bernard was young, loading boxes onto trucks for the equivalent of about $40 a month at today's rates. The pay wasn't great, but he was occasionally able to bring home clothes for Bernard, Eric, and their younger sister, Josephine.

The company eventually laid off Bernard's father, and he spent months unemployed before finding a lower-paying job as a security guard at a local guest house. It was a tough time for the family. A good chunk of his pay was spent on rent for their home, where they all slept together in a single bedroom. The house also had a small living room with a picture of Jesus on the wall and a narrow porch where Bernard's mother cooked meals on a coal stove. Bernard's favorite was banku, a mixture of fermented corn and cassava dough, paired with okra stew. He would help out by fetching water in large plastic jugs since their home didn't have a tap. When his mother wasn't cooking or cleaning, she sold secondhand clothes in the market to help pay for the kids' school fees and the occasional plastic soccer ball.

Bernard had a lot more interest in the school's soccer field than its classrooms. "When I was in school, I was not clever," said Bernard. But he was intelligent on the pitch. He would bolt from his wooden desk when class was over and head out to play. There was a small field for younger kids like Bernard, with weathered wooden goalposts that leaned at an angle. The older kids had a full-size pitch with rusty metal goals that had lost most of their white paint. These fields teemed with kids in the afternoons and on weekends. Women set up wooden tables selling drinks and grilled corn. Those kids who weren't playing stood around in their brown and yellow school uniforms and watched.

They weren't the only ones watching. Local coaches prowled the fields looking for the best young talent in the area. Seth Ali first spotted Bernard playing soccer at the school in a pair of old tennis shoes when he was about 8 years old. Even then, he stood out for his speed, control in tight spaces, and ability to take on players with his dominant left foot. Ali convinced Bernard and his parents that he should join his team, the Top Stars, and the midfielder quickly impressed his new teammates. Tornado, they called him, because of his work rate in practice. It was a nickname he shared with one of Ghana's most famous players, Stephen Appiah, a midfielder who played for Juventus and captained Ghana's national team, the Black Stars, in the 2006 World Cup. Bernard also dreamed of playing for the national team one day. A red, yellow, and green Ghanaian flag with its distinctive black star waved in the courtyard of Bernard's school, where the Top Stars practiced.

Ali had more enthusiasm than resources, a constant problem for soccer coaches in Africa. He only had two balls for the 50 kids he was training, so they spent a lot of their time simply running around in the dust. But he clearly knew who his best player was. "People were always talking about Bernard," said Ali. "He was the best player in every game, always the best player." It was clear to his teammates as well. "He was raised from nowhere to become a star," said his good friend and teammate Joshua Lartey. "His free kicks, penalties, passes, are all incredible." But Ali had a problem. He needed money to buy jerseys and equipment. That's how Justice Oteng, the coach who told Bernard about the Football Dreams tryout, came into the picture.

Oteng was putting together a new team, Unique FC, to play in Ghana's youth Colts League, and he needed players. He spotted Bernard playing in the schoolyard and approached Ali to buy him and over half a dozen other players from the Top Stars for his team. It was an example of the booming economy for even the youngest soccer players in Africa. Local coaches, many of whom have no formal training, hope to get rich by finding a kid who is good enough to play at a top club in Europe. Some people see these coaches as villains out to exploit young players. Others believe they're vital because they help fund grassroots soccer throughout Africa. There's truth on both sides, but the potential for abuse is very real.

Oteng not only had Bernard join his team but also had the player come live with him. It's a common practice by youth coaches in Ghana when it comes to dealing with their best players. It helps to strengthen the bond in two ways. It proves the coach's loyalty to the player and his family by taking on some of the financial burden of raising him. It also makes it more difficult for a competing coach to

Bernard (second from right) lined up with members of his Colts League team, Unique FC.

steal away the player, and Oteng definitely didn't want to lose Bernard. "He was very small, but he had the talent," said Oteng. "He was the best striker and offensive midfielder we had." Bernard knew it as well. He was an affable character off the field, quick to crack a joke. On the pitch, he was pure confidence and determination. "By God's grace, I have that kind of talent," said Bernard. "I know how to dribble. I know how to give a pass. I have a lot."

Bernard's family was happy to do anything they could to support his soccer career, even if it meant him living outside the house. His father, also a passionate soccer fan, was sure his son was going places. "Whenever I saw him playing soccer, I had this feeling that my boy was going to become somebody someday," his father said. "I believed in him because of the way he played and the passion he had." Bernard didn't forget about his family either. Whenever he won a packet of FanIce (ice cream) or some boflot (Ghanaian donuts) in pickup games, he always shared the spoils with his parents and siblings.

Bernard and two other players slept on the floor of Oteng's one-room home. Oteng took care of them like they were his own kids. He bought them cleats and jerseys, cooked for them, and even paid some of their school fees. When they weren't in class or playing soccer, they helped out at Oteng's welding business. It was run out of a tattered wooden shack with Oteng's cell phone number scrawled across it in white paint. He used the proceeds from the business to fund his Colts teams. In addition to jerseys and equipment, he had to pay for transportation to games and hospital bills if a player got injured.

Oteng also got support from his local church, the same one Bernard was cleaning the day Colomer came to town. His teams often slept on foam mattresses under a large mosquito net at the church the night before games so they could pray for victory. One of the church's ministers, Rev. James Mensah, used to play fullback in the Colts League himself. "But I was born again at 17 and eventually stopped," he said. Bernard moved in with Rev. Mensah and his wife in 2007 because Oteng got a welding contract in the central city of Kumasi and could no longer take care of him. That's why Oteng went to look for him at the church the day of the Football Dreams tryout to tell him to grab his cleats and head for Star Park. Neither of them had ever heard of the group holding the tryout, but that didn't matter. It was an opportunity.

Scouting for soccer players is often a shoestring operation, even toward the upper echelons of the sport. Scouts in England, for example, endure long hours behind the wheel driving to places like Yeovil and Hartlepool to watch a steady parade of games. They subsist on ham and mustard sandwiches, or perhaps rice, curry, and chips, frequently eaten on the run. They constantly worry about job security, especially amid the oft-promised data revolution looming over the soccer world. For their troubles, they are often paid a measly 40 pence a mile or so, as chronicled by Michael Calvin in *The Nowhere Men*, a touching portrait of this largely invisible clan. "Scouts may be marginalized, professionally, but they possess the power of dreams," wrote Calvin.

The pay can be significantly better at the world's top clubs but not necessarily for scouts chasing youth players. And those youth scouting operations definitely don't include paramilitary police protection or covert intelligence agents. They don't feature talk of procuring satellite phones for secure communication while out for a boat ride with a Nigerian militant. That's because Colomer wasn't traveling across Africa to scout for Barcelona, Chelsea, or any of the other big teams that might come to mind. Colomer's backer made them look like paupers. He wasn't in Africa for one of the richest clubs in the world, but one of the richest countries: the tiny desert kingdom of Qatar. A country most people in Africa had likely never even heard of. Many people in the rest of the world, too.

That changed in dramatic fashion a few years later when Qatar shocked the world by winning the bid to host the 2022 World Cup. The country's qualifications looked paper thin. Qatar is smaller than Connecticut and has so few citizens that the exact number is considered a national secret. Its team was ranked 113th in the world at the time and had never qualified for a World Cup. Temperatures regularly soar above 110 degrees in the summer, when the tournament is normally held. But Qatar did have one powerful weapon: money. Oil and gas reserves worth trillions of dollars sit beneath the country's desert sands and offshore in the Persian Gulf. Combine that wealth with a population of only 2 million people, a mere 300,000 of whom are citizens, and you get a lot of excess cash.

Qatar's ruling sheikhs were determined to use this wealth to seize a place on the world stage and knew few things could have as much impact as success in international soccer, especially the World Cup. But the tournament turned out to be a public relations nightmare for Qatar. The country was soon battling allegations that it had bribed officials to win the bid. It faced serious concerns about the health risks of playing soccer in the Gulf's searing summer heat, prompting FIFA to make the controversial decision to move the tournament to winter. The country also grappled with withering criticism about its treatment of migrant laborers, who make up much of Qatar's population and are tasked with building the tournament's many stadiums. The uproar was so intense that many called on FIFA to revote on which country would host the 2022 World Cup.

Despite this newfound attention, Qatar's mammoth search for the next generation of soccer stars has remained shrouded in mystery. Perhaps the only thing more shocking than the size of Football Dreams is how few people know about it. Most seem to have no idea that years before Qatar won the right to host the World Cup, it decided to dispatch Colomer to Africa with a mandate to bring back the best young players he could find. The program was launched by Aspire Academy, a colossal, state-run institution built by Qatar at a reported cost of over a billion dollars.

Even those familiar with Football Dreams have struggled to understand Qatar's goals and why it has spent so much money on the program, well over $100 million according to one source. Is the nation trying to build a crack team of Africans to compete in a future World Cup? Does the country see a path to even greater riches by harvesting the continent's best players and selling them to the highest bidder? Aspire has presented Football Dreams as a humanitarian project to help young Africans achieve their goal of joining the world's top clubs, but that hasn't quelled suspicions in the media and elsewhere that Football Dreams is yet another chapter in the long history of rich nations stripping Africa of its most valuable resources. "Is this the academy of dreams or exploitation?" said one newspaper headline.

This is an important question, but it only scratches the surface of a much broader story, one that centers on the boys Colomer plucked off dirt fields across Africa and took to Qatar. Their journeys not only peel back the mystery surrounding Football Dreams but also provide a revealing glimpse into the increasingly global search for young soccer talent. It's a side of the game that largely sits in the shadows. Millions of kids around the world see making a life in soccer as the ultimate dream, but the small number of players who succeed dominate the headlines, not the millions who fail. Fans rarely see just how daunting the odds are for children to make it, even when they're marked for greatness at a young age, like Bernard, or how challenging it is for scouts to pick the right kids, even when they know what to look for, like Colomer. Science and technology can help, but only so much. Nigerian militants normally don't.

Bernard quickly dressed in his best soccer gear after his coach told him a foreign scout was coming to town. Bernard loved Nike and always said the company would be his sponsor if he hit it big. He looked like a Nike advertisement as he walked out the door, albeit one that probably wouldn't have made the company very happy since it was all knockoff gear sold on the black market. It was all Bernard could afford. He covered his lithe, five-foot frame with all the Nike gear he could get. On that day, he wore a white Nike T-shirt, black shorts, and white socks and carried his black and white Nike cleats. He set off in the direction of Star Park, the public field where the Football Dreams tryout was being held.

The park was located down a red dirt road that branched off one of Teshie's main thoroughfares. The crowded street was a riot of activity. Traders hawked a multitude of goods from small, wooden stalls: stacks of dried fish, large brown yams, and mounds of green mangos. Women walked by with plastic laundry buckets on their heads filled with peanuts and dried plantain chips. The din receded as Bernard walked away from the main street toward the park. He prayed God would help him in the tryout, known as a "justify" in Ghana. The term helps explain one of Bernard's favorite Bible verses, Romans 10:10. "For it is with your heart that you believe and are justified, and it is with your mouth that you profess your faith and are saved."

Bernard wouldn't have had to look far for religious inspiration on his walk. The short road to the park now hosts the God's Time Beauty Salon, the God Is Good Beauty Salon, and the God Is Grace Beauty Salon. Pretty much every business in Ghana has some reference to Christianity in its name, a testament to the strength of religion in the country. The road also sports the Girls Girls Pub. Its sign features a woman in tight jeans and high heels next to a row of liquor bottles. What's virtue without a little vice?

The scouts were nowhere to be seen when Bernard arrived at Star Park. Its name was grander than the reality. The park was simply an open expanse of dirt bookended by a pair of goals. Their white paint was chipped badly, exposing the metal underneath. Players used crushed-up coal meant for cooking stoves to mark the field, leaving an uneven black line that meandered around the pitch.

Bernard had already done an initial Football Dreams tryout at the park. All around Africa, Colomer used locals to conduct a first set of trials to weed the players down to the best 176 kids at each field. He and the other European scouts would show up a few days later for the second stage. Bernard was so eager for that first tryout he showed up before dawn, hours before it was scheduled to start. But like many players, he was still dubious that Football Dreams was a legitimate opportunity. African soccer is filled with people of all stripes who make big promises they never intend to keep. For this reason, Bernard grew disillusioned as he sat waiting for the scouts, who were late showing up for the second tryout. He eventually got fed up, figured the whole thing was a fraud, and decided to leave.

On his way home, he ran into Oteng, who insisted he turn around and head back. Reluctantly, Bernard retraced his steps past the clamorous stew of traders and down the red dirt road to the park. Soon after he returned, he saw a truck approaching that said Aspire Africa Football Dreams on its side. It was emblazoned with the image of a small African boy heading a soccer ball and the slogan "Your Dreams Come True." Perhaps the whole thing was legitimate after all.

Colomer stepped out of the truck into Ghana's bright sunlight, and the tryout was soon under way. The organizers had set up a tent and plastic chairs so spectators could watch the games in the shade. But Colomer didn't sit. He moved up and down the field and sometimes stood right in the center, slowly turning in a circle as the play developed around him. The dirt pitch was uneven and littered with stones, causing the ball to bounce in unpredictable directions, but the best players were able to reel it in like it was on a string. Their cleats provided flashes of color against the drab, sandy background. Shouts of joy and despair welled up from the crowd in response to a classy step-over or a fluffed shot. These moves sent puffs of red dust into the air, records of the plays that lasted an instant before the wind erased them.

Soccer increasingly seems like a game in which every action on the pitch is now recorded, catalogued, and processed for review, but the matches Colomer witnessed across Africa were very different. His eyes were the recording device, his brain the processor. That's a challenging reality for a game as complex as soccer and a task as difficult as picking the next Messi. It's a reality that science and technology are now changing. Analysts have moved far beyond basic statistics like assists, shots, and goals to scout for talent. The latest models even analyze how players think. That's a quantum leap from where the technology was even a few years ago, but today's advances obviously meant nothing to Colomer in 2007 as he stood on the side of Star Park in Teshie.

Many of Bernard's teammates from Unique FC also showed up for the tryout, so he took the field with them when it was his turn to play. Shorter than many of the other kids, he certainly wouldn't have caught Colomer's eye based on his physical presence. He was about five feet tall, around the same height as Messi when he first arrived at Barcelona as a 13-year-old. Like Messi, Bernard likely looked downright small in his black and white Nike gear, but he was brimming with confidence. He knew he had the talent needed to impress Colomer and make it to the final tryout in Ghana. Plus, he was sure he could count on help from a powerful friend. "I knew that definitely I would be among the final 50 players because I have always been praying to God that he would help me," said Bernard.

Perhaps God took the game off. Colomer didn't select Bernard. He didn't select any of them. They walked off the field dejected after their 20-minute game. "The scout said he didn't see anyone," said one of Bernard's teammates, Shadrack Ankamah. Disappointed and confused, Bernard told his friends he was leaving. Shadrack and the others tried to get him to stay but had no luck. Bernard took off his cleats, changed out of his Nike gear, and headed for the exit. For the second time that day, he was leaving Star Park without so much as a nod from Colomer.

Just then someone called his name. He turned around and saw

it was Eugene Komey, the local coach who had organized the tryout for Aspire in Teshie. "I called him back because I wanted him to play again," said Komey. He knew how good Bernard was and didn't feel like his talent had shown through in the first game. Maybe he didn't get enough touches. Maybe his teammates hogged the ball. Maybe he was just unlucky. Soccer is a game of luck as much as skill sometimes. Komey decided to put Bernard on his own team, Dragon FC.

In a twist of fate, it turned out Dragon would play against Bernard's team, Unique. His original teammates had convinced the organizers to give them another chance, but Komey was confident the best player was now on his team. The other players on Dragon thought so as well. "That side, they knew him as a great player, so every ball they got, they gave it to him," said Shadrack. "He knew our weaknesses, too." Bernard shredded his old teammates. With the ball balanced on his left foot, he danced around players in a way that was eerily similar to a small Argentine who has grown into a giant of the game.

Messi wasn't as famous back then as he is now. He placed third in the Ballon d'Or and second in the FIFA World Player of the Year voting in 2007. He was only 20 years old, and his dominance of the sport was yet to come. As his fame increased, many people began to see similarities between Bernard and Messi. But there was one person at the field who already knew Messi's skill and style of play intimately. He was standing in the middle of the pitch with a notebook in his hand.

Komey believes he knows the exact moment when Colomer decided Bernard was a special talent. The speedy midfielder received the ball on the right side of the field near the halfway line. He sprinted inside with the ball on his left foot, as Messi has done so many times. A defender approached as he neared the center of the field. Bernard did a quick step-over and called out to a teammate on his left, pulling the defender with him. With the defender off balance, he played a no-look pass to a teammate on his right. Colomer jotted something down in his notebook and came to speak with one of his assistants on the sideline.

Komey told the people around him he was sure Bernard had been selected as one of the top 50 players in Ghana who would participate in the next set of tryouts in Accra. They disagreed. There was no way he could know, they said. Plus, Bernard was so small. But anyone who simply focused on physical characteristics like his size, or even his speed, was making a mistake. They could be forgiven, though. It's a mistake scouts around the world make all the time, potentially missing out on the next Messi.

Youth scouting has long been a fairly subjective process, with coaches and scouts relying mostly on instinct to determine which kids have the most potential. But in recent years, researchers have increasingly investigated whether there's a better way. They've tried to identify which specific characteristics are most useful in determining whether a young player has what it takes to make it. How much should scouts focus on size and strength? What about speed and agility? How about technique and game intelligence? The aspiration of this research is to make youth scouting more science than art.

In some sports, scouts can simply focus on a small number of key physical traits like size or speed to get a good idea of whether an athlete has the potential to be world-class. These sports are often described as more nature than nurture since genetics play an outsized role in determining who has the ability to succeed. One example is rowing. In 2007, the United Kingdom launched a program called Sporting Giants to identify tall men and women who could potentially become Olympic athletes in rowing, volleyball, and handball, all sports in which height plays a powerful role in determining success. Men had to be a minimum of six feet, three inches tall, and women five feet, eleven inches. Candidates also had to be between 16 and 25 years old and have some sort of athletic background, but not necessarily in the sports being targeted. One of those picked in 2008 out of more than 4,000 applications was Helen Glover, a 22-year-old PE teacher who had never rowed before. She was just below the required height but stood on her tiptoes when measured to make the grade. Four years later, she won a gold medal at the 2012 Olympics. She repeated the feat in 2016 and has won a slew of other international competitions, catapulting her to the number one ranked female rower in the world.

Australia achieved a similar feat in the winter sport of skeleton, which certainly isn't for the faint of heart. An athlete begins by running down the ice with one or two hands on a sled, dives on board, and then careens down the track headfirst at more than 70 miles per hour. Officials at the Australian Institute of Sport learned that the beginning sprint accounts for about half the variation in total race time, so they conducted a nationwide hunt for new female athletes in 2004, based largely on a 30-meter sprint test, according to David Epstein's book *The Sports Gene*. The women had never tried the sport before but were recording the fastest runs in Australian history within three slides. One woman beat half the field at the Under-23 skeleton world championships only 10 weeks after she first set foot on the ice and won the title in her next try. Another made it all the way to the 2006 Winter Olympics.

But soccer is different. The calculus for scouts is much more complex. First of all, they could never target adults who haven't played soccer before. Researchers have shown that elite soccer players across the world start playing from a very young age, often around 5 years old, and accumulate thousands of hours of playing time before they even turn 16 years old. Players who haven't put in this time have no hope of ever competing at the highest levels. That means scouts trying to identify the sport's next stars have to focus on children, a more difficult prospect given how much kids change physically and mentally during childhood. Clubs have compounded this complexity by focusing on younger and younger kids, with many academies targeting children as young as 5 years old. That gives coaches more time to train them and prevents other clubs from snatching them up. But the younger a player is, the more difficult it is to assess his potential.

Physical traits like height and speed can certainly help soccer players, but scouts need to be careful about how much they weigh these factors when evaluating kids. Height can be especially important in certain positions like goalkeeper and central defense, but it's not a prerequisite in soccer like it is in rowing or volleyball. The sport is much more democratic. A pair of Australian scientists found that 28 percent of men have the height and weight combination that could fit in with professional soccer players, even as athletes' bodies have become more specialized over time. That's over five times the number they found could play in the NBA.

In fact, being short can actually be an advantage in soccer. One study published in 2012 found that shorter players with lower centers of gravity are better at performing the sharp changes of direction top players use to elude defenders. Shorter legs and lower mass are also advantageous for acceleration, as Epstein pointed out in *The Sports Gene*. That may be why NFL running backs and cornerbacks have gotten shorter over the last 40 years, even while humanity has grown taller, Epstein speculated.

Speed can, of course, be a big advantage for a soccer player. Look no farther than the winning goal Real Madrid winger Gareth Bale scored against Barcelona in the 2014 Copa del Rey final. With the score tied 1-1 in the 85th minute, Bale, one the fastest players in the sport, received a pass at midfield near the left sideline and kicked the ball into open space far down the pitch past Barcelona defender Marc Bartra. Then he turned on the afterburners. Even though Bartra shoved Bale several yards out of bounds at one point, the winger proved far too fast and was several feet ahead of the defender by the time he collected the ball just outside the penalty box. With a few more touches, Bale put the ball between the goalkeeper's legs and into the back of the net. Even Usain Bolt, the fastest man in history, was impressed. "It's a goal any sprinter in the world would like to score one day," he told a Spanish newspaper.

Multiple studies looking at youth academy players of different ages have found that kids who eventually become professionals tend to be faster than others. Researchers have also found they tend to have greater endurance, agility, and leg power, although the differences were often relatively small and the utility of the measures differed depending on a child's age.

But scouts can't rely on these physical traits to predict who will become a star like they do in rowing or the skeleton. Speed may be the most useful metric of the bunch, but even it has relatively little predictive power to reveal which kids will make it. That's because coaches are producing soccer players, not track stars. Choosing the fastest kid in a group would, of course, always make sense if the players were equal in every other way, but that's rarely ever the case.

At the other end of the spectrum, players may require some minimum level of speed, endurance, and agility, especially as the game has gotten faster and more physically rigorous. But it's unclear what those minimums might be, and players can often compensate for relative weaknesses by having better technique or game intelligence. Those skills are bigger differentiators at the top level of the sport than a player's time in the 50-yard dash. Technique and game intelligence come from putting in thousands of hours of training, not from simply having a predetermined genetic build.

"As one example, I'm sure Messi isn't the greatest athlete in the world," said A. Mark Williams, editor of the book *Science and Soccer* and chair of the Department of Health, Kinesiology, and Recreation at the University of Utah. "He's probably a decent athlete, but he's not a super athlete. Maybe what stands him out is he spent all those hours training, a lot of it initially in street football, developing the key technical competencies that are important to progress."

Soccer is thus much more nurture than nature, and simply picking the biggest, fastest, and strongest kids on the field wouldn't be a very successful strategy for a scout. But many make precisely this mistake. One way to see this is to look at when professional players were born. The relative age effect is a widely recognized problem in talent identification. It basically means coaches and scouts often choose young athletes born earlier in a sport's selection year because they are more physically mature, and this advantage can result in better performance at an early age. After all, a gap of up to twelve months can make a huge difference in the height, weight, and speed of a 13-year-old boy. These older kids are often the ones who receive the best training opportunities, potentially leaving behind an athlete who has greater potential but just needs to catch up physically.

Many studies have shown the relative age effect is a big problem in soccer. There's significant overrepresentation of players born early in the selection year on top youth and professional teams across the world. For example, around 60 percent of professional soccer players in England were born in the first quarter of the selection year. Scouts seem to be choosing current performance over future potential by picking older and more physically mature players, potentially missing out on the next big star. "In this way, talent spotting becomes an attempt to avoid failure rather than an ambitious quest to find truly exceptional raw material." That's how former soccer coach Rasmus Ankersen put it in his study of elite athletes, *The Gold Mine Effect.* He pointed out that the club Flamengo passed on future Brazilian superstar Ronaldo in the early 1990s when he was 15 years old because coaches thought he was too small and slight. Ronaldo was born in September. To find the next star, scouts must be prepared to take greater risks than many have in the past.

Younger and smaller players who do make it into the right training environment may have an advantage when they get older because they have developed skills to compensate for their size. Think of Messi. When he first showed up at Barcelona as a 13-year-old, he was only four feet, ten and a quarter inches tall. The young Argentine had been drawn to Barcelona because his home-town club couldn't afford the expensive hormone treatment needed to battle a growth disorder. He was so little that when Barcelona's future sporting director, Txiki Beguiristain, ran into Messi and his father in the elevator that first day, he ruffled the young player's hair and said, "This boy must be good, he is small," according to Guillem Balague's biography, *Messi*.

The Flea, as they would later call Messi, was never going to overpower bigger players his age at Barcelona, like the tall central defender Gerard Piqué. Instead, he left Piqué and others in the dust with his speed and control. Messi's coach once warned Piqué and his teammates not to injure the fragile new player, and the defender shouted, "How can we be careful? We can't even get close to him!"

A study published in 2011 found that award-winning athletes in soccer and a handful of other sports were actually more likely to be born late rather than early in the selection year. The soccer players included in the study were those who finished in the top three spots in the FIFA World Player of the Year and Ballon d'Or awards over a period of 20 years. Messi has won the Ballon d'Or a record five times, and he's far from the only little guy to make soccer history.

The relative age effect is further complicated by the fact that a young athlete's biological age, or physical maturity, can differ significantly from his chronological age. For example, two 13-year-old

boys can have biological ages six years apart because they are growing at different rates. That would mean the early maturer has a body
of a 16-year-old and the late maturer a body of a 10-year-old. Much
like players who are chronologically older than their counterparts,
early maturers have a physical advantage and are often favored by
scouts. Imagine if Barcelona had passed on Messi because he was
too small. He was clearly a late maturer given his growth deficiency
but was lucky enough to be at a club willing to take chances on
small, technical players. In fact, they would eventually become the
club's calling card, with Messi, Xavi, and Iniesta all topping out at
no more than five feet, seven inches tall.

Technique is likely a better indicator of a young player's potential,
especially the kind of dribbling prowess Messi exhibited as a child.
One study published in 2009 that looked at a group of teenage players at a pair of top Dutch academies found that those who ultimately became professionals were consistently 0.3 seconds faster on
average when dribbling 30 meters than those who didn't make the
cut. They were also a second faster on average when repeating the
drill three times in a row. Other studies have found that players at
youth academies who progressed over the years were also better at
passing, shooting, and crossing, although the differences were often
relatively small.

Colomer certainly knew the importance of focusing on technique. He spent time in the 1990s studying the training methods
at France's best-known youth academy, Clairefontaine, which made
technique its driving focus and helped the country win the World
Cup in 1998 and the European Championship in 2000. "I had the
opportunity to really learn how they were working for the World
Cup and how they were working with children," said Colomer. "At
the time, Clairefontaine was maybe the reference for youth development in the world."

The French federation first started its youth academy system in the 1970s after years of underperforming on the world stage. Initially, the focus was on improving players' physical conditioning. The training was brutal. Coaches made players run in bulletproof vests laced with metal, according to an article in the soccer magazine *The Blizzard*. That changed when officials realized they were producing players who were incredibly fit but technically inept. If a kid can't control and pass the ball like it's second nature, he'll never become a star. Technique became the mantra, not endurance. They made players practice technical drills over and over again and never sent kids on a run without the ball. The strategy worked. Clairefontaine, which is located on the sprawling grounds of a French chateau outside Paris, ended up producing France's leading goal scorer, Thierry Henry, as well as many other top players. This success sealed Clairefontaine's reputation as one of the best youth academies in the world at the time.

But focusing on a young player's technique still tells a scout relatively little about whether the kid will reach the top level, even when the observations are paired with physical measures of speed and agility. A study published in 2016 looked at the results from a battery of five tests conducted by the German soccer federation on over 20,000 of the top Under-12 players in the country. The tests measured speed, agility, dribbling, passing, and shooting. The researchers assessed the utility of the tests in determining how high the kids would progress once they reached the Under-16 to Under-19 level. The study found that players who scored in the 99th percentile or higher in the tests still only had a 6 percent chance of making the youth national team. "This makes the task of searching for future national players similar to searching for a needle in a haystack," the study said. To improve the predictive power of the tests, the researchers recommended the federation include psychological factors like game intelligence and personality, which are likely the biggest drivers of success. But that's easier said than done since they are much harder to measure than qualities like speed and technique.

To Colomer, Bernard certainly looked like one of those needles in the haystack. After traveling thousands of miles across Africa, the Spanish scout had finally found a player who reminded him of Messi. And Colomer wasn't the only one who saw similarities between the left-footer from Teshie and the Flea. One of the scouts working the final Football Dreams tryout in Ghana in 2007 was Pere Gratacós, who coached Messi on Barcelona's reserve team when Colomer was at the club. Watching Bernard in Accra clearly brought back memories. "Pere called me over in the final 50 and said, 'Sit beside me,'" said Bernard. "He told me that I reminded him of a player at Barcelona. He was talking about Messi, who was not as famous then." Gratacós may have been thinking about Bernard a few years later as well when he told a Spanish newspaper that Football Dreams made him realize that "in Africa, there are many Messis."

Gratacós's words gave Bernard a needed boost of confidence. He was a little dazzled by the array of talent Colomer had assembled at the University of Ghana, where the tryout was being held. The Spanish scout planned to select the three best field players from Ghana to attend the final tryout in Doha. Bernard also felt a bit lonely because his coach Oteng didn't come to the tryout. "Bernard called me and said the other managers had come and asked me to come too," said Oteng. "I said, 'God is there with you. God is your manager, so you shouldn't worry.'"

Bernard certainly spent plenty of time praying but didn't have to rely on God alone. He could also turn to Komey, the coordinator who helped engineer his selection at Star Park. Komey gave Bernard a ride to the tryout and got a room across the hall at the university to keep an eye on him. "I kept his bag and kit in my room so nobody could steal anything," said Komey. "Sometimes he said breakfast was not enough, so I gave him my breakfast."

Whatever he ate, it worked. Bernard mesmerized the crowd with his moves on the university's clumpy grass field. "Everybody was like, 'Your boy is so good. Can he play for me?'" said Komey. "He was a much more intelligent player than most of the kids on the pitch." University students crowded around the edges of the field and applauded especially good plays. The matches weren't the only spectacle, though. The Football Dreams staff had also invited a variety of performers, including men banging on traditional wooden drums; dancing children wearing hats the color of the Ghanaian flag, red, yellow, and green; and a trickster juggling a soccer ball in every way imaginable, even keeping it balanced on his head while he removed his cap.

Over the first three days of the tryout, the scouts chose the best 22 players and then pitted them against each other in a final 25-minute game on the last day. Colomer made sure to let the players know just how high the stakes were at that point. "Everything you did until now was only a test. What is really important is today," said Colomer at a more recent final. He told the players that simply having great technique wasn't enough. They needed to show that they could bring something special to the game. "The best players in the world, Messi and Cristiano Ronaldo, these players, they show in the important games they have personality," said Colomer. "They don't hide themselves. They show that they want the ball."

When the final game rolled around, Bernard took his place in midfield alongside the other top players in the tryout. He suffered an unexpected setback during the match when he blew out one of his cleats. But he simply hopped off the field, quickly donned a replacement, and jumped right back into the fray, skipping past

Colomer speaking with players at a Football Dreams tryout.

players with the ball glued to his left foot. Komey bragged to the other coordinators on the sideline that the scouts were bound to choose Bernard, but they pushed back, just like the coaches had in Teshie. "They were telling me I was lying because Appiah was so small," said Komey. "I told them Appiah is intelligent. They will pick him on any given day."

Komey was right. The Ghana country director, Andy Sam, called Oteng a week or two after the tryout ended to tell him that Bernard was one of the three Ghanaians headed to Doha for the final test, which would include the other top players found across Africa. "It was amazing," said Bernard. "I called my mom and dad, and we prayed together." Bernard's parents were ecstatic, especially his father, who always believed his son would become a star. But there was a tinge of sadness as well as they prepared to watch their son leave. He may have lived with Oteng for several years growing up, but this was the first time he was leaving the country, the first time anyone in the family had ever left the country. First passport, first plane trip, first time at a proper academy: Bernard's life quickly transformed into a procession of firsts.

On the eve of his trip, Bernard's family threw him a party at their home in Teshie. His mother cooked his favorite meal, banku and okra stew, and they ate together on the narrow porch outside their house. Bernard also played one final game with his good friend Shadrack and other members of his Colts team on the dirt pitch at Star Park where Colomer first saw him. Several months later, the Spanish scout would stand at a press conference in Doha and tell the story of spotting Bernard. "When I saw him, I remembered Leo Messi in Barca because he was playing like him," said Colomer. "He is a good player, and I think he will be somebody in football."

CHAPTER 2

The Skipper

Diawandou Diagne took off at a full sprint, his skinny arms and legs pumping furiously. Beads of sweat quickly sprouted on the young player's forehead and streamed down his face. The heat of the afternoon sun was relentless, but he kept up the pace. Diawandou was determined to make the most of the Football Dreams tryout being held that afternoon in his hometown of Thiès, Senegal's third largest city. He had dreamed of becoming a professional player like his father since he was a young boy. There was just one problem. He wasn't at the tryout. He was late.

Diawandou had an exam the day the tryout was being held and knew his uncle would kill him if he missed it. That wasn't always enough to prevent him from skipping school to play soccer. Sometimes he hid his cleats under the books in his backpack and took a shower at his best friend's house so his uncle wouldn't know he had been playing. But the deception didn't always work. Diawandou's uncle, Cheikh Gueye, was a lot more interested in his education than his soccer career and even paid for him to attend a small private school in Thiès called Mababa. It was a pretty humble operation. The school only had a handful of classrooms filled with scratched wooden desks, cracked chalkboards, and bare concrete floors. Paint peeled off the walls. But it was better than the public schools in town, and Gueye would give Diawandou a serious beating whenever he found out he was playing hooky. He even injured his wrist pounding on Diawandou one day when he discovered the young boy had gone out to play soccer instead of doing his homework. The message finally sank in, and Diawandou didn't dare skip his exam on the day of the Football Dreams tryout, even though he knew it would be tough to make it there after school. His only chance was a full sprint, so he tore out of the gates as soon as the test was finished.

Gueye took over responsibility for raising Diawandou after his parents divorced and moved away from Thiès when he was young. Diawandou's mother, Khadidiatou Gueye, left for the Ivory Coast to live with her new husband and run a restaurant selling traditional Senegalese food. His father, who once played professional soccer in Thiès, moved to the coastal city of Mbour to work for the railroad. Diawandou stayed put and grew up in his mother's large ancestral home with his uncle's family and dozens of other relatives. The rambling concrete house was originally built by Khadidiatou's grandfather, the most successful jeweler in Thiès, a city of over 600,000 people.

Subsequent generations of Diawandou's family prospered in the city as well. Khadidiatou's father was a senior director of a large printing business, and her brother Cheikh studied architecture at a university in Saint-Louis. Many of the other family members attended university as well, a notable achievement given that less than half of Senegal's population can read. Diawandou's uncle never finished his degree because family problems forced him to return to Thiès, where he ended up running a construction company. But he continued to believe in the importance of education and presided over the family like a stern headmaster.

The family's prosperity enabled them to expand their home over the years until it grew to include over a dozen rooms built around a small tiled courtyard shaded by a large ficus tree. There were limits to their wealth, though. The main building's white paint job faded and grew dark with grime over time, and some of the new additions had an unfinished look. But the house was significantly bigger than others that lined the patchwork of dirt streets that made up their crowded neighborhood of Bayal. Many were one-story structures built with crude red bricks slapped together with cement. A few were simple reed huts topped with rusted sheets of metal held down with stones.

The neighborhood is located off a busy paved road where cars and motorcycles compete for space with a stream of pedestrians and horses pulling wooden carts. The street hums with the buzz of small-scale commerce common throughout Africa. Merchants hawk their wares out of cracked concrete buildings and makeshift wooden shacks leaning at precarious angles. There's a convenience store with dried spices hanging from the ceiling in small plastic bags, a shop selling old printers that spill out into the street, and a tailor with a single sewing machine operating out of a room the size of a broom closet. Men in white robes stream out of a small concrete mosque after prayers, a scene played out five times a day across Senegal since most of the population is Muslim. Not far away, a baker sells loaves of French bread wrapped in newspaper, a reminder of the French colonization of Senegal that began in the seventeenth century. The French brought soccer as well, and shops throughout Diawandou's neighborhood sell cheap rubber balls suspended from the ceiling in red netting and colorful knockoff Adidas cleats hanging by their laces.

Diawandou first started playing soccer with his cousins in the courtyard of his home and eventually migrated to the dirt streets outside. He played three on three with his best friend, Baye Laye, and other neighborhood kids, sometimes for money. He was stick thin, but his talent quickly stood out. So did his feet. Many of the kids played barefoot or in plastic sandals, but Diawandou's family could afford to buy him cleats at a young age. To this day, he believes his legs would be stronger if he had been forced to play barefoot like the other kids. These neighborhood games not only honed his skills but also earned him his first break when he was about 10 years old. That's when Bousso Ndiaye, a coach at a local soccer academy, first spotted him playing in the street. "When I saw Diawandou, I knew he had talent," said Ndiaye.

The coach lived in the neighborhood and would often roam the streets looking for young players to recruit to his academy, the Centre National d'Education Populaire et Sportive, which was run by the government. CNEPS, as it's widely known, was a far cry from the academies operated by top clubs in Europe but was considered one of the best in Senegal at the time. Two of the academy's three fields were grass, a rarity in the country. The school also had a few buildings that could house players, although most of the boys were from Thiès or had family in the city and didn't normally live at the academy. They usually trained in the afternoon after school.

When Ndiaye spotted Diawandou, he asked why he was playing in the street when he could be training at CNEPS. Diawandou told him he would have to speak to his family to get permission. Normally it wasn't much of a challenge for Ndiaye to convince a family to say yes. Nearly half of Senegal's population lives on less than a dollar or two a day, and many kids view soccer as their best chance for a better life, even though only a tiny percentage actually achieve their dream of playing in Europe. That's true in many other parts of Africa as well, and there's a problem with kids dropping out of school hoping to make it as professional players. Sometimes their parents even support the decision or simply don't have the money to continue paying school fees.

Few players end up succeeding, but those who do often come

from relatively poor backgrounds. These kids have few other opportunities, so they end up playing soccer for thousands of hours, the
kind of training that is necessary for success but certainly doesn't
guarantee it. The dynamics are the same in many other parts of
the developing world. Rasmus Ankersen, the author of *The Gold
Mine Effect*, found that 90 percent of Brazil's top players grew up
in poverty.

It's less common for a child like Diawandou, who comes from a
relatively prosperous family and attended private school, to gamble
on becoming a professional soccer player and commit to the training necessary to give him a chance. Diawandou's uncle wanted
him to focus on attending university one day. That's why Ndiaye
had some convincing to do when he showed up at Diawandou's
house seeking the family's permission for the young boy to attend
his academy.

It wasn't the only time someone had come to talk to Gueye about
Diawandou's soccer talent. The head of the boy's private school
once appeared at the house, and Gueye thought he was going to
praise Diawandou's performance as a student. Instead, the headmaster pleaded for Gueye to let Diawandou play on the school's soccer team. "I asked him, 'Is Diawandou in school to study or play
football?'" said Gueye. But he eventually agreed, and school officials
still speak wistfully about how many trophies Diawandou helped
them win. The young player also impressed his fellow students by
juggling lemons picked off a tree in the school's courtyard. Diawandou's passion was clear. Not even breaking his leg twice as a kid
diminished his love for the sport. Thus, Gueye ended up agreeing
to Ndiaye's request for the boy to attend his academy, although he
continued to hound him about his education.

Diawandou was excited to begin his training at CNEPS, but it
didn't start so well. The first time he showed up at the green metal
gates that mark the academy's entrance, Ndiaye sent him home.

"His hair was too long," said the coach. The kids were supposed to have buzz cuts, but Diawandou arrived sporting dreadlocks. "He said I needed to cut my hair, so I went home and came back the next day," said Diawandou. It wasn't the last time Ndiaye sent him home without playing. Diawandou had to run for 15 minutes to make it from school to the academy every afternoon and sometimes showed up late. Many of the other kids had already dropped out of school, so they didn't have the same challenge of turning up on time. But Ndiaye was a stickler for the rules. Whenever Diawandou showed up late, he sent him packing.

Otherwise, Diawandou excelled at the academy. He normally played in center midfield and was especially good at passing and free kicks. His idol was the famed attacking midfielder Zinedine Zidane, and he had a poster of the Frenchman on his bedroom wall at home. But it was Diawandou's leadership on the field that impressed Ndiaye most. He began shouting instructions at the other young kids on his team as soon as he arrived at the academy, and the coach quickly appointed him captain. "He always talks with the players," said Ndiaye. "He's the second coach of the team." Diawandou is much less vocal off the field and exudes a quiet intensity. He speaks when necessary but often refrains from participating in the constant banter among his teammates. But they look to him for guidance when the chips are down and know they can count on his judgment and determination.

Diawandou hoped to impress the Football Dreams scouts with these same qualities, if he could just make it to the tryout on time. He certainly knew the way. The tryout was being held at his academy, so the route from school was burned into his brain. He took a hard right as he ran out of the gates and quickly picked up speed along the paved street outside. He eventually hung a left onto a dirt road, passing a small convenience store selling cold drinks and a basketball court where kids dressed in school uniforms often played after class. He willed his legs to go faster, even though he knew the chance of being selected for Football Dreams was tiny.

Ndiaye was the one who told him Qatar was sending scouts to pick the three best field players from Senegal for the final tryout at Aspire in Doha. Diawandou was dubious and said, "Three players in all of Senegal? No, I cannot do this." But Ndiaye insisted, "No, just come try, nobody knows what's going to happen." Neither of them had ever heard of Qatar before. Diawandou was familiar with Saudi Arabia since Mecca was the center of Islam and he was Muslim. Qatar was a mystery, though.

Diawandou finally agreed to attend the tryout and now didn't want to miss his chance. As he headed into the final stretch of his sprint, he ran past a small butcher shop and a long white wall that radiated purple when the bougainvillea was in bloom. Finally he could see the academy in the distance. He burst through the green gates and sped past the school's crumbling concrete stand. He could see the tryout was still being held on the academy's dirt field, but it was almost over. There was only one match left.

The team Diawandou was originally supposed to join had already played its game, so he had to scramble to get in front of Colomer, who was running the tryout. Luckily, there was a single spot open for the last match, but it was in central defense, not his normal position in midfield. Not ideal, but Diawandou had no choice and took up his place in the defensive line. As it turned out, it didn't take long for him to impress Colomer enough to be invited to the next set of tryouts, in Dakar, and Diawandou thinks he knows why.

Diawandou was fast and had impressive technique. In fact, he scored from a free kick soon after taking the field. He was also a natural leader. But those weren't the things Diawandou thought put him over the top when he was unexpectedly thrown into the team's defense. In his mind, the critical edge came from years of playing matches in the dirt streets outside his home. "Sometimes when we

Players battling for the ball at a Football Dreams tryout in Thiès.

played with friends, we put money on the game," he said. "And if I was winning, I would go defend because I didn't want them to score and lose my money."

Back then, the only reward seemed to be pocket change for ice cream. Little did Diawandou realize these pickup games were helping him develop arguably the most vital skill in soccer, something that truly separates the greatest players in the world from the rest, not just in defense, but everywhere on the field. Not coincidentally, it also happened to be the most important thing Colomer was looking for as he scouted hundreds of thousands of kids across Africa.

The magic ingredient wasn't size or strength. Those things couldn't tell you very much about a young player's potential. It wasn't speed either, although it could be a big asset. Technical ability was vital, but even it played second fiddle to the trait Colomer truly wanted to see: game intelligence. After all, being the fastest dribbler on the pitch or the best passer isn't going to do a player much good if he doesn't know what to do with the ball or where to position himself to be effective.

"A talent, if there is a way to describe it, is the player who understands the game, who understands instantly what the game is asking," said Colomer. "Many players know how to dribble. They know how to shoot. But you realize that when the game is asking for dribbling, they pass. When the game is asking for a pass, they shoot." Other players do exactly what the game requires. "These are the talented players," said Colomer.

He likes to give the example of Andrés Iniesta, Spain's World Cup winner and Barcelona's sprightly midfield genius. "Iniesta is not quick, is not good in one-on-one, is not excellent at shooting, and is not strong physically. But he is doing exactly what the game is asking," said Colomer. Iniesta makes better decisions on the field than he can manage watching the star's games from the comfort of his couch, he said.

It's not just soccer. Colomer's observations about game intelligence apply to every sport where fast-paced, complex decision making is involved. Think of Tom Brady picking out a receiver as 300-pound linemen sprint toward him, or LeBron James playing a no-look pass to a teammate as he dribbles full speed toward the hoop. The ability to evaluate a dynamic situation and execute the right decision almost instantly is the hallmark of sporting genius.

Colomer intuitively knew to look for game intelligence after years of scouting for talent, but scientists learned of its importance in soccer in a different way. They assessed the game intelligence of players by freezing match footage at different moments and asking players to predict what would happen next or what decision a player on the field should make. Elite players were faster and more accurate in their ability to scan the field, pick up cues from an opponent's position, and recognize, recall, and predict patterns of play.

One of the first studies in the early 1980s examined attempts by goalkeepers to predict the direction of penalty kicks. This study, which employed simple static images of penalty takers and recorded observations using pen and paper, found that skilled goalkeepers had a more structured visual search process, restricting their gaze to the right side of the body and shooting leg, in the case of a right-footed penalty taker. Subsequent studies using match footage and more advanced technology like portable eye trackers have examined players in a wide range of game scenarios, such as one-on-one, three-on-three, set plays, and so on.

A study in 2011 recorded the eye movements of players when interacting with life-sized video sequences of 11-on-11 situations filmed from the perspective of a central defender. It found that skilled players had better anticipation because they spent more time focused on the opposing team players and areas of space, as opposed to the player in possession and the ball. Similar studies found that skilled players were better at recognizing familiar patterns of play, such as a two-on-one situation or a triangle or diamond shape forming between players, and using this information to predict the best course of action (for example, where a player should pass the ball).

One of the best stories illustrating the power of game intelligence involves another little Argentine who became a giant of the game, Diego Maradona. It was told by Jorge Valdano, who was on the field when Maradona scored his famous goal in the 1986 World Cup by dribbling through half the English team. As Maradona sprinted from the halfway line to goal, Valdano kept pace alongside him in the center forward position, expecting a pass but never receiving one. After the game, Maradona came to see Valdano in the locker room and apologized for not giving him the ball. Maradona said he had originally planned to pass, but as he neared goal, he remembered a similar situation against the English keeper seven years earlier. He failed to score then, and as he weaved through the English team at the World Cup, he realized where he made his mistake. Maradona concluded he didn't need Valdano and could score by himself. Amazingly, he was able to call up this memory, process it, and execute the right decision in just seconds, while dribbling at full speed in one of the highest-pressure environments in soccer. The story, published by the soccer magazine *The Blizzard*, prompted a former Ajax team manager to note that "the seconds of the greats last longer than those of normal people."

Stars like Maradona build up the database of memories needed to drive this game intelligence, as well as the technical skill to put it to work, by playing soccer for thousands of hours. But not all play is equal. Scientists have discovered that one type of training in particular is most useful in developing game intelligence and preparing young players to become professionals. Maradona and Messi both did it. So did Diawandou, Bernard, and the other players Colomer plucked off fields across Africa.

Researchers have found that the key ingredient is not how much formal practice or how many official games players had as kids, but how much pickup soccer they played in informal settings like the street or schoolyard. One study published in 2012 looked at two different groups of elite players from English Premier League academies who were about 18 years old. One group scored higher than the other for game intelligence based on a series of tests using match footage. They found that the two groups accumulated about the same number of hours of formal practice and official competition during the previous six years. But the players with better game intelligence engaged in almost one and a half times as much pickup soccer than the other group. A similar study published the same year found that over 20 percent of the difference in game intelligence was accounted for by the amount of pickup soccer kids played between the ages of 6 and 12. Researchers believe this type of training helps build game intelligence and hone technique because it creates the opportunity for players to experiment with different skills and tactics in an unstructured environment, leading to better anticipation and decision making.

Another group of researchers published a study in 2009 comparing players at a Premier League academy who received full-time professional contracts at the age of 16 with those who didn't and were let go. They also found that the two groups had accumulated about the same numbers of hours of formal practice and competition between the ages of 6 and 12. But the players who were given contracts engaged in more than twice as much pickup soccer as those who were let go. A similar study in 2012 looked at the playing histories of elite Under-16 academy players in several countries, including Brazil, England, France, Ghana, Mexico, Portugal, and Sweden. Brazilian players accumulated the most number of hours of pickup soccer, four to five per week, which helps explain why they've been so successful on the world stage. Kids also logged plenty of hours playing pickup soccer in Ghana, where Colomer found Bernard, the player who reminded him of Messi. Pickup soccer is often the most popular in poor countries where kids have little else to do and see the sport as their only ticket to a better life. As the venerated Dutch striker Johan Cruyff once said, "Every disadvantage has its advantage."

Scouts certainly understand the importance of assessing game intelligence when judging a young player's quality and potential, but it's much harder to measure in an objective way than factors like height, speed, and even technique. One way is to simply watch a player's head when he's on the field. A study of Premier League midfielders found that the ones who scanned their surroundings the most completed almost twice as many forward passes as the least visually active. But this is a pretty inexact measure.

It may not simply be where players look either, but how much they can physically see. A group of researchers in Germany and the United States recently developed a computer test to determine a person's "attention window," the maximum visual area consciously perceived with one glance. It's tested by measuring the area in which people can quickly and accurately perceive two objects on the edge of their peripheral vision. This is vital in soccer because a striker, for example, has to keep an eye on opposing defenders, the goalkeeper, his teammates, and the ball simultaneously.

Researchers found that athletes have a 25 percent larger attention window than nonathletes. They also discovered that athletes who play team sports like soccer that demand a greater horizontal distribution of attention perform better in this respect than those who play sports like volleyball that require more vertical attention. The club Red Bull Salzburg has started measuring the attention windows of its youth players and has found a clear correlation with their performance on the field. "The first results are really great," said the club's academy director, Ernst Tanner. "If they have a broader attention window, they are usually the better players."

Other researchers have used brain games in the lab to see if they could determine which players have greater game intelligence. One recent study conducted by a group of Scandinavian scientists tested the "executive function" of players from the top three divisions in Sweden or, to put it more simply, their skills in problem solving, planning, multitasking, cognitive flexibility, and the ability to deal with novelty. During one test, for example, players had to draw a series of nonrepeating geometric patterns on paper to test their "design fluency," a well-known evaluation of creativity under pressure. The researchers found that both senior-elite and semi-elite players had significantly better measures of executive function than the general population. Also, executive function was able to predict which players would do better in terms of goals and assists over the following two years.

The researchers also tested two of the world's most intelligent players, Barcelona stars Xavi and Iniesta. Iniesta was in the top 0.1 percent for design fluency and also scored incredibly well in what neuroscientists call "inhibition," the ability to alter one's learned behavioral responses in a way that makes it easier to complete a particular task. Xavi also had very high scores in tasks involving scanning ability, analysis, and imagination.

These kinds of tests are promising, but they are far removed from the real world of soccer. Even the process that researchers have used to gauge game intelligence by showing match footage to players and asking them about their perceptions and decision making is imperfect because it doesn't measure performance in real game settings. Even if better tests were available, scouts would still need to evaluate game intelligence alongside a player's physical and technical qualities. That's what makes soccer scouting so difficult. There are so many variables to consider and no specific mix that's guaranteed to produce a star. Think of talent identification in terms of a series of dials a scout uses to evaluate a potential athlete. In a sport like rowing, a scout may be primarily concerned with just a few dials, like height, wingspan, and VO_2 max (which helps measure aerobic fitness potential). They're easy to measure, and the minimum settings needed to produce a star are clearer than in soccer.

In contrast, soccer scouts must focus on a whole host of dials, which could vary depending on position. They include speed, agility, endurance, dribbling, passing, shooting, crossing, heading, tackling, and of course game intelligence, just to name a few. Only a few of these are easy to measure in a comprehensive fashion, and the minimum settings needed to produce a star are much less clear. That means scouts are grappling with a multitude of combinations that could produce success or failure. They're also trying to assess individual performance in a team setting, no easy task. Plus, they're dealing with children, who present moving targets since their bodies and minds are in a state of flux. It's extremely challenging to identify which kids have a greater capacity to learn and improve over time, which will ultimately determine who ends up on top.

The preceding list of variables doesn't even include what might be the most important factor in determining a young player's potential: personality. It's also one of the toughest things for a scout to gauge, especially at the initial stages of evaluating a potential talent. "In 25 minutes, you cannot know the personality of anybody," said Colomer. "We don't fail too much with their football level, but we fail sometimes with their personality." A kid might have blistering speed as well as impressive technique and game intelligence for his age, but does he possess the discipline and motivation necessary to succeed? That doesn't just include the drive to train day after day and the emotional control necessary to handle match pressure and deal well with coaches and teammates. It also involves the ability to cope with potential distractions off the field like family problems or pesky agents.

Messi is often described in the press as more of a "natural talent" when compared to his Real Madrid rival, Cristiano Ronaldo, who is frequently painted as a product of sheer determination and hard work. But this storyline masks the psychological factors behind the Argentine's success. How many 13-year-olds would have the mental and emotional toughness to thrive despite moving to a foreign land at such a young age and watching the decision break up his family? Messi had to deal with his mother moving back to Argentina with his little sister, while he stayed in Barcelona with his father. He also had to decide each night which of his skinny legs to stick with a needle to inject the hormone he needed to grow. Despite these challenges, Messi persevered.

Psychologists call this kind of perseverance to achieve long-term goals grit. Grittier individuals are more likely to stay married, keep their jobs, and pursue further education. A study published in 2016 looked at the role grit played in the performance of elite youth soccer players in Australia. Using questionnaires, researchers found that grittier players accumulated significantly more hours of training over the years, including playing pickup soccer, and had correspondingly higher game intelligence when tested with match footage.

But grit is just one of a multitude of psychological traits that could influence a player's potential, and researchers have struggled to figure out which ones are most vital to future success. Another study published in 2016 examined a much wider set of psychological traits among Under-12 players in the German talent development program to determine their impact on future success (defined as whether they were selected for professional clubs' youth academies at the Under-16 level).

Using questionnaires, researchers looked at seventeen different psychological scales related to traits like motivation, concentration, self-confidence, and anxiety control. Ten of the scales demonstrated predictive power, but the size of the impact was small (each explained only 1 to 3 percent of the difference in future success). That led the researchers to conclude that the tests weren't powerful enough to use for talent identification. "There are probably about a million inventories out there that you could measure players on to isolate some aspect of personality disposition, but historically these have been proven not to have great predictive utility," said A. Mark Williams, the editor of *Science and Soccer*.

Despite this uncertainty, some clubs have sought to become more rigorous in their evaluation of players' personalities. Mark Allen, the former head of Manchester City's academy, said the club had begun using a test developed by Stanford University psychologist Carol Dweck to determine whether youth players have the right outlook to succeed. Dweck calls this a "growth mindset," which means a person believes success is based on hard work rather than innate ability. She has found that children with growth mindsets are more motivated to learn and get better grades than their peers. Allen said early results indicated the test was useful in identifying players who didn't have the mentality to cut it at the academy and beyond. But even if the club could establish a direct link, it would still face the challenge of figuring out how to weigh the results against all the other factors that must be taken into account.

To help soccer scouts cope with the multidimensional nature of talent identification, many clubs have created formal criteria to guide them in evaluating young players. They're often expressed as acronyms. The most famous, TIPS, was developed by the Dutch club Ajax and stands for technique, insight, personality, and speed. Scouts in England have used TABS (technique, attitude, balance, and speed) and SUBS (speed, understanding, personality, and skill).

Clubs often tweak their evaluation criteria, but historically technique at Ajax was broken down into skills like dribbling, passing, crossing, shooting, heading, and tackling. Insight covered vision and decision making when it came to positioning, making runs, selecting passes, and covering opponents. Personality included leadership ability, match mentality, attitude toward others, receptivity to coaching, and ability to withstand pressure. Speed was measured off the mark, from zero to 10 meters, 10 to 30 meters, above 30 meters, and with the ball. Twice a year, all players were assessed and given one of three marks that determined their future at the academy (A = stay, B = doubtful, C = go).

But many of these observations at clubs continue to be quite subjective based on the views of scouts and coaches standing on the sidelines. That's especially true when it comes to game intelligence and personality, which are the hardest qualities to measure and may have the most bearing on whether a young player will succeed. It's perhaps no surprise then that the success rate of picking kids who make it to the sport's top level is incredibly low, even at the best academies.

James Bunce, the former head of sports science at the Premier League, said only half a percent of the kids who join a Premier League academy at the Under-9 level end up making it to the club's first team, according to an article in the *Guardian*. That's one in 200 kids. The numbers aren't much better for young players hoping to make a living in the sport at any level. An education and welfare officer at a top European academy told the authors of the book *Youth Development in Football* that only about 5 percent of the kids there would have a career as professionals. "If this was the success rate in a school, it would most likely be closed down," the authors concluded.

Five percent might even be high. In *The Nowhere Men*, Michael Calvin said only around 1 percent of the 10,000 kids in the entire English academy system would make a living in the game, and two-thirds of those given a professional contract at age 18 are out of professional soccer by the time they're 21 years old. That hasn't stopped clubs from aggressively recruiting kids as young as 5 years old. Much like venture capital investing, the money made from one home run, or saved by not having to buy an equivalent player, can make up for a high number of failures.

But kids aren't companies, and there's a serious personal cost for the thousands who don't make it. Plenty of players who are identified as the next big star at a young age dedicate thousands of hours to training and then watch their career prospects peter out over the years. Perhaps the initial scout's assessment was wrong, or the player got injured or simply didn't have the personality to succeed. Multiple paths can lead to dead ends. Along the way, players are forced to sacrifice time with family and often end up neglecting their schoolwork. Many struggle to figure out a new path forward when a professional career doesn't work out. Of course, there can be real benefits to academy life as well: camaraderie with teammates, learning the importance of hard work, and so on. But the sting of failure can be painful and lasting. The sad reality is an industry built on dreams ends up dashing almost all of them.

What about the kids Colomer was selecting across Africa? Would they fare any better? He certainly thought so. In fact, Colomer predicted around half the kids he picked for the final tryout in Doha that first year would become professionals, 50 times the percentage that makes it from the English academy system. "Many, many names you will see in professional leagues, top leagues," he said at the time. His confidence was fueled by the fact that Football Dreams had a much larger pool of young players to choose from than any club in the world. "Look, Barcelona is selecting from a small country, Catalonia. They take one or two from Spain and a rare one from outside. In Football Dreams, we select from a continent, and a continent full of football."

Like many scouts, Colomer was sure he could sift through this vast pool to find the hidden gems because he had spent so many years hunting for talent. "A cook sees a steak and knows the flavor, level of salt, level of cooking," said Colomer. "A doctor knows symptoms in a patient. It comes from experience. It is the same for us. Our job is to anticipate the future of these talents. But like any doctor or any cook, we make mistakes."

One way Colomer tried to limit the number of mistakes was by using sports scientists to estimate the biological ages of the boys at the final tryouts in the African capitals to avoid picking players simply because they were more physically mature. This was done using the peak height velocity test, which determines the age at which a child is growing fastest. For example, the test may say a 13-year-old boy will hit peak height velocity at the age of 15, meaning he's a late maturer. Alternatively, it could say he was growing fastest at 11 years old, meaning he's an early maturer. The test is based on a boy's date of birth, height, sitting height, and weight. But using it in Africa can be challenging because it's often difficult to pin down a child's exact date of birth. Aspire required players to bring a copy of their birth certificate or a document from school, but they weren't always accurate.

The sports scientists also carried out several physical tests at both the tryouts in the capitals and in Doha. They included a 40-meter sprint; a standing vertical jump, which measures leg power; and an endurance run. Colomer didn't use this information as a primary decision-making tool since these physical traits don't have much predictive power. He might look at the data when comparing two players with a similar level of talent, especially to get an idea of their speed. But he was much more focused on technique, game intelligence, and personality. Science says that's the right strategy, but it's far from a foolproof one. Having a massive pool of players was great, but it wouldn't do Colomer any good if he picked the wrong ones.

A few days after Colomer first spotted Diawandou in Thiès, the young player headed to Dakar to compete against the other top 50 players from Senegal for the chance to go to the final in Doha. The tryout in Dakar was held at one of Senegal's largest stadiums, Léopold Sédar Senghor, named after the country's first president. The stadium is home to Senegal's national team and can pack 60,000 screaming fans into a sea of red, yellow, and green plastic seats, the colors of the country's flag.

The venue was a far cry from the dirt pitch where Colomer discovered Diawandou in Thiès, but the young player wasn't fazed. The setting actually gave Diawandou an advantage since he was used to playing on grass and wearing cleats. Many of the other players had spent most of their time on dirt fields kicking the ball around barefoot or in plastic sandals. At least one boy tried to play in borrowed cleats during the tryout and quickly switched back to sandals because he didn't feel comfortable.

Diawandou may not have been as flashy as Bernard but still impressed Colomer, especially with the composure and leadership he displayed on the pitch. From the beginning of the tryout, Diawandou took up his natural role as captain and directed the movement of players around him. Colomer wasn't the only one who was impressed. "At the end of the four-day test, all the coordinators thought Diawandou should be chosen," said his coach, Bousso Ndiaye, who attended the tryout. "All the coordinators said this boy is in the academy." And he still wasn't playing his regular position. After Diawandou's performance in the first tryout, Colomer continued to play him in central defense, even though at roughly five and a half feet, he was far from the tallest player on the field. Senegal sometimes feels like an entire population of NBA players since so many people are strikingly tall.

Despite this disadvantage, Diawandou felt confident he would be one of the three players to make it to Doha. That wasn't what he sensed from many of the others. They were never far away because the players all stayed in spartan rooms inside the stadium complex during the tryout. "I heard people saying, 'Hey, this guy is very good, huh?'" said Diawandou. "You know that means they weren't having so much confidence to believe they can make it." He felt just the opposite. Football Dreams seemed like destiny. "Over the four days, I believed I would make it because this dream needs to come true," he said. "I needed to make it because this is my time."

It was indeed. The Football Dreams staff would normally wait several days after the tryout is over to notify the players who have been selected to go to the final in Doha. That was true for the other Senegalese boys who made the cut and received calls after they returned home. But Colomer didn't wait to tell Diawandou. "When the tryout finished, Colo told me, 'Don't go, stay,'" said Diawandou. "The other players were leaving, but he told me they picked me to go to the tryout." Diawandou didn't want to brag, so he didn't tell anyone when he got home. He waited for the Football Dreams staff to call his family. "It was amazing in the house that day," said Diawandou. "Everybody was happy, saying I wish you good luck, I know you love football and can succeed."

When the day finally rolled around for Diawandou to travel to Qatar, he celebrated with his family and half a dozen friends at his home in Thiès. They tucked into a large bowl of chicken yassa and then played a pickup game on the dirt street outside in the harsh afternoon sun, pinging the ball against the concrete walls of surrounding homes. After the game, a friend who was an especially devout Muslim stopped Diawandou in the street to offer him a special prayer to protect travelers. The two stood face to face, heads bowed, hands out, palms turned to the sky. When his friend finished praying, he smiled, shook Diawandou's hand, and wished him good luck in Doha.

CHAPTER 3

The Target

Soccer players come in all sizes—small, medium, and large. With Bernard and Diawandou, Colomer had checked the first two boxes, small and medium. No surprise there. Many of the game's greatest players sit in those same boxes: Maradona at five feet, five inches; Messi at five feet, seven inches; and Pelé at five feet, eight inches. But there's also no denying the potential value of a classic target man, a big striker who can manhandle opposing defenders, hold up the ball for his teammates, and rain in goals himself. Think of Didier Drogba at six feet, two inches, or Zlatan Ibrahimović at six feet, five inches.

With those images in mind, it's no mystery why the Football Dreams scouts liked what they saw when they first laid eyes on Ibrahima Dramé in the sleepy town of Ziguinchor in southern Senegal. He was already nearly six feet tall, had a nose for goal, and a level of self-confidence that matched or even exceeded his height. But that wasn't always the case. When Ibrahima first showed up at his neighborhood soccer school as an 8-year-old, the coach told him he couldn't play. He was too small and might get hurt, the coach said. But that didn't stop Ibrahima. He hadn't yet grown, but his confidence was already Size Large. And for him, soccer was the ticket out of a life already defined by hardship.

Ibrahima's father, Moussa, came to Ziguinchor from neighboring Gambia when he was around 18 years old, hoping to make enough money to escape from Africa to Europe. He took a job in Ziguinchor's small port, carrying sacks of rice and other supplies to the long wooden boats that make their way along the mighty Casamance River that runs alongside the town. Many are brightly painted in the colors of Senegal's flag, red, yellow, and green. With over 300,000 people, Ziguinchor is the largest town in Casamance, the area of southern Senegal separated from the rest of the country by the Gambia. The town was once an important colonial outpost for the Portuguese and French, but economic growth has slowed considerably in recent years, partly because of a decades-long separatist insurgency that racked Casamance, now one of the poorest regions of Senegal.

Whitewashed colonial buildings that sprang up near the river long ago have since crumbled and grown dark with grime, giving Ziguinchor the feel of a faded postcard. A stack of old red roof tiles made in Bordeaux sits in the dirt next to one building. It's easy to imagine French soldiers sitting on the veranda years earlier, sipping wine as the sun set over the river. Dotted with palm trees and bright red and purple bougainvillea, Ziguinchor feels much more tropical than the concrete jungles of Dakar and Thiès. That's true even as you move away from the river toward the more densely populated part of town, where the red dirt roads are lined with poorly constructed concrete homes often set behind walls made of rusted sheets of metal. Life moves at a more languid pace than in Senegal's other big cities, and birds can still be heard chirping in the trees. Even at the town's port, fishermen seem in no hurry as they haul in their catch or sit and mend their nets. Pods of river dolphins occasionally break the surface of the water nearby.

Ibrahima's father eventually gave up his job at the port and acquired a wooden pushcart, which he used to eke out a meager living transporting goods around town. He also met Ibrahima's mother, Oumou, and the short stay he had planned in Ziguinchor became permanent when the two married. But the marriage didn't last. They divorced when Ibrahima was around 7 years old, leaving his mother with the difficult task of trying to scrape together enough money to raise him and his three siblings. His father used everything he earned to support his second wife and their many kids.

Only months after the two separated, life got even harder for Ibrahima's mother. The small mud house she was living in with her kids collapsed after a heavy rain, and they had to move in with her own mother, all sleeping in a single room made from crude concrete blocks. They cooked meals on a coal stove outside, shielded from the elements by a few rusted sheets of metal held up by a slender wooden pole. To make a little money, Ibrahima's mother set up a table beside a nearby road to sell mangoes and small plastic bags of peanuts. "It was very difficult for me to raise Ibrahima and his brothers by myself," said his mother, who often has trouble holding back tears when reliving the memory.

Ibrahima's brother, Sekou, was only about 12 years old at the time but felt like he needed to do something to help since he was the oldest son. Against his mother's wishes, he dropped out of school so he could work with the fishermen at the port and ended up earning enough money to buy the family basic goods like rice and cooking oil. Sekou insisted Ibrahima stay in class, even though his school, housed in a run-down French military barracks, was nothing to write home about. Ibrahima mostly listened to his brother, although as he got older, he occasionally skipped school as well so he could go down to the port and help the family. "It was so difficult, but that's life in Africa," said Ibrahima. "Your family doesn't have power, you go fight for them."

When Ibrahima wasn't in school or skipping class to work, he was playing soccer. He started playing barefoot in the courtyard of his family's home, running around with his brothers and whatever they could come up with for a ball, usually rags or plastic bags tied together with string. His mother would sit in the shade and watch the kids dribble around plastic laundry tubs under lines filled with drying clothes. As Ibrahima got older, his obsession with soccer only increased. His mother could barely get him to sit down for a meal without hearing protests that he didn't have time because he needed to be out on the field improving his game. She couldn't even get him to stop playing when he was sick and should be recovering in bed rather than running around in Ziguinchor's heat and suffocating humidity. "I would tell him to stop playing football, and he would say, 'No, it's my life,'" said his mother.

Luckily for Ibrahima, he had an uncle, Amadou Traoré, who lived around the corner and decided to start one of Africa's many informal neighborhood soccer schools. The kids trained on an uneven dirt field in front of a local primary school, where they lashed the ball past rickety wooden goalposts while trying to avoid a large pair of trees that dominated one side of the pitch and a concrete building that jutted into the other. Boys who weren't playing sat in a row on a concrete walkway outside the school or perched themselves on a wall on the opposite side of the pitch, their skinny legs dangling over the edge. Girls wearing brightly colored dresses and long, flowing headscarves sometimes got pinned against the wall by the run of play as they tried to cut through the field.

Ibrahima showed up at Traoré's soccer school one afternoon when he was 8 years old and demanded to play, but his uncle told him he wasn't big enough yet and would have to sit and watch. Ibrahima unhappily took a seat and kept his eye on the game. After a few minutes, he marched back over and defiantly told Traoré he was better than the kids on the field. Once again, his uncle told him to

Ibrahima (right) posing with a teammate from his soccer school in Ziguinchor.

sit down. "He said, 'You are so small. You cannot play football here. They are going to hurt you,'" said Ibrahima. This time Ibrahima simply ignored him and took the field. Even though he was playing in cheap plastic sandals, not proper soccer cleats like many of the boys, he quickly proved his uncle wrong. "Once he saw how I was playing, he said, 'OK, you can come train,'" said Ibrahima. Even at that age, he was a natural goal scorer and would go on to become the best player the school ever produced.

Years later, when Aspire contacted Traoré to work as a Football Dreams coordinator and told him the academy was looking for the best 13-year-old boys Senegal had to offer, he knew exactly which kid had the best chance of making the cut. This was 2008, the second year of Qatar's massive talent search. Ibrahima had grown like a weed and was no longer the little kid who first showed up at Traoré's school. He now stood nearly six feet tall and was lanky and strong. Traoré asked Ibrahima to give the tryout a shot, and he agreed, even though he had never heard of Qatar.

But when the day of the tryout arrived, Traoré looked around the sandy public field in Ziguinchor where it was being held and saw no sign of the young boy. "Where on earth could he be?" thought Traoré. "This was the chance of a lifetime." It turned out a friend had borrowed Ibrahima's cleats, and he was frantically trying to track him down so he could use them at the tryout. He finally succeeded and took off at a sprint to make it to the field before the tryout ended.

Traoré was relieved to see him run through the gap in the concrete wall that surrounded the field and pressed Ibrahima to throw on his cleats and jersey as quickly as possible. The striker did as he was told and didn't disappoint when he took the pitch. He quickly scored two goals and caught the attention of the Spanish scout who had traveled to Ziguinchor to watch the tryout while Colomer was holding trials elsewhere in Senegal. "The scout told me he hadn't seen talent like this anywhere in the country," said Traoré. There was little doubt Ibrahima would be headed to Dakar in a few days' time to compete against the top players found across Senegal for a chance to attend the final tryout in Qatar.

Colomer may not have been at Ibrahima's initial tryout in Ziguinchor, but he had been to the town before. In fact, it was where he first dreamed up the idea for a massive talent search in Africa while working as Barcelona's youth director. Colomer traveled to Senegal in 2005 on a pair of fateful scouting trips at the invitation of Lamine Savané, the gregarious son of a government minister who was working as a sports agent in Dakar. The two of them traveled to several of Senegal's major cities, where Savané arranged a series of games so Colomer could look for talented young players. It was an eye-opening experience.

During one of the sessions in Dakar, Colomer spotted a kid named Serigne Abdou Thiam who hadn't even reached his teens but wowed the Spanish scout against a group of much older, bigger players. Colomer invited him to Barcelona to play a tournament with one of the club's youth teams. The team won, and Serigne Abdou was a big reason why, said Savané. That got Colomer thinking about what kind of talent he could find for Barcelona in Senegal if he could cast his net even wider. "Savané put around 50 players in front of me, and I found one who was very good," said Colomer. "I started to think to myself that if among 50 players, there is one very good player, what can happen with 1 million players?"

But it was the second trip to Senegal that really got the creative juices flowing. Colomer and Savané made the long journey south from Dakar to Ziguinchor. They stopped at several cities along the way, and Colomer grew more and more impressed by the level of talent. Senegalese kids from the ages of 13 to 20 zipped around in front of him trying to catch his eye. "When Colomer came, he was like, 'Wow!' He was even more impressed than expected," said Savané, who would later become the Senegal country director for Football Dreams.

Of course, Colomer knew there was talent in Africa before he got on the plane. He only needed to look as far as the Camp Nou, where the Cameroonian Samuel Eto'o helped Barcelona win the league in 2005 with 25 goals. It wasn't the fact there was talent in Senegal that impressed Colomer, it was the sheer quantity of it. "I saw the potential of the players there," said Colomer. "It was amazing."

Colomer witnessed this firsthand because he was doing something that most European scouts weren't: traveling outside Dakar looking for skilled young players. Most stuck to Africa's capitals, if they came at all, and were often shown older players at the major clubs. Or they relied on tournaments where Africa's youth national teams played. There were a couple reasons for this. Traveling across Africa as Colomer was doing was difficult and took both time and money. Also, transferring players under the age of 18 to Europe from Africa and other countries wasn't easy. FIFA had placed extensive restrictions on the practice, although they weren't ironclad. Many European clubs pushed the boundaries on the rules or simply broke them. That would get some into trouble later, including Barcelona.

One of FIFA's goals was to crack down on the illicit trade in young players by unscrupulous agents in Africa. They regularly dupe under-age kids by claiming they can get tryouts with top European clubs in exchange for money and then disappear with the cash. Those who do make it to Europe often find themselves abandoned when the tryouts fail to materialize or they don't make the team. Some end up living on the streets, either because they don't have the money to go home or can't face the prospect of returning a failure. It's a tragedy for them and their families, who often pay thousands of dollars in the hope that their son will be the next Drogba. FIFA has tightened its restrictions over time, but it hasn't stopped this abuse.

Some in the soccer world have criticized FIFA's rules as being too heavy-handed, saying they are preventing young African players from getting a chance to train with reputable European clubs. It's often extremely difficult for an 18-year-old African kid to slot into a major European team because he hasn't received the same level of training as players from that club's academy, who have spent years practicing there.

There aren't that many high-quality academies in Africa offering the kind of training a player might find in Europe. The most famous is run by Ivory Coast's top club, ASEC Mimosas, which produced stars like Yaya and Kolo Touré. Others include Diambars and Generation Foot in Senegal and Right to Dream in Ghana. The shortage of top-notch academies is mainly driven by a lack of resources, a problem exacerbated by corruption at all levels of African soccer.

Several European clubs have set up their own academies in Africa over the years, but many have failed. Critics say the missing ingredient was often adequate knowledge of the local soccer scene and how much it differed from Europe. The absence of a large academy infrastructure helps explain why only four of the *Guardian's* top 60 young players worldwide in 2017 were from Africa. It has also contributed to the failure of African teams to live up to expectations on the international stage.

Pelé famously predicted in 1977 that an African nation would win the World Cup by the year 2000. It probably seemed like a safe bet given the continent's passion for soccer, the number of kids playing in the street, and their motivation to use the sport to improve their lives. But it hasn't happened. The farthest African teams have gotten in the tournament is to the quarter-finals: Cameroon in 1990, Senegal in 2002, and Ghana in 2010. What's driving this underperformance? Simon Kuper and Stefan Szymanski looked at this question in their book *Soccernomics.* "To win at sports, you need to find, develop and nurture talent," they wrote. "Doing that requires money, know-how, and some kind of administrative infrastructure. Few African countries have any."

Most African kids train at the thousands of informal soccer schools that dot neighborhoods across Africa, under the guidance of coaches who often have no formal training and very few resources. The situation at major African clubs can be somewhat better, but they haven't historically targeted kids much younger than 16 years old. Also, these clubs can miss talented young players who live outside the major cities where the clubs are located because youth soccer in Africa is much less organized than in Europe.

Savané and his partner George Sagna, who was one of the first Senegalese to play professional soccer in Europe, realized all this. They knew that if European teams wanted to see the real talent Senegal had to offer, they must look at younger players outside the major clubs. They believed that if they traveled across Senegal to look for talented young kids, especially at the small soccer schools that dot almost every neighborhood, they would find undiscovered gems who could be trained to play at the highest levels in Europe. "The best players are playing on their local teams or their school teams, not necessarily in the clubs," said Savané.

These were the kids they were showcasing for Colomer in Ziguinchor and other cities across the country. But they were operating with very limited resources. In essence, the process consisted of Sagna tapping his contacts around the country for talented players and then traveling personally to see them. Colomer wondered what would happen if they went much bigger, canvassing the country in an organized fashion to uncover the best young kids Senegal had to offer. If he had been impressed by the players assembled by Savané in a piecemeal fashion, imagine what they would find if they left no stone unturned. "If you have the chance to find the best young kid in Senegal, he must be unbelievably good! Imagine if you got to see all of them!" said Savané.

Colomer's mind was spinning with the possibilities of what he had seen as he jumped into the car in Ziguinchor for the 12-hour return trip to Dakar. He chatted excitedly with Savané and Sagna as they made their way along bumpy, rutted roads. They passed through the lush green landscape of the southern Casamance region, cut through the Gambia, which juts into Senegal like a crooked smile, and made their way past the many baobab trees that dot the road to Dakar. They likely passed barefoot kids playing soccer in the dirt beneath their nubby branches. Along the way, they mapped out a blueprint of what it would take to conduct a blanket talent search in the country.

Upon arrival in Dakar, Colomer took a short rest at his hotel before reuniting with Savané for a grilled fish dinner at the city's most famous live music venue, Just 4 U. "Even in the car from the hotel to dinner, Colomer was saying, 'We have to find a way to do this! It would be unbelievable!'" Savané said. They arrived to find the joint jumping. Dakar is a musical hothouse and has produced one of Africa's biggest stars, Youssou N'Dour. The distinctive mbalax music he popularized in the 1970s, combining percussive Senegalese drumming with jazz, soul, and rock, has spread far beyond this concrete metropolis nestled next to the Atlantic.

But Colomer and Savané weren't focused on the music. They were captivated by their scouting idea. "We were crazy excited!" said Savané. They stayed out until 2 a.m. talking, raising their voices to be heard over the music. At one point, Savané got worried they were simply indulging in fantasy. "I said to Colomer, 'Take it easy. Maybe we are just dreaming and don't know what we're saying. We have to find someone to talk to, explain, and get feedback,'" said Savané. They ran the idea past Savané's father, Senegal's industrial minister, the next day at lunch to make sure they weren't crazy. "My father said, 'No, it's not crazy. There is existing demand, but some talent is being missed,'" Savané said.

What Senegal and many other African countries lacked was the organization and resources to fully tap into this talent pool. Colomer and Savané had addressed the first issue by coming up with a blueprint for the process. But it was unclear where they could get the resources. At this point, they were just focused on Senegal. Extending the talent search across Africa seemed too outlandish to even contemplate. The only groups that seemed to have the cash that would be needed were major European clubs like Barcelona. But it was unclear if the plan was too ambitious even for them. Plus, they might be excluded from doing it altogether because of FIFA's restrictions.

As Colomer boarded his flight back to Barcelona, the dream seemed like it might be out of reach. "We assumed we couldn't get the money," said Savané. "You were conditioned to thinking this is so expensive that it wouldn't make sense."

A fabulously wealthy Qatari sheikh would soon take care of that problem. He had seemingly endless riches but not the talented young soccer players necessary to assemble the kind of world-class national team he had always envisioned. Soon their paths would cross, and Colomer would discover that there was indeed someone rich and ambitious enough to carry out a program as massive as Football Dreams.

In the spring of 2008, a few years after Colomer made his Qatari connection, the big striker Ibrahima jumped into a car with a local coach for the 12-hour drive from Ziguinchor to Diawandou's old academy in Thiès. That's where Colomer was holding the tryout for the top 50 players found in Senegal during the second year of Football Dreams. Ibrahima began raining in goals as soon as he arrived and was certain before the final Senegal trial was even over that he was headed to the last tryout, in Doha. "The final was so easy for me because everybody knew they were going to pick me," said Ibrahima. That included the kids he was competing against who approached him in the cafeteria between sessions. "They would say, 'Don't worry, they already picked you,'" said Ibrahima. "They told me that I was the best."

Making it into Aspire would be life changing for Ibrahima. The families of the boys who entered the academy received a stipend of several thousand dollars a year. That money would take the burden off Ibrahima's mother and older brother and could, of course, be a tiny prelude to the riches he would earn if he made it to a top European club.

Not long before Ibrahima left for Doha, he heard that his brother Sekou was thinking about taking a risky journey to Spain to find a better job to support the family. At the time, thousands of West Africans were using small wooden boats with single outboard motors to cross the Atlantic to the Canary Islands, located off the coast of Morocco. Hundreds had already died when their boats capsized, and Ibrahima told his brother it wasn't worth the risk now that he had the chance to join Aspire. "Ibrahima told me, 'Don't go,'" his brother said. "'I'm going to the tryout now. I think when I'm at the academy everything will change for the family.'"

That was the dream of all the boys Colomer plucked off dirt fields across Africa and took to Doha. They were different sizes and played different positions, had different skills and personalities, came from different countries and backgrounds. But all hoped Football Dreams would be a life-changing opportunity. Diawandou and Bernard would get the first shot, along with the other boys found during the first year of Football Dreams. Ibrahima would soon follow.

PART TWO
TRAINEES

CHAPTER 4

The Academy

With its smoothly curved walls and high-tech metallic sheen, Aspire Academy looks like a giant futuristic space station that somehow ended up on Earth. It radiates a brilliant royal blue and cool gray, the academy's official colors, which seem especially intense in Doha's bright desert sunlight. Even major clubs like Bayern Munich and Manchester United that come to train at Aspire are often dazzled by its facilities, especially the academy's signature feature: a massive air-conditioned sports dome marketed as the largest of its kind in the world. The dome is about the width of the Eiffel Tower lying on its side and required more steel to build than the iconic French landmark, about 7,000 tons. Its 290,000 square meters of floor space house an Olympic-size swimming pool, a regulation soccer field, an athletics track, eleven tennis courts, and many other sports facilities.

The complex, which took thousands of workers two years to build, also includes upscale dorm rooms to house athletes and classrooms where they attend school. It cost a reported $1.3 billion, almost twice what Arsenal paid to build its 60,000-seat Emirates Stadium in London at about the same time. Over the years, the Aspire complex has grown to include two five-star hotels, one of which looks

A youth team from Manchester City playing a match at Aspire in Doha, with the academy's massive dome and the five-star Torch hotel looming in the background.

like a giant torch; a top sports science hospital; a 40,000-seat stadium; a luxury mall; and six outdoor soccer fields. The green spaces and running trails that surround the complex make Aspire a welcome oasis amid the sand, asphalt, and concrete that make up much of Doha's landscape. Speakers across the campus even pipe in the sounds of birds chirping throughout the day.

The first time Diawandou walked into Aspire's dome, he decided that even if he wasn't one of the players chosen to train at the academy, he wanted to be buried there. "I looked up and thought, 'This is amazing!'" said Diawandou. "I never saw anything like this in my life. This facility, if you don't play football here, you need to die here!"

Diawandou wasn't alone. All the Football Dreams kids found the scene that greeted them in Doha to be mesmerizing. Their first glimpse came as they descended into the city's airport. Below them, a forest of ultramodern skyscrapers blanketed the coastline. The buildings' curved lines and varied geometric forms make them look like some sort of giant urban art installation. At night, they're lit up like Las Vegas with flashing red, blue, and gold lights. For the kids, it was like staring into the future, a sensation both wonderful and disorienting. Doha often had that effect, even on Qatar's own citizens, especially the ones who were old enough to remember what the country looked like only a few generations earlier. Back then, it was nothing more than an impoverished patch of desert dotted with crumbling mud homes that had no plumbing or electricity and very little access to fresh water. The leap from that to one of the richest countries in the world had occurred in a historical blink of an eye.

Modern-day Qatar, a finger of sand jutting into the Persian Gulf, didn't even have permanent settlements until well into the nineteenth century. The country's future rulers migrated from the vast central desert area of what is now Saudi Arabia. Qatar was technically under control of the Ottoman Empire until the early twentieth century, but it was a restless territory, and the Ottomans vied with the British for influence in the region. Pirates holed up in Doha regularly attacked ships in the Gulf, angering the Brits, who bombarded the town in retaliation. Despite these periodic disputes, the local ruler signed a treaty with Britain in 1916 that placed Qatar under the country's protection.

But life for Qatar's small population was difficult. There were only about 20,000 people in the country toward the end of the nineteenth century. Most of them lived in modern-day Doha on the peninsula's eastern coast. They relied on pearling or fishing to make a living. Large wooden boats with high, V-shaped hulls lined the beach in town. Their edges had distinctive grooves worn by the ropes pearl divers tied around their waists before jumping in the water. It was tough work and not very profitable.

The locals lived in small, dingy mud homes huddled closely together on narrow, winding dirt alleyways. They fetched water from brackish wells in the desert using bags made out of goatskin. The center of activity in Doha was the marketplace, Souq Waqif, where fishermen went to sell their catch. Bedouins who lived in the desert also came to the market to buy and sell camels, as well as camel hair carpets and blankets.

Life got even tougher in the 1920s and 1930s. The Japanese perfected the ability to grow cultured pearls, and the bottom fell out of the market. The worldwide economic depression that struck at about the same time made matters even worse. These were the "years of hunger" that the oldest Qataris still remember. Poverty forced many people to leave the peninsula or live in dire conditions. Even Qatar's ruler at the time struggled. He was forced to take out a mortgage on his house in 1935 to cover a debt of 17,000 Indian rupees. But the country's fortunes were about to shift.

Qatar signed its first oil concession later that same year with the Anglo-Persian Oil Company. Workers finally struck crude in 1939, but the country didn't begin exports until 10 years later because of World War II. The pace of change was slow at first. People in Doha still didn't have electricity, telephones, or adequate clean water in the early 1950s. The weekly plane that brought the mail often didn't bother to land. It would circle two or three times and drop its load by parachute. Even when the mail did come, there were only about 600 Qataris who could read. But the oil money eventually began to have an impact. The country built roads, schools, and a desalination plant to produce clean water. It also said goodbye to the British when it declared independence in 1971.

But it wasn't oil that drove Qatar's dizzying transformation from a penniless backwater to a nation of mind-boggling wealth. It was natural gas. Qatar's oil reserves aren't that big compared to many of its Gulf neighbors. But the country does have the third largest natural gas reserves in the world, enough to heat all U.S. homes for more than a century. Most of that gas is located in one large field off Qatar's northeastern coast that covers an area nearly the size of the country itself. It shares the field with neighboring Iran. The winds of change really picked up speed in the 1990s when Qatar began to export liquefied natural gas. Its largest tankers are each the size of an aircraft carrier and can hold enough gas to heat every home in the United Kingdom for a day. Those shipments made Qatar the largest exporter of liquefied natural gas in the world and sent the nation's wealth soaring.

Qatar's oil and gas sales regularly generate over $100 billion a year, a significant amount given the country only has a population of about 2 million people. Its average income per person (GDP per capita) is around $100,000, one of the highest in the world. That's close to double U.S. GDP per capita and over a hundred times greater than the level in many of the African countries targeted by Football Dreams. But GDP per capita doesn't really capture Qatar's true level of wealth because the state only has about 300,000 citizens. The rest of the population is mostly composed of poor migrant laborers who hardly receive any state benefits. Qatar's GDP per citizen is closer to $700,000. That's over 10 times higher than the equivalent figure in the U.S. Qatar's staggering leap in wealth prompted the U.S. Embassy in Doha to write a cable in 2008 saying, "Qatar will soon—literally—have more money than it knows what to do with."

That wealth has transformed Doha. Gone are the crumbling mud homes of pearl divers that once dotted the city's coastline. Gleaming skyscrapers now stand in their place, and construction cranes, ready to build more, poke their skinny heads into the sky across the city. The towers rise on the backs of South Asian men who often live and work in terrible conditions. They're filled with white-collar workers from the United States and Europe who are responsible for building the country's foundations in a different way. As for the Qataris themselves, the country's cradle-to-grave welfare system means they don't have to work that hard at all.

Outside the city's skyscraper forest, Doha feels like a rambling ode to poured concrete. Vast gated communities catering to white-collar expats are filled with identikit, two-story villas. Those owned by Qataris are often three or four times larger and are built with elaborate facades. Fleets of white Toyota Land Cruisers, the Qatari vehicle of choice, dominate Doha's notoriously clogged streets. Ferraris and Maseratis are popular as well. They buzz between opulent five-star hotels and palatial malls filled with stores like Gucci and Valentino. In fact, much of the city feels like a duty-free shop in a modern airport. Luxury brands, a nice display, but a bit soulless.

Even the parts of the city that are supposed to look old are new, like Souq Waqif. The government completely renovated the market so it looks historic but posh. A group of men in traditional Arab dress are paid to ride white horses back and forth through the souq, past patrons sipping tea and smoking shisha at outdoor tables. It may seem artificial, but it's certainly better than the real version of that life Qataris were living only a few decades earlier. The locals definitely aren't hungry and scrounging for pearls anymore. They're buying them.

Qatar's newfound riches have dramatically transformed its place in the world as well. People used to joke that the country was best known for not being known at all. But the emir who presided over Qatar's massive increase in wealth, Sheikh Hamad bin Khalifa Al Thani, wanted to change that and spent billions of dollars to raise the country's global profile. One of the first things he did was launch Al Jazeera in 1996, and it quickly became the most important news service in the Arab world. Qatar also engaged in a flurry of international mediation efforts in places like Libya, Lebanon, and Yemen; snapped up some of the world's most iconic businesses and valuable real estate, like Harrods department store in London and Europe's tallest skyscraper, the Shard; and became one of the world's biggest buyers of art, spending hundreds of millions of dollars on works by major artists ranging from Paul Cézanne to Damien Hirst.

These were certainly effective ways to attract attention, but media, politics, business, and the arts weren't enough. What Qatar's rulers truly craved was success in the world's most popular game. Soccer offered a route to market the country to billions of people around the globe in a way that could transcend differences in politics, culture, and religion. In fact, to many people, the sport is a religion. It offers its own culture, and the only politics that matter are which team you support. Qatar's rulers knew that if the country could make a splash in international soccer, the rest of the world was bound to stand up and take notice. Aspire Academy and Football Dreams fit squarely into that vision.

Aspire was the brainchild of one of Qatar's richest and most powerful men, Sheikh Jassim bin Hamad Al Thani, son of the emir who had transformed the country. Sheikh Jassim was slated to follow in his father's footsteps, but the two couldn't have been more different, even down to their looks. A portly mountain of a man with a bushy black mustache, Sheikh Hamad looked as much like the Hollywood version of a powerful Arab ruler as his son did the dashing young prince. Sheikh Jassim's square jaw, perfectly trimmed beard, and tall, slim figure gave him movie-star looks. Also, unlike his father, the reserved, soft-spoken sheikh didn't want to spend his time tending to matters of state. Soccer, not politics, was his true passion. He renounced the throne in 2003 at the age of 24 and threw himself into the game in a way few others could.

Sheikh Jassim (center) and his father, Sheikh Hamad (left), standing before a soccer match in Doha.

There's a story told in Doha that illustrates just how passionate Sheikh Jassim is about soccer. He was battling insomnia several years ago and summoned a doctor to the palace. When the doctor arrived, the reason for his lack of sleep was immediately clear: rows of television sets covering the wall, all tuned to soccer day and night. The doctor told him to turn off the televisions and his insomnia would be cured. The story might be complete fiction, but the fact that it's told at all is revealing.

Sheikh Jassim didn't just watch soccer. He played as well, and not just anywhere. He had a private, perfectly manicured pitch hidden away within the royal palace complex in Doha. The field is regulation size but seems small compared to the palaces around it. At least a half dozen of them are set amid elaborate gardens filled with palm trees and trickling fountains. Elegant horseshoe arches typical of Islamic architecture grace the palace facades. Inside, ornate Persian carpets and oversized crystal chandeliers fill cavernous rooms the size of tennis courts. Paintings by Manet and Chagall hang on the walls. Servants attired in traditional white robes and headdresses attend to the royals and their guests. They serve lobsters the size of small dogs and tea out of gracefully curved, golden pots.

Sheikh Jassim was used to this kind of luxury. Qatar's oil and gas riches meant he had more money than he could likely spend in a lifetime. The emir enjoys absolute control in the country, and there's no real difference between his family's bank account and the state treasury. "Qatar is a family business with a seat at the United Nations," a former U.S. ambassador once said. But Sheikh Jassim didn't have the one thing he truly wanted: a national soccer team that could compete on the international stage. Qatar had never qualified for a World Cup, and he wanted to change that. The odds were definitely against him. No state with so few citizens had ever made it to the tournament.

Qatar didn't have much soccer history either. Foreign oil workers first brought the sport to the country in the late 1940s. They played in the sand near the western city of Dukhan, where the first well was located, and reportedly used oil to line the field. The country officially started its league in 1973, but relatively few Qataris played. Soccer had to compete with traditional sports like camel racing and falconry. Many players in the league were from other Middle Eastern countries and the Indian subcontinent, definitely not soccer powerhouses. Over time, soccer became the most popular sport in the country, but that mainly meant locals watching European games on TV. There were still relatively few Qataris who played or watched the country's mediocre clubs. These teams often competed in front of a couple hundred fans in gleaming stadiums built for much larger crowds, even after the government pumped millions of dollars into the league in the early 2000s to attract aging stars like Pep Guardiola, the former captain of Barcelona who would go on to become the club's most successful coach in history.

These certainly weren't the ingredients to produce a world-class

Qatari soccer team. But the country did have plenty of cash. Could it simply buy one? Qatar certainly tried. The nation offered three Brazilian players reportedly more than a million dollars in 2004 to play for Qatar in the 2006 World Cup. All three played in Germany, and one was the top scorer in the Bundesliga at the time. None had previous connections with Qatar. The move prompted a rebuke from FIFA and caused the organization to tighten its rules on players switching nationalities. But that didn't stop Qatar from naturalizing players. When the country surprisingly won the 2006 Asian Games, its best players were a Uruguayan striker, a Senegalese defender, and a Senegalese goalkeeper.

But Sheikh Jassim had a different idea. Could Qatar train its own world-class soccer players by building a state-of-the-art academy and recruiting the best coaches and sports scientists? There were certainly significant obstacles. Qatar's local population is not only one of the smallest in the world, it's also one of the most overweight. Nearly half of Qatari adults and adolescents are obese, according to government studies. Physical activity is often kept to a minimum, with servants catering to their every need and Toyota Land Cruisers whisking them wherever they need to go. Qatar's lack of soccer culture didn't help either. Many boys in Argentina grow up dreaming of becoming Messi. It wasn't the same in Qatar. Becoming a professional soccer player in the country wasn't seen as very glamorous.

None of this deterred Sheikh Jassim. He had billions to spend and wanted to see how far that could take him. The sheikh also wanted his academy to capture the world's attention. Money could certainly do that. For the international launch of Aspire in 2005, the academy hired Cirque du Soleil acrobats, kung fu fighting Shaolin monks, and two of the greatest soccer players in history, Pelé and Diego Maradona. They put on a show for Qatar's royal family and 120 international journalists under Aspire's massive air-conditioned dome. Not surprisingly, headlines followed. The organizers even

handed out $15,000 gold medals to VIP guests that were designed
by the French mint that makes the ones for the Olympics.

But splashing out cash on eye-catching buildings, celebrity guests,
and pricey mementos was the easy part. Now Aspire somehow had
to produce a world-class soccer team. A big part of that challenge fell
to Andreas Bleicher, a steely, angular German with a buzz cut who
was hired as Aspire's sports director. He was responsible for sports
science and talent identification, among other things. Before joining
Aspire, Bleicher worked as a director at the German Sport University
in Cologne and at one of the country's Olympic training centers.

One of his first tasks at Aspire was trying to figure out just how
much young soccer talent there was in Qatar, so he held tryouts for
basically every young boy in the country. At least that's one benefit
of Qatar's size. They could test everyone. There were only a few
thousand boys in each class at school, and only a little over 2,000
registered soccer players in the whole country. That's the equivalent
of a few Manhattan city blocks. Slim pickings.

Not surprisingly, Bleicher only found a small handful of Qatari
kids in each age group who he thought had the potential to become
decent national players in the future. That wasn't good enough
because those players weren't challenged by the other kids their age,
thus stunting their development. They also lacked the motivation to
work hard since they were better than everyone else. Imagine young
Messi trying to develop into a world-class player by only competing
against kids his age on the Pacific island nation of Vanuatu, and you
get the idea. Bleicher tried to address the problem by inviting top
youth teams from around the world, like Arsenal and Ajax, to play
against the Qataris, but that wasn't enough because the competition
was intermittent.

Bleicher realized he needed a larger pool of players if Sheikh Jassim's multibillion-dollar experiment was going to work. "We thought
it would be better to increase the quality by integrating better play-

ers with very high motivation and the ability to be role models for our kids," said Bleicher. They could bring the players to Aspire on scholarships, and they would provide the kind of competition the Qataris needed to improve.

The country was certainly no stranger to using migrant workers to build its future. But where should they go to find the players? Ideally, it would be a place that was the polar opposite of Qatar. Somewhere with a large population of incredibly fit, highly motivated kids who spent most of their time playing street soccer, weren't getting the formal training they needed to develop, and were poor enough that they would jump at the opportunity to come to Aspire with the hope of becoming professionals and transforming their lives. It didn't take much digging to realize that many places in Africa fit the bill.

When Aspire began its African recruitment, Bleicher and others simply reached out to contacts they had on the continent to find kids. They brought their first African player to the academy in the fall of 2005, a powerful defender from the town of Obuasi in southern Ghana, the site of one of the largest gold mines in the world. John Benson had loved soccer since he was a young child, when he would ride on his mother's back carrying a small ball in his hand. His father worked in the mine, but there were periods when he was out of work, making life tough for John and his three siblings. They all lived together in a one-room house, and John spent as much time as possible outside playing soccer on a patch of grass near his home.

He impressed the local coaches enough to join an academy run by Ajax in Obuasi. It was later taken over by a local team, Ashanti Gold, when the Dutch club pulled out. The head soccer coach at Aspire, Michael Browne, knew the CEO of Ashanti Gold, Andy Sam, a retired army captain, so he called him in 2005 saying they were looking for young players. Sam agreed to help, and Aspire sent one of its coaches to Obuasi to scout players at Ashanti Gold's academy. He ended up inviting six of them, including 14-year-old John, to Doha for a trial in the fall of 2005. Sam, who would later become the Ghana country director for Football Dreams, came along as well.

It just so happened that Josep Colomer was at Aspire at the same time for an interview. Bleicher had heard he left Barcelona and contacted him about possibly leading Aspire's effort to scout foreign players. While Colomer was in Doha, officials asked him to take a look at the group of young Ghanaian players on trial. He said John was the only one who caught his eye. "I told them, look, my opinion is John Benson can stay. He has enough of a level to become a professional someday," said Colomer. "I don't think he will be a top ten player, but he can play professionally."

It was a wise choice. Aspire invited John back a few months later, and he helped lead one of the youth teams to victory in a tournament held in conjunction with the academy's international launch. The other squads were from major European clubs like Barcelona, Arsenal, and Ajax. Aspire's team may have been a year older, but it was still considered a major triumph when the academy beat Barcelona in the final. Sheikh Jassim came on the field to congratulate the players after the game, and John became the first African player to get a scholarship to Aspire.

The academy brought Colomer on board as well, and he quickly added another African player to Aspire's roster. It was Serigne Abdou Thiam, the young Senegalese boy Colomer found in Dakar in early 2005 when Lamine Savané invited him to scout players. Colomer also tried to expand Aspire's recruiting efforts to Brazil because of his connections in the country. Before joining Barcelona, he had worked with Brazil's national team coach, Luiz Felipe Scolari, during the country's winning World Cup campaign in 2002. But it was a tough sell to convince Brazilian players to move to Qatar.

One of the Aspire staff remembers asking players from a visiting Brazilian youth national team whether they would be interested in a scholarship. Even though many came from poor backgrounds in Brazil's favelas, they had one thing on their minds. "The Brazilians wanted to know whether there were women they could sleep with in Doha," said Roberto Solano, laughing at the memory. "If not, they didn't want to stay." The Brazilians weren't excited to learn that Qatar was a conservative Muslim country where sex out of wedlock was illegal. "In Brazil they may be poor, but many have a really good life," said Solano.

Colomer's initial scouting for Aspire in Africa and South America was piecemeal, but he hadn't forgotten the ambitious plan hatched with Savané over dinner and music in Dakar months earlier. They had mapped out a scheme to scout all of Senegal's players in an organized fashion, but with backing from Qatar, Colomer now thought they should aim much higher. "Josep called me up and said, 'I think there is a possibility of doing what we talked about,'" said Savané. "'But we can't just think about Senegal. We need to think about all of Africa.'"

That was the vision Colomer and Bleicher presented to Sheikh Jassim in his stately office in Doha in 2006. Given Qatar's goal of attracting the world's attention, it's perhaps no surprise that the sheikh liked the idea of carrying out the largest soccer scouting project in history. It could help achieve his dream of assembling a world-class national team, and they could pitch it as a humanitarian program helping African players. Also, if they could find and develop the sport's next superstar, it would catapult Qatar to the forefront of international soccer. Sheikh Jassim was quick to say yes, and Football Dreams was born. Aspire even brought Pelé back to Doha to announce the program's launch in April 2007 as Colomer set off across Africa to find the first class of kids.

CHAPTER 5

Final Tryout

Colomer spent a lot of time at the Doha airport in January 2008 as the players he found all over Africa trickled into the city for their three-week tryout. When Diawandou arrived, he wasn't sure where to go when he got off the plane. The airport looked like a labyrinth fit to hold the Minotaur compared to the four-gate version back in Dakar. But Diawandou came up with a solution. "If you are a little clever, you just watch the direction people are going," said Diawandou. "When I went outside, I met Colo downstairs. He said, 'You are very clever to travel by yourself and come here.'"

Bernard showed up with the other two players from Ghana who had made it to the final, Hamza Zakari and Adama Issah. When they entered the arrivals hall, they also found Colomer waiting for them. He greeted Bernard by saying he remembered watching him play back in Ghana. "I asked why," said Bernard. "He said the way I play seems like Messi." Others came from South Africa, Nigeria, Cameroon, Kenya, and Morocco, a stream of wide-eyed boys who couldn't quite believe where they were and had no idea what new wonder awaited them around the next bend.

Colomer had sifted through nearly 430,000 kids from seven

African countries to choose the best 24 players: three field players from each country and three goalies. All the kids were undoubtedly good, but Colomer needed to find out who was the best. The plan was to offer the top three players scholarships to the academy. To find out who those players were, he planned to put them up against some of the best youth teams in the world, including top Spanish clubs Real Madrid and Valencia, one of the best sides in Portugal, Porto, and even a national team from Germany. That may have seemed daunting enough for a bunch of kids who were recently running around dirt fields in Africa, but Colomer didn't think it was enough of a challenge. He was so confident that the 13-year-old African players he found were better than their European counterparts that he planned to pit them against kids who were one or two years older.

The organizers had originally contemplated turning this stage of the tryouts into a reality TV show. "Every week we would invite a different European team for them to play," said Lamine Savané, the Football Dreams country director in Senegal. "People would vote, and a certain percentage of the vote would count in the selection." Months earlier, they opened talks with a TV channel in Dubai, ART, to develop the show and came up with the name "Football Dreams," which Savané had based on the documentary "Hoop Dreams," about two teenagers from inner-city Chicago trying to make it as basketball players. But they eventually abandoned the idea because of well-founded ethical concerns about turning the hopes and dreams of African children into a TV spectacle. They did keep the Football Dreams name though.

The reality show idea may have been scrapped, but the kids were still going to take on some of the best youth players in the world while they were in Doha. Before they could do that, though, they needed to do a little adjusting to the world around them. It wasn't just Aspire's massive dome or its half dozen pristine soccer pitches that amazed them. It was also the more pedestrian things like the all-you-could-eat buffet in the academy's cafeteria, a revelation for kids who may not have grown up hungry but certainly had never experienced that kind of abundance. They discovered with delight that they could not only eat until stuffed but also could stockpile more food in their rooms for later.

The rooms themselves held wonders for the kids as well. They were similar to those you might find at an average hotel in the West but seemed luxurious to boys who grew up in much more cramped and spartan conditions back home. "Everything was perfect," recalled Yobou Thome, an Ivorian defender discovered during the second year of Football Dreams. "When I slept, everything was clean. When I went to the toilet and took a shower, my towel was clean. The TV in your room, free. I said to my family, 'Hey, this place is very nice. I don't want to come back. You stay in the Ivory Coast. Me, I stay here.'"

When the kids weren't marveling at their rooms or shoveling down food in the cafeteria, they were navigating new challenges like operating elevators and hot-water showers for the first time. "The reaction is very similar across the kids," said Wendy Kinyeki, a Football Dreams staff member from Kenya. "For most of them, this is the first time they owned a passport. It's the first time they traveled outside their village, let alone their country. They are visiting a place where streets are clean, people observe traffic rules, water comes out of taps, and there is no rationing of electricity. It's a very foreign concept for them."

The local coordinators traveling with the boys had some adjusting to do as well. One sat in his room in the dark for two days because he didn't know he had to insert his key card to operate the lights and figured Doha was experiencing power shortages. But the coordinators were just as impressed by Aspire as the boys. "The environment was fantastic," said Diawandou's old coach, Bousso Ndiaye. He soaked in Aspire's dome, its fields, and its food. But what truly blew him away was the academy's high-tech sports medicine hospital, Aspetar, the same facility that treated Ivorian star Didier Drogba when he was injured. "After visiting the hospital, I trusted that Diawandou could grow up in this academy," said Ndiaye.

All the Football Dreams kids who attend the final in Doha visit Aspetar to get a physical exam and vaccinations for diseases like polio and whooping cough. A Senegalese goalkeeper from the 2008 tryout was sent home early because they discovered he had hepatitis, reducing the group to 23 players. Other kids have been found to have more serious medical issues, like life-threatening heart problems requiring surgery.

Aspire was more spectacular than anything the Football Dreams kids could have imagined, but they needed to focus on the battle that would play out on the field to have any hope of staying. Three scholarships. That's what the Aspire staff said was up for grabs. Three spots for 23 kids, all of them bristling with talent and determined to grab an opportunity that would transform their lives. Diawandou tried to shut out the distractions from his new world by transporting himself back home. He sat on the bed in his room, headphones clamped over his ears, listening to the same Quranic music he relied on back in Thiès to center himself and get focused on game day.

But the tryout started badly for the skinny midfielder-turned-defender. He rolled his ankle at the beginning of a game against the Under-16 German national team. Diawandou was in serious pain, but the head soccer coach at Aspire, Michael Browne, told him he needed to push through to have any chance of winning a scholarship. "Coach Michael told me there was no time to get injured here, so I played with it," said Diawandou. They went on to lose the hard-fought match 2-1, but it wasn't a bad showing for a bunch of kids who had just started playing together and were hobbled by an injured central defender.

Diawandou was stuck with a bad ankle for the rest of the tryout. The trainer would tape it before every session, but it was still painful and hampered his play. He was often left out of the starting lineup for games because of the injury, but Browne was still impressed by his performance, even though he wasn't one of the tallest defenders. "He was quick, he read the game well, he can pass, he tackled, he was brave," said Browne, who previously ran the academy at the British soccer club Charlton Athletic. Browne's opinion was critical. He not only coached the boys during their tryout in Doha but also had a big say in who would receive a scholarship.

Browne was also impressed by Diawandou's determination to play through his injury and the leadership he showed among his teammates, even though he couldn't communicate with all of them that easily. Most of the kids spoke French and English since they were largely from Francophone and Anglophone countries in Africa. Diawandou grew up speaking French and Wolof and only knew rudimentary English, but always managed to get his point across. "Great kid, great attitude, he was always first class, everything he did," said Browne. "Any situation he was in, you could rely on him. In training, in matches, he wanted to make sure he was the best."

None of these comments would have surprised Diawandou's old coach, Bousso Ndiaye. They were the same qualities he noticed when Diawandou first showed up at his academy back home, prompting Ndiaye to appoint him captain. Colomer and Browne followed suit in Doha, despite Diawandou's injury. He may not have been able to perform at 100 percent, but it quickly became clear to anyone who spent time with Diawandou that the team was best off when he was at the helm. "He is a born leader," said Forewah Emmanuel, a Football Dreams staff member from Cameroon. "He is a very good example and knows when to talk to the guys. In the field, you can see how he is commanding."

Bernard also had a rough start to the tryout. He was left out of the starting lineup for the first game against Germany in favor of another small, speedy midfielder, Happy Simelela, whom Colomer found at the first field he visited in South Africa. "When they came to Ghana, I was the one they chose first," said Bernard. "So when I went to Doha and was not in the first team, I was very sad." He chalked it up to Michael Browne not having seen him play enough, but knocking Happy off his perch wasn't going to be easy. Happy was from Soweto, the sprawling black township in Johannesburg that was plagued by violence when he was growing up. His father was stabbed to death in an attempted robbery when Happy was young, an experience that hardened his character and drove him to stand up to any challenge. "Happy asked me one time, 'Why do you think I'm never afraid?'" said one of the Football Dreams staff, Ndongo Diaw. "He said, 'Maybe it's because I saw people kill my father.' He is very strong."

Happy was tough, but Bernard was just as determined to succeed and pushed himself even harder in training. "Bernard is a strong guy, mentally strong," said John Benson, the first African player Aspire recruited. He would watch the Football Dreams kids play when he had a break in his schedule and was astounded when he spotted his fellow countryman, Bernard. "When I saw him playing, I just said to my friend, 'Look at this guy, he is going to be one of the best,'" said John. "I saw the way Bernard moved, the way he passed the ball, and how seriously he was playing."

John was also impressed by another Ghanaian, Hamza Zakari, a defensive midfielder from Tema who had sublime skill but sometimes let his temper get the better of him, and by Anthony Bassey, a lightning-fast striker from southern Nigeria who had developed an amazing ability to manipulate the ball from years of juggling for money on the streets of his hometown, Uyo. But Bernard's skill left the strongest impression, and the playmaker soon won over Michael Browne, even though he was one of the smallest kids on the field.

"Bernard was technically very, very talented," said Browne. "Excellent with the ball, great in small areas, he could do anything." The days of sitting on the bench were over for Bernard. Browne shifted him into the starting lineup for the next game, one that would stand out in the players' minds for years to come.

It wasn't the opponent, FC Porto, that made the game so memorable. Nor was it the setting, the full-size pitch inside Aspire's space station–like dome. It wasn't even the result, a thrilling 3-2 victory over Porto's Under-15 side. It was the guy with shoulder-length brown hair sitting next to Colomer in the stands, dressed casually in jeans, a white button-down shirt, and black and white Adidas sneakers. Lionel Messi didn't say much but attracted everyone's attention, just as Colomer knew he would when he invited him to Aspire to meet the Football Dreams kids.

Messi even ruffled a few feathers back home to make the trip because he skipped a rehab session for a thigh injury that had sidelined him for a month. The bond between Messi and Colomer was clearly strong, and few players could inspire the African boys and attract attention to Football Dreams quite like him. The Football Dreams kids reveled at the chance to meet the Barcelona star, and Messi was quite taken by them as well. He certainly knew what it was like to be discovered at the age of 13 and was impressed by what he saw when he led the African players in a training session ahead of their game against Porto. "Aspire Academy is an astonishing facility, and the team I trained with today all have a great future in football," he said.

The Football Dreams kids made sure to grab a photo with Messi while he was there, crowding around him as he knelt on the field. The smiling star's white shirt stood out against the wall of dark blue Nike jerseys worn by the boys. Diawandou smiled as he crouched down next to Messi in the middle of the frame, his right arm resting on the star's knee. The other players spilled out around them, some

The Football Dreams kids posing with Messi at their final try-out in Doha in 2008.

of them laughing and leaning forward in an attempt to get as close to Messi as possible. But Bernard was all business. He stood as tall as his five-foot frame would let him almost directly behind the Barcelona star and cast a somber, tough-guy expression at the camera. There was work to be done on the field, and Messi's presence had further raised the stakes.

Colomer even called Bernard over as he was talking to Messi. "Colomer was telling him in Spanish, 'This is the guy I was talking about,'" said Bernard, who relied on Colomer to translate. "I heard Messi telling him I was very good but I should work hard, keep calm, and obey the coach." Those weren't the only items on Bernard's to-do list. He had also been praying to God to help him play well during the tryouts. "Sometimes when I was sleeping, I would wake up and pray to God that he should help me, that I should be the best," said Bernard. He stepped up his prayers ahead of the Porto game. At first, it was simply because it was his initial shot at the starting lineup. Now he had the added pressure of performing in front of Messi. "I prayed to God that if he ever gave me any luck in football to give it to me that day," said Bernard. "By God's grace, I had a good day."

Bernard's performance was good enough to keep him in the starting lineup for the final two games of the three-week tryout, a narrow 4-3 loss to Real Madrid's Under-15 team and a scoreless draw against Valencia's Under-15 side. The score of the last game didn't reflect how much the Football Dreams players controlled the match. "The performance of the players was nothing short of outstanding," said Michael Browne at a press conference the day after the Valencia game. "They absolutely dominated the game from start to finish, restricted the opposition's position, and proved how talented they are."

Aspire had scheduled the press conference at the end of January to announce the three players who would receive scholarships to the academy. Colomer even wore a suit for the occasion. Journalists scribbled notes as the Spanish scout stood onstage and shared anecdotes about discovering the players. He started by describing how he spotted Diawandou at his academy in Thiès, wound his way around the African continent, and concluded with the last country he visited, Morocco. As Colomer went along, he called out the names of each of the boys at the tryout, and they assembled one by one at the front of the room in matching white Nike T-shirts and blue sweatpants.

One of the most memorable stories Colomer told was about visiting the small Ghanaian town where he discovered the tall central defender, Adama Issah. Colomer arrived the night before he was scheduled to hold the tryout and couldn't quite believe what he found. "All 176 players that were supposed to be tested the next day were already waiting for me on the field," said Colomer. "I said, 'What are they doing?'" It turned out the boys had traveled from all over the area and were so intent on showcasing their skills that some had been sleeping on the field for two days.

Bernard dribbling by a pair of Valencia players at the final Football Dreams tryout in Doha in 2008.

The players' determination clearly left an impression on Colomer, but not just in that small town. He recalled how Hamza battled his way through the final tryout in Accra even though he was fasting because it was Ramadan, the holy month for Muslims. But Colomer saved his highest praise for Bernard, telling the crowd at the press conference that the little midfielder reminded him of Messi. "He is a good player, and I think he will be somebody in football," said Colomer.

Michael Browne stepped up to the podium next to describe how impressed he was that the boys had been able to coalesce into a team in such a short time. "When they arrived, my first impression of them was that individually they were very talented, but collectively they were quite poor," said Browne. "When I saw the games we were scheduled to play, against the Under-16 German national team, the Under-15 sides from Porto, Real Madrid, and Valencia, we were a bit concerned. But as time went on, the progress the boys made was exceptional. They were always good individually, but now they function very well together. Sometimes it's easy to lose track that these kids are not a team. They are 23 kids from seven different countries. For me personally, it has been a privilege to work with the boys because their application and dedication have been first class. I'm very sure many of them are going to have very successful careers in football."

This was the moment the crowd had been waiting for. With the 23 players assembled at the front of the room, journalists who had flown to Qatar for the press conference prepared for Browne to announce the names of the three winners. The boys stood together in their matching Nike outfits and cast determined looks at the TV cameras in the front row, each seeming confident that he would be one of the chosen few to stay at the academy.

But the names of the winners never came. The plan had changed behind the scenes, or at least was in the process of changing. Colomer couldn't stomach the thought of only taking three players and watching the rest slip away. They were just too good. He had been lobbying Sheikh Jassim's right-hand man, Tariq al-Naama, to keep far more players. "I said, 'Tariq, look, the level of the players we are finding is amazing," said Colomer. "I don't think we should take only three. I think we can take 20 and put them in an academy and develop them until they go to big clubs, and Aspire can have the best youth academy in the world."

Taking more players certainly made sense if Colomer really hoped to find the next Messi, since predicting which 13-year-old would become a star was such a complicated calculus. A kid might seem exceptional today, but myriad things could go wrong on and off the field to derail his progress. He might get injured, lack the motivation to work hard enough, get distracted by his personal life, or simply not progress as fast as his teammates. There was one certainty, though. No matter what the probability was that any one kid would make it, Colomer's chance of identifying a future star would rise if he could take more players.

Andreas Bleicher, who first dreamed up the idea of recruiting Africans to Aspire, agreed with Colomer. "By choosing 20, we increase the likelihood to really find the next top football player," he said. But he didn't think they could flood Aspire with so many foreign players, so they began brainstorming about setting up a separate academy run by Colomer in Africa for the kids who wouldn't be staying in Doha. It was still a work in progress by the time the press conference rolled around, and they would need Sheikh Jassim's approval before they could move ahead. "We do not have everything finalized yet, but we are very positive we will get the right decision so we can support the other players in Africa," Bleicher told the crowd.

Even though Aspire was thinking about taking more than the three boys initially planned, Colomer and Browne still needed to whittle the group down to the best players and figure out which ones would be staying in Doha versus training in Africa. Their method of doing so was surprisingly basic given that they were working at a gleaming new $1.5 billion sports academy. They didn't employ the kind of sophisticated data analysis that has become increasingly common in the sports world and largely relied on what their eyes and years of experience told them was the right decision. That certainly wasn't uncommon in soccer, especially at the time. The sport has a history of dragging its feet into the data world.

Michael Lewis popularized the notion of data-driven analysis in sports with his 2003 book *Moneyball*, which described how the Oakland Athletics were able to challenge much richer teams through the innovative use of statistics. General Manager Billy Beane realized that the traditional statistics used to gauge players, such as their batting average and runs batted in, weren't actually the most effective. Through rigorous statistical analysis, he discovered that alternative measurements like on-base percentage and slugging percentage were more useful indicators of a player's offensive success. He used this insight to find undervalued players in the market who would provide Oakland with the kind of talent the team needed at a price it could afford.

Since then, the use of sophisticated data analysis to find a competitive edge has exploded throughout the game of baseball and expanded to other sports, particularly basketball. But the pace of change has been relatively slow in soccer as veteran coaches and scouts have resisted the notion that statistical analysis can compete with old-school intuition derived from years of experience. "In comparison to historical medicine, soccer analytics is currently in the time of leeches and bloodlettings." That's what the founder of one soccer analytics firm, Mark Brunkhart, told the authors of *The Numbers Game*, which was published a decade after *Moneyball*. Several years later, one of the authors, Chris Anderson, said, "There's still a lot of leeching going on."

That's not to say all clubs have resisted the move toward a more analytical approach. Many of the top clubs in the world now employ analysts who have access to reams of data that can be used to evaluate recruiting prospects, monitor their own players, and scout opponents, although this is happening much more at the senior level than on youth teams. Arsenal even bought a U.S.-based soccer analytics firm, StatDNA, for more than 2 million pounds in 2012. But many clubs have yet to fully embrace the potential of data analysis. "The purist analytic types want to use the data as a filter to identify undervalued talent, the classic *Moneyball* story," said Anderson. "But it's not really used to identify players from scratch. It's mostly used to confirm or deny the choices that scouts or heads of recruitment wish to make." At the senior level, those opinions are often formed by watching a player as many as twenty times over a period of several years. Then the number crunchers are called in to figure out how the player compares to others on the market and what the club should pay for him.

Even then, the metrics are fairly simple. "It's the common stuff you would imagine," said Anderson. "A central defender needs to have very good defensive positioning, be good one-on-one, be able to head the ball, and be calm under pressure, and you can put some basic numbers against that kind of stuff. A number nine needs to be good on the ball, shoot really well, and have good finishing skill. In part, because geeks haven't really arrived in full force in soccer at all, we're still talking about relatively basic metrics."

That doesn't mean metrics haven't evolved at all, though. Many analysts have shifted from using simple statistics like assists, shots, and goals—the kind Colomer and Browne were focused on in 2007—to more advanced stats that have greater predictive power in determining the performance of players and teams from season to season. For example, statistics like expected goals and expected assists aim to decrease the elements of luck and chance that can reduce or magnify a player's perceived talent. It's easy to imagine how luck or chance could affect an individual shot. It could deflect off a defender or be saved by a particularly good goalkeeper. It also matters whether the ball was served up to a striker on a silver platter by a midfield maestro like Xavi or hammered in by a Sunday league duffer.

The expected goals statistic seeks to reduce the effects of luck and chance by measuring the number of goals a player would have scored given the probability that shots taken during a match would normally go in. Different models exist to determine these probabilities, but they normally factor in the type of shot, location, and possibly a few other factors. A shot from very close to the goal might go in about 50 percent of the time, making it worth 0.5 expected goals. A strike from far out might only be worth 0.1. As shots are taken during a game, these probabilities are added up to produce an expected goals figure that can be compared to actual goals for an individual player or entire team. The new statistic gives a clearer view of whether a player is getting into good goal-scoring positions, regardless of whether an individual shot goes in or not. That's what matters most. Analysts have determined expected goals more accurately predict a team's performance over the course of a season and a player's quality from year to year than actual goals. Expected assists operate in the same way.

Advocates of more sophisticated data analysis in soccer don't necessarily aim to replace the traditional network of scouts clubs have in place as much as provide them with additional information to enhance their decision making. Daniel Altman, founder of the soccer-focused firm North Yard Analytics, offers a service that can digitally clone a club's best scout, thus allowing a team to assess players in dozens of leagues irrespective of where its favored scout is located. He does this by building a computer program that filters players based on the characteristics the scout deems most important. Perhaps the scout likes pacey midfielders with high expected assist numbers who rarely give away the ball. The program uses this information to spit out a list of players likely to be of interest to the club who can then be evaluated by the organization's scouts in person. Altman, who has a PhD in economics from Harvard University, believes spending 200,000 euros on this kind of data analysis could save a club at least 50 times that amount in the transfer market, but generating interest has still been an uphill battle. "The number of clubs that are interested in being serious about analytics is still a minority," said Altman. "But it's growing."

The fact that Colomer and Browne didn't have access to this kind of technology clearly made their job of picking the best players more difficult, but that wasn't the only challenge they faced. Football Dreams also encountered criticism from those in the soccer world who didn't think it should be happening at all.

To Jean-Claude Mbvoumin, Football Dreams seemed less like a dream and more like a nightmare. A former professional player from Cameroon, Mbvoumin runs a Paris-based NGO, Foot Solidaire, that fights the illicit trade of underage soccer players out of Africa. He embarked on his mission in the late 1990s when the Cameroonian Embassy in Paris called him asking for help with a group of teenagers who had been invited to France by an agent, supposedly for trials with a professional club, and then abandoned. Mbvoumin showed up at the embassy to find the kids sleeping on the floor and was told they didn't have return tickets to Cameroon even though each of them paid the agent 3,000 euros. "So you can imagine the money he made on this dirty business," said Mbvoumin.

He set off on a search across Paris to track down the agent but had no luck. Instead, he discovered that the teenagers at the Cameroonian Embassy were far from an isolated case. He ran into scores of young African players who had paid agents to travel to France for professional trials that weren't successful or never materialized and were now living in the country illegally, sometimes on the streets. "I was shocked," he said. He set up Foot Solidaire to provide the kids with support, including food, access to medical care, and tickets home, although some are too ashamed to return to families that made huge sacrifices to pay the agents in the first place. Mbvoumin has also lobbied FIFA to do more to deal with the problem but has often been frustrated by the response. "It is very difficult if the main stakeholders try to close their eyes and don't want to see."

European clubs have long relied on imported African players, especially in countries that have colonial ties with Africa, like France, Belgium, Portugal, and England. This migration, and the associated problem of trading in underage players, ballooned in the late 1990s and early 2000s due to a confluence of factors. One was a ruling by the European Union in 1995 that improved the bargaining position of players and helped send compensation soaring. Many European clubs responded by looking for more affordable players from the developing world, especially Africa. The sorry state of professional soccer in many parts of the continent meant that even the best African players were often only earning a few hundred dollars a month and were ripe pickings for European clubs growing richer from spiking TV revenue. This exodus has further weakened African soccer to the point where relatively few people go to local league matches, preferring instead to watch the continent's best players battle in Europe on TV.

In 2003, FIFA President Sepp Blatter wrote a column in the *Financial Times* saying European clubs that had benefited most from the trade in African players had behaved like "neocolonialists who don't give a damn about heritage and culture, but engage in social and economic rape by robbing the developing world of its best players." He may have been playing politics since he relied on Africa for much of his political support at FIFA, but many people agreed with his statement. He also described European clubs' recruitment of young Africans as "unhealthy if not despicable." FIFA tightened its regulations on the recruitment of minors in the first half of the 2000s, stipulating that clubs could not transfer players under the age of 18 across international borders.

The only exceptions were if a player's parents moved to the new country for non-soccer reasons, the transfer took place within Europe, and the player was at least 16, or the player already lived within 100 kilometers of the new club. Some decried the new rules as too heavy-handed, saying they prevented Africans from training at the best academies in Europe. But many people say European clubs often break the rules with little consequence, and the flow of young players out of Africa has continued. Foot Solidaire estimates that thousands of underage players are shuttled out of West Africa every year with dreams of making it at clubs in Europe and elsewhere. Almost all fail, and many find themselves stranded.

Mbvoumin was alarmed when he visited Cameroon in 2007 and learned Aspire was recruiting 13-year-old African boys on an unprecedented scale. "Trafficking is institutionalized in Africa because now everyone comes to these countries and takes the children abroad," he said at the time. "It looks like a kind of exploitation and modern slavery." He thought Aspire should be held to the same FIFA regulations that prevent clubs from transferring players under 18. "Even though Qatar has the best conditions, they must respect the rules," he said. "FIFA needs to do something to prevent this."

Aspire argued it wasn't bound by the rules because it wasn't a professional club and the kids weren't playing in an official league. The academy also highlighted that Football Dreams was supported by local African soccer federations and the United Nations Office on Sport for Development and Peace. But the answers didn't satisfy Mbvoumin, and he teamed up with members of the European Parliament to send a letter to Blatter in mid-2007 demanding that FIFA stop the program. At the time, FIFA refused to comment officially on Football Dreams, saying instead that it welcomed "any initiatives of solidarity between the more affluent countries and those who have less for the development of sport and of football." But in a personal reply to the letter from the European Parliament, which was leaked to the media, Blatter expressed serious concern about the project, saying "their establishment of recruitment networks in these seven African countries reveals just what Aspire is all about. Aspire offers a good example of . . . exploitation."

Many people were also worried that the real goal of Football

Dreams was to improve Qatar's national team by finding talented Africans who could be given Qatari nationality, just as the country had done in the past. This suspicion intensified when Qatar won the bid to host the 2022 World Cup. The country had never qualified for the tournament before, but as the host, it was guaranteed a spot. That meant there was a risk Qatar would be humiliated by soccer's giants on its home soil. To many observers, filling out the country's team with players found through Football Dreams seemed to be a logical way to try to prevent that from happening.

Bleicher, who oversaw talent identification at Aspire, said in January 2008 that the academy didn't require the Football Dreams kids to play for Qatar, but indicated they might end up getting passports. "We leave it up to them," said Bleicher. "A player might be here for five years, and if he wants to play for Qatar, we would not say it is impossible." Many people disapproved of the idea of Qatar skimming off the best African talent for its national team and worried the country could simply dangle enough money in front of the kids to make it happen. "In the beginning, most people thought they were choosing the players to play for Qatar," said Diawandou's old coach, Bousso Ndiaye.

Mbvoumin arranged a meeting with Blatter at FIFA headquarters in Zurich in June 2008 to express his concerns about Football Dreams and the trade in underage African players more broadly. But by that time, the FIFA president had changed his tune under pressure from Qatar. The flip-flop came after Blatter visited the country in February 2008 at the invitation of the emir, Sheikh Hamad, and Mohamed bin Hammam, a Qatari who served on FIFA's powerful executive committee. Blatter visited Aspire during his trip and surprised reporters by praising Football Dreams only months after he had criticized it. "This visit has provided me with the opportunity to learn about the Aspire Africa program firsthand, and I have to say that I am very relaxed and supportive about the project now that I understand how it works," said Blatter. Mbvoumin's concerns were sincere, but he was no match for Qatar's growing influence in the soccer world. Football Dreams was here to stay.

The Football Dreams kids were still in limbo when Blatter visited Aspire, since Colomer and Bleicher were still exploring the idea of setting up a satellite academy in Africa. They also needed to convince Sheikh Jassim that the kids were good enough to make it worthwhile. But the players took care of that themselves about a month later. At least that's how some people in the program tell it. All the sheikh needed to do was see them play one match, but not just any match. This one was against arguably the world's greatest soccer power: Brazil.

The kids were understandably a little daunted. Brazil had visited Aspire several times before, and not surprisingly, no academy team had ever defeated them. "Everybody said Brazil was going to beat us," said Adama, the Ghanaian defender. But Aspire had never had a team like this before, and the coach, Michael Browne, thought the African kids could give Brazil's Under-16 side a run for their money. "Michael told us, 'They are very strong, very big, but you have to work hard and score against them because every time Brazil comes to Aspire, they beat us,'" said Bernard. "'We have to break that record.'"

Bernard took the field with Browne's words ringing in his ears, dressed like his teammates in a blue and white striped jersey emblazoned with Aspire's logo, a capital A with silver wings on a royal blue background. He certainly had his work cut out for him in center midfield. Lining up opposite Bernard, dressed in Brazil's iconic yellow and green, was Philippe Coutinho, who would later earn the nickname the Little Magician when he became a star for Liverpool and Brazil's senior national team. Fellow Ghanaian John Benson stopped by to watch the match at one of Aspire's outdoor fields and was impressed by how Bernard was holding his own against one of Brazil's biggest youth stars. "Bernard was competing very well," said John. "You could see that they have one player, and we have one player: Bernard and Coutinho, great competition."

Bernard and his teammates poured on the pressure and conjured up a moment of magic in the first half. Arabo Bakary, a midfielder from Cameroon's far north who had to travel 17 hours to make it to the tryout in the capital, threaded a pass through Brazil's defense. Running onto it was Jasper Uwa, a searingly fast striker who convinced Colomer of his skill back in southern Nigeria despite playing on completely waterlogged fields. He latched onto the ball and managed to slot it past Brazil's keeper, prompting wild celebrations among the Football Dreams kids. As the first half drew to a close, the score remained 1-0.

When the Football Dreams kids resumed their battle in the second half, Brazil's coach threw a new striker on the pitch. The thin, baby-faced player meant nothing to the Football Dreams kids at the time. In fact, it was his first call-up to the national team. But it wouldn't be long before the world knew his name: Neymar. His silky footwork and nose for goal were already attracting attention back at his Brazilian club, Santos. He would eventually move to Barcelona and help form one of the most fearsome attacking tridents in history, alongside Messi and Luis Suárez, before moving on to Qatar-owned Paris Saint-Germain for the highest transfer fee in history.

Neymar and Coutinho had never played together before traveling to Doha but now linked up effortlessly and ran at the Football Dreams kids. Bernard and his fellow countryman Hamza sprinted like madmen to smother their creativity in midfield, while Diawandou, Adama, and the other defenders tried to maintain a solid back line. Again and again, the Brazilians came at them, but the defense held firm. So did the goalkeeper, John Felagha.

Colomer first selected John after testing his skills personally on a rain-soaked field in the Niger Delta. The Spanish scout kept him at the pitch after the tryout ended and fired shots at him that skipped off the water at unpredictable angles, forcing quick reactions as John slid around in the mud. Colomer lost track of the number of times he fired the ball at the goal, probing for a weakness. But he remembers how many times he scored: none.

Neymar and Coutinho had just as little luck getting the ball past the Nigerian keeper. "That was the best game I ever played," said John. The Brazilians never found a way through, and the Football Dreams kids held on to win 1-0, a huge victory. They now enjoyed the reputation as the first Aspire team to ever beat the Brazilians.

It's easy to imagine Sheikh Jassim watching the Africans beat soccer's golden boys and realize Aspire was really onto something with Football Dreams. That's how Forewah Emmanuel, a Football Dreams staff member from Cameroon, tells the story. However it played out, Colomer got his wish: an academy in Africa for the kids who wouldn't be staying in Doha. It was the chance for him to build the soccer school of his dreams with a pool of players he believed was more talented than any he had ever encountered, Colomer's own African La Masia. All that was left now was to announce who was going where.

The kids all stayed in Doha until the end of May, and Aspire waited until they were packing up their rooms to head home for the summer before notifying them of their fate. Michael Browne got first dibs on deciding which kids would be based in Doha since the primary purpose of Football Dreams was to improve the Qatari players. That meant Bernard was staying put, along with fellow Ghanaians Hamza and Adama. Colomer would have to watch his African Messi bloom from afar. Aspire had originally planned to keep only three kids from the first class in Doha, but Browne added the Nigerian keeper John as well after his performance against the

Brazilians. They would get the chance to train in an environment they couldn't have imagined a few months earlier.

Diawandou would be leading the group of players headed to Senegal with Colomer. He had impressed Browne during his time in Doha but was left off the list to stay. Perhaps it was his ankle injury at the beginning of the tryout. Whatever the reason, Diawandou was disappointed. Staying in Qatar was certainly seen as the bigger prize among the boys. They didn't know exactly what the academy would be like in Senegal but were sure it wouldn't be nearly as spectacular as Aspire. At least Diawandou would be on his home turf and could help many of the other boys adjust to life in a new country. They were saying goodbye to Aspire's air-conditioned dome and manicured fields, but at least they were keeping their captain.

CHAPTER 6

Sent Off

Bernard looked up toward the sky and panicked. He was back in Doha following summer vacation and was supposed to be at the academy by 6 p.m. curfew, but the darkened sky and lit street lamps indicated he was running late. He set off at a sprint, dodging Qatari men wearing white robes and headdresses and women in black abayas and veils, taking care not to bump into the Filipino nannies pushing baby carriages behind them. He passed rows of luxury stores and a canal filled with swimming pool blue water, where shoppers took rides in wooden gondolas painted black and gold. Anxious to make it back to the academy in time, he burst through a doorway and was momentarily confused by the bright sunlight that struck his face. Then he started laughing. It turned out he wasn't late after all. The sun was still high in the sky. Life in Doha could certainly be disorienting.

The Villaggio mall was a case in point. They definitely didn't have places like this in Bernard's neighborhood in Ghana. Located next door to Aspire, it was built to resemble some sort of idealized version of Venice, with a canal snaking past shops set inside pastel-colored facades meant to resemble Italian villas, complete with faux balconies topped with potted flowers. The mall had high ceilings painted to look like a blue sky filled with puffy white clouds, dimmed just enough to make Bernard think he had missed his curfew at the academy. The glowing street lamps that line the mall's walkways added to his panic, until he emerged into the sunlight outside and realized his mistake. Good thing his friends from Aspire weren't around to make fun of him.

In the months since joining the academy, Bernard and the other Africans there had fast become a tight-knit group. They included the other Football Dreams kids, Hamza, Adama, and John Felagha, as well as three others: John Benson, the first African player recruited by Aspire; Serigne Abdou Thiam, the Senegalese boy Colomer discovered in Dakar while he was at Barcelona; and Antoine Messi, a Cameroonian goalkeeper the Spanish scout found for Aspire before launching Football Dreams.

Bernard had been thrilled when Aspire told him he would be one of the boys staying in Qatar, but he wasn't surprised. Five feet of pure self-confidence, that was Bernard. He was sure by the end of the tryout his performance had been good enough to make the cut. "I will not lie to you," said Bernard. "I was amazing." By his telling, Sheikh Jassim even requested personally that he remain in Doha. "Colomer called me and said the king likes only me," said Bernard. Truth or fiction, the story is revealing. Bernard felt entirely in command on the field at Aspire, unbowed by any competition thrown his way.

The other Africans respected Bernard's immense talent on the field, but that didn't stop them from teasing him off it. His fellow Ghanaian John Benson especially liked to needle him about his poor English, particularly when he had to read out loud in class. Even though English is Ghana's official language, Bernard grew up speaking Twi at home, and the English he studied at school did little to help him master the language. Studying was never his forte.

"Whenever it came time to read, I would shout, 'Hey, Bernard, it's your turn!' and he would say, 'No, no, no!'" said John Benson.

John was a couple years older than the other kids but was often stuck in the same class because many of Aspire's teachers spoke Arabic, not English. Bernard would often tap John's shoulder in class, point to English words, and ask, "What's this? And this? How about this?" He even showed up at John's door one day asking how to spell the Microsoft web portal, MSN. "I said, 'M - S - N,'" said John. "He started laughing and went back to his room. We did have fun."

Bernard may have had trouble with English, but that didn't stop him from jabbering away with his buddies. He talks the way he plays, in rapid-fire bursts, the words flying out of his mouth like they're skipping past a defender. He may be all business on the field but otherwise loves cracking jokes, trying to get a laugh out of his teammates. "Off the pitch, he is very funny, so everybody loves being around him," said Hamza, his closest friend at the academy.

Bernard could get by in English, despite the taunts from his friends. But he felt much more comfortable in his mother tongue, one of the reasons he and Hamza became so close. They both grew up speaking Twi less than 20 miles from each other in Ghana, although the drive between Teshie and Tema could take hours thanks to Accra's notoriously bad traffic. Other than Hamza being Muslim and Bernard Christian, the two came from similar backgrounds.

The youngest of six kids, Hamza grew up in a simple three-room, concrete house wedged into a crowded neighborhood near Tema's busy port. Lines filled with drying laundry run from house to house like some giant urban spider web. Women squat on the ground pounding cassava with long wooden poles and grilling corn and fish over coal fires. Sewage runs through open gutters that line the alleyways between the buildings, and the occasional goat wanders by munching on a cast-off scrap of paper.

Hamza's father grew up in northern Ghana, where his education was largely limited to studying the Quran. He moved to Tema before Hamza was born to look for work and managed to get a job driving a truck at the local port. Life wasn't easy, but the job put food on the table and paid for his children's school fees. "Sometimes we struggled a bit, but it was ok," said Hamza. Years later, his father decided he had had enough of the city and moved back north to become a farmer. Hamza's mother ran a small open-air restaurant near their home in Tema that consisted of a few wooden benches nestled in the dirt by the roadside, protected from the elements by a patched canvas roof. Bernard would have approved of the menu since she served his favorite, banku and okra stew. Hamza sometimes helped out washing dishes when his mother asked but spent most of his time outside school playing soccer.

Hamza got his start playing barefoot with a small rubber ball in a patch of dirt in front of his home and soon joined a neighborhood team. Like Bernard, he became part of Africa's booming trade in extremely young players when he was sold to another coach around the age of 10 and joined the man's team, Great Palmas, where he played central defense. His coach signed up to work as a coordinator when Aspire launched Football Dreams and convinced Hamza to give it a shot even though neither of them had ever heard of Qatar.

The tryout took place on a dirt field outside a nearby primary school, just around the corner from the God's Grace barbershop. Hamza only managed to touch the ball twice during his match. "But these two balls were incredible," said Colomer, who was convinced he wanted to see more. The Spanish scout took Hamza along with him to the next field, and even though he only touched the ball three times there, Colomer was convinced. He called one of his assistants over, pointed to Hamza, and said he was one of the best players in Ghana. The final tryout in Accra was no different, and Hamza could tell he was headed to Doha as soon as the last match ended. "Everybody was talking about me, mentioning the number on my jersey," said Hamza.

As with Diawandou, Colomer and Michael Browne decided they could get more out of Hamza by changing his position. Whereas Diawandou moved from midfield into defense, Hamza migrated in the other direction. He was a solid defender, but his ability to hold the ball and distribute passes made him even more valuable as a defensive midfielder, as evidenced by his performance in the win against Neymar and the rest of the Brazilian squad. Hamza's commanding presence on the field also led Browne to appoint him captain of the team the kids trained with in Doha. Bernard may have been the flashier player, but Hamza was more of a conductor on the field, barking out commands and directing other players where to go.

Hamza didn't hold back from speaking his mind off the field, either, a tendency that led to occasional clashes with the Aspire staff and earned him a reputation as a player who could be difficult to coach. Hamza didn't see any problem with his behavior, but one of the staff compared him to Mario Balotelli, the talented Italian striker whose career has been hamstrung by his mercurial personality. "Like Balotelli, he is great on the field and difficult off it," said Forewah Emmanuel, the Aspire staff member from Cameroon. "You have to choose your words carefully with him."

That may have been true of the staff, but Hamza and Bernard got along like peas in a pod. Sometimes they even slept in the same room, although Bernard had the habit of getting up in the middle of the night and praying out loud, disturbing everyone else. "He didn't care that everyone had to get up and go to their own room," said John Benson, who sometimes joined in the slumber party. They were all religious to some extent, but Bernard was by far the most devout and expressive of his faith.

One of the downsides of Aspire was that Bernard couldn't attend

Qatari players praying at dusk at one of the fields at Aspire Academy in Doha.

church, a tough blow since it had been such an important part of his life back in Ghana. There are several churches in Doha, but none of them were easily accessible for him and the other Christian boys, John Benson and John Felagha, so they had to pray in their rooms. Even if the churches had been nearby, John Benson was too scared to go. He had heard too many stories about Christians being persecuted and even killed in the Middle East. That wasn't common in Qatar, but John wasn't taking any chances.

In general, there wasn't that much for the boys to do when they weren't training or in class. The biggest treat was to get a pass to go next door to the Villaggio, which not only had luxury shops and a meandering canal, but also a 235,000-square-foot indoor amusement park, Gondolonia, with bumper cars, a mini Ferris wheel, and a bunch of other rides. Not far away was an indoor ice skating rink with a large banner proclaiming it to be the home of the Doha Ice Skating Club, which was likely a pretty small group since temperatures in Doha don't normally drop much below the mid-50s. If that wasn't enough, there was always the plethora of fast-food joints: McDonald's, Hardee's, Pizza Hut, Baskin-Robbins, Krispy Kreme, you name it. Serious competition for the healthy fare served in Aspire's cafeteria.

The kids were armed with around $300 in "pocket money" given to them each month by Aspire as part of their scholarship, often more than their parents made working back home by a significant margin. Aspire also sent around $5,000 every year to their families, money used for everything from buying food and paying school fees to building homes and starting businesses. Flush with their newfound cash, the boys roamed the Villaggio buying up clothes to show off back at the academy, snapping photos of each other in the process. One shows Bernard standing in a T-shirt shop inside the mall, with a white fedora jauntily perched on his head. He's back in his room at the academy in another, dressed like he's headed to one of P. Diddy's white parties, with a long-sleeve Billabong shirt, capri cargo pants, and Adidas sneakers. But they could only get permission to go to the Villaggio every so often, and even that got a bit old after a while. Otherwise they mainly hung out in their rooms, listening to music or challenging each other on PlayStation. "It was often really boring," said Bernard.

But all this was just a sideshow to the real action at the academy, which took place on the field. Aspire hadn't spent millions of dollars combing Africa so the kids could wander through the Villaggio or play PlayStation in their rooms. They were there to motivate Qatari players who had grown up with life delivered on a silver platter. Some were even dropped off at training in Bentleys and Ferraris. That's not a recipe for producing players with the grit and determination to become world-class, as Sheikh Jassim dreamed when he founded Aspire, especially since Qatar had such a small talent pool to begin with.

The Qataris were a far cry from the players that many of Aspire's coaches were used to training at academies back in Europe. One coach, Luis Miguel Silva, showed up at Aspire from Porto, where he coached players who helped make up Portugal's national team alongside superstar Cristiano Ronaldo. "When you coach these kinds of players and then you move to Qatar and coach Qatari players, it's a shock," he said.

When Aspire first opened, the coaches noticed the Qatari players went down at the slightest hint of contact and rolled around the field like they had been shot. "We couldn't quite get it," said David Burke, who had been at Fulham's academy before coming to Aspire. "It was completely over the top compared to the exaggerations you see on TV." Kids also sobbed after matches if things didn't go their way and were ready to blame anyone but themselves. "It was eye opening for me," said Michael Browne, Aspire's head coach. "We said, 'Look, we don't want to see anyone crying after games. Look at areas you think you can improve and don't blame anyone else. Don't blame the referee, don't blame the conditions, don't blame this, and don't blame that.'"

It's easy to understand why Aspire's top brass decided they needed to drop a few African players into the mix. Bernard and the others were not only far more talented than most of the locals, but they also possessed a relentless drive to succeed. There were no silver platters in their childhood, just dirt, sweat, and competition. They showed up at Aspire ready for more of the same and were surprised to discover many of the Qataris lacked their hunger. Sometimes they didn't even bother coming to training. "Maybe five or six would show up and you have to train like that," said Hamza. That likely wouldn't have impressed Sheikh Jassim, who sometimes showed up unannounced at the academy and stood on a grassy knoll next to the field to watch the boys play.

Some of the Qatari players didn't take too kindly to the African imports, worried they were going to lose their spot on Qatar's national team. "They were not happy," said Bernard. "They thought we had come to take their positions." It was a legitimate concern, and the naturalization question had sparked growing controversy around Football Dreams. Qatar had a long history of using its wealth to lure foreign athletes into taking Qatari citizenship and representing the country at international competitions like the Olympics. The list included Kenyan runners, Bulgarian weightlifters, Montenegrin handball players, Chinese chess grandmasters, and yes, African soccer players. The Football Dreams kids had been selected as the elite of the elite, and some of the Qataris at Aspire wondered how they could ever compete. Many outside the academy were also convinced Qatar was going to give the Africans passports.

The issue was fuzzy to the African players as well, and several of them spent time training and playing friendlies with Qatari national teams of various age groups. John Benson traveled to Germany with one of the country's youth teams to play in a friendly tournament, and the coach of Qatar's Under-23 team repeatedly told John he wanted him to help them qualify for the Olympics. "I didn't speak with Aspire because I didn't know what was going on," said John. Antoine Messi, the goalkeeper from Cameroon, also traveled with one of Qatar's youth sides to play in Malaysia, and Bernard said he once trained with the national team at Aspire at the request of one of his coaches.

At the beginning of Football Dreams, Andreas Bleicher had said the kids in the program might end up playing for Qatar, but Aspire eventually reversed course and insisted the boys would play for their own national teams. The shift came after FIFA made it a lot harder in June 2008 for countries to naturalize foreign players, although Aspire insists this had nothing to do with its new stance and now says there was never any plan for the Football Dreams kids to play for Qatar. FIFA acted in 2008 after President Sepp Blatter expressed concern about the number of Brazilian players taking foreign citizenship. At the time, a player only needed to live in a new country for two years, at any age, before changing nationality. "There is a danger that in 2014 half the players in the World Cup could come from Brazil," Blatter told the media then.

Qatar, of course, had tried to naturalize three Brazilians before the 2006 World Cup and became embroiled in a controversy over its naturalization of another Brazilian player, Emerson, in the fall of 2008. To stem such moves, Blatter pushed through a rule stating a player had to live in a new country for five years after reaching the age of 18 to change nationality. That made it a lot less feasible to naturalize the Football Dreams kids since they dreamed of playing in top clubs in Europe when they graduated, not staying in Qatar until they were 23 years old.

Many continue to suspect Qatar will find a way to naturalize the Football Dreams kids despite Aspire's denials, but the academy's new stance helped ease fears among the local players there, to the point where some eventually warmed up to the Africans. Bernard became close enough friends with one of the Qataris, Nasser Al Meshadi, to visit his house on the weekend. Nasser's father was a die-hard fan of one of Qatar's clubs, Al Rayyan, and spent the weekend trying to convince Bernard he should join the team. But Bernard had his heart set on Barcelona or one of Europe's other top clubs.

In general, making it to Europe was the overwhelming focus of the Football Dreams kids. They gave little thought to their role in helping Qatar improve its own players. In their mind, they were at Aspire to receive the training necessary to become European stars. Bernard grew especially close to Paul Nevin, who came to Aspire in 2007 after heading Fulham's academy and ended up coaching the Football Dreams kids. He even invited Bernard and the other Africans over to his house for dinner. Nevin, who would go on to become head of academy coaching at the Premier League, saw great promise in the left-footer from Teshie. "He told me that like Ronaldhino, I have a lot of skills," said Bernard.

Nevin sought to shape Bernard's decision making on the field to make him an even more effective player. He wanted Bernard to push the ball forward more often, rather than simply looking to pass, so he could become more of a goal scorer like Messi. Bernard was hesitant at first, thinking about what happened to players back in Ghana who held the ball too long. "In Ghana if you do that, they will kill you," said Bernard. "But in Europe, people are afraid they will get a card."

The Aspire coaches focused much of their training for the Africans on these kinds of tactics, helping them understand how their decisions fit in a team's game plan and how they should position themselves relative to their teammates and opponents. While the coaches were generally blown away by the Africans' technical skill, physicality, and drive, they found tactics to be the weakest part of their game. That's understandable given that many of their coaches in Africa had little if any formal training, but that wasn't what some of the Aspire coaches thought.

They wrongly speculated that the Africans were tactically weak because they had only played in the street and never on a full-size field. That might seem like a sensible conclusion to someone who had never visited Africa, but this type of thinking revealed how little the coaches actually knew about the conditions that had shaped the development of the African players back home. They might have a relative shortage of well-trained coaches in Africa, but they do have full-size fields, even if many of them are dirt.

Other theories strayed even closer to the kinds of stereotypes that have long dogged Africans. Some coaches speculated the Africans were better at short passes than long passes because they could lose the ball in the bushes if they kicked it too far. They also

guessed that the African players weren't always the strongest finish-
ers because someone might steal their ball back home if they shot it
past the goal. These theories underscore just how little most of the
officials at Aspire really knew about the backgrounds of the Africans they had drafted into the academy and what the experience
was like for them to be there.

Since the African players were so much better than the Qataris,
they had to rely on competition with each other to really push themselves forward. John Benson remembers what it was like in training
when he had to go up against Bernard, who had bulked up from a mix
of weightlifting and a steady stream of healthier food from the cafeteria. "When I met Bernard one-on-one, it was crazy, it was like war,"
said John. "I wouldn't let him take the ball from me, and he wouldn't
let me take the ball from him. Sometimes we just kicked each other,
but after the game we would go take a shower, and it was normal."

John, Hamza, and Adama weren't the only Ghanaians Bernard
went up against at the academy. Ghana sent a couple of its youth
national teams to Aspire for training, and they played against the
academy side that included Bernard and the other Football Dreams
kids. The Under-20 team showed up in September 2009 to prepare
for the Under-20 World Cup, which it won later that month after a
penalty shoot-out with Brazil in the final.

The national team players were blown away when they watched
Bernard showcase his talent for the first time. "When we played
against them, even our Under-20 boys said, 'Hey, this guy is going
to be one of the best,'" said John Benson, who ended up joining the
national team for the World Cup. "They said he was going to be one
of the best because the way he was playing was unbelievable." The
Ghanaian team had a pretty good reference point since the squad
included the son of one of Africa's most famous players, Abedi Pele,
who surprisingly got his start playing for a club in Qatar before moving to Europe.

It's easy to understand why the Ghanaians were so impressed with Bernard based on a highlight video of a game a couple months later that he played against Ghana's Under-17 team. Bernard is everywhere, skipping past defenders, feeding passes, and tracking back to muscle an opponent off the ball to avert a fast break. He has hinges for ankles as he changes direction on a dime, always a few paces faster than the players around him.

In one memorable clip, he steals the ball in the center of mid-field, and as his opponent lunges to get it back, he gracefully moves the ball past him with a flick of his left foot behind his right. The next player dives in, studs-up, but Bernard nonchalantly taps the ball to his left and jumps over the defender's legs. A third player moves in for the kill with just as little luck. Another flick of his left foot behind his right and Bernard is past him. Finally, he slides a pass to a teammate on his left at the top of the box, but a defender just manages to intercept the ball. The defender may have stopped a clear goal-scoring opportunity, but not before Bernard had made several of his teammates look like fools.

Colomer spent relatively little time in Doha during this period, but the progress that Bernard was making at the academy didn't go unnoticed. When Colomer was in Accra for the second year of Football Dreams in the fall of 2008, he raved about Bernard's per-formance at Aspire to Eugene Komey, the coordinator at the field in Teshie where the Spanish scout first spotted his little Ghanaian Messi. "He said the boy was doing very, very well," said Komey. "He said Bernard was even smarter than Messi was when he was in Bar-celona's academy."

Others began to take notice as well, especially the coaches of European teams that played against Bernard. Aspire often flew clubs to Doha to play against the academy teams, and the kids also traveled to tournaments in Europe. After Bernard played a match against the Spanish club Valencia in Doha in 2009, one of the coaches approached him in Aspire's cafeteria and gave him his business card. "He told me that I should be playing with him because I have the quality," said Bernard. On another occasion, Bernard's coach, Paul Nevin, called him into his office at Aspire after they returned from a trip to Italy, where they played against one of the country's top clubs, Lazio. "He told me that after the game, Lazio said they liked me," said Bernard. "I said, 'Why don't you sell me over there?' And he said, 'No, I can't do it unless Aspire gives me an order.'"

After less than two years at the academy, Bernard was getting impatient. With European coaches whispering in his ear, he decided he was wasting his time at Aspire and was ready to move to a club in Europe, where he could earn a lot more money for himself and his family. "My heart was boiling," said Bernard. He sat in his room at Aspire and watched young players in Europe on TV, thinking to himself, "The ones playing over there, I can play better than them."

Training with the Qataris only strengthened his belief it was time to move on since they didn't provide much competition. Aspire brought in the Africans because they realized the best Qatari players would lose the motivation to push themselves if they weren't sufficiently challenged. Coaches insisted the program was working, but Aspire simply transferred the problem to the Africans since they were now the ones who lacked a proper challenge day in and day out. Even Colomer grew disillusioned with the strategy because it was impeding the progress of the African players. "Three players cannot raise the level of the team," said Colomer. "These three players will get the level of the rest. I don't think this is the way."

Bernard finally ran out of patience and began badgering Andreas Bleicher and other Aspire officials involved with Football Dreams to let him transfer to a European club. "They would tell me no, I have to wait, I have to wait, I have to wait," said Bernard. They told him FIFA regulations prohibited him from moving to a club in Europe until he was 18 years old. Bernard didn't know much about the rules but thought a club could simply appoint someone to look after him until he turned 18. That wasn't true, but many clubs danced around the regulations or broke them outright to get foreign players they wanted, even major teams like Barcelona and Real Madrid, according to FIFA. In any case, Aspire told Bernard the rules were the rules and he wasn't going anywhere until he was 18. He would stay and train with the Qatari players as planned.

Aspire's head soccer coach, Michael Browne, began to sense something was wrong with Bernard but didn't know exactly what it was since he wasn't as close to him as some of the others. Bernard's performance on the field began to drop off. "There was something that held him back," said Browne. "He lacked that self-drive to really push on and make it." The conflict with Aspire over moving to Europe was taking its toll.

But that wasn't the only thing troubling Bernard. There were problems at home as well. Tension was growing over the roughly $5,000 Aspire sent to Bernard's parents every year. They were tremendously grateful for the money, which amounted to roughly ten times what Bernard's father made as a security guard, and used it to begin construction on a house of their own for the first time.

But as aid organizations have experienced, injecting money into African communities can spark conflict over the newfound resources. Bernard's old coach, Justice Oteng, felt he should get some of the cash since he had raised Bernard like a son for several years, but the player's father only gave him about $125. "In Teshie, everybody was annoyed with the man," said Oteng. "Many people were saying he should have given me a proper share of the money." This wasn't an isolated case. Other Football Dreams kids experienced the same: coaches fighting with families over the cash and families bickering among themselves.

Bernard told Oteng he should forget about the money from Aspire since he had something potentially far more valuable: the player's license. The coach effectively owned Bernard. Oteng had registered the player with the Ghana Football Association when the boy first joined his Colts team, and the coach expected a cash windfall when Bernard finally transferred to a European club. This is the dream that fuels the trade in young players across Africa, although so few actually make it to Europe that many coaches fail to earn back the money they spend on their teams and watch the cash dribble out of their pockets for years.

Oteng viewed Bernard as his only real chance to turn the tide. By his estimate, he had spent thousands of dollars on his teams over nearly a decade, using cash from his small welding business and getting help from his church to fill the gaps. Oteng had never been able to sell a player for much money and didn't have any others like Bernard. The coach was convinced the midfielder was his ticket to making back what he had spent and earning a tidy profit on top. At least that's how he felt before a showdown with Aspire at the Coconut Grove Hotel in Accra in the fall of 2009. After that, everything changed.

It all started when the Football Dreams country director in Ghana, Andy Sam, contacted Oteng to say Aspire wanted Bernard's license. The request came as a surprise to the coach. When Aspire first selected Bernard, Oteng's understanding was that the academy wasn't interested in owning the players and simply wanted to help them achieve their dream of becoming professionals. After all, Aspire repeatedly said Football Dreams wasn't a money-making scheme. Now that Oteng was hearing something different, he was suspicious Sam was trying to profit from Bernard personally.

Sam said Aspire simply needed to protect itself and the investment it was making in the players. The country director estimated the academy spent around 1 million euros on each of the Football Dreams kids it trained. It's unclear why Aspire waited until 2009 to ask for Bernard's license, but the scholarship agreement the player signed in 2008 when he first joined the academy indicated Aspire was interested in his license all along. It stipulated that Bernard agree to register and transfer his rights to any team chosen by Aspire in Qatar, Ghana, or elsewhere. But the agreement was co-signed by Bernard's father, not Oteng.

The coach told Sam he would only hand over the license if they drafted an agreement saying he would benefit when Bernard was finally sold to a club. Major academies in Africa usually offer local coaches a few hundred dollars for a player plus 5 to 10 percent of his future value when he's sold, and Oteng demanded something similar. But Aspire didn't want to share any future windfall, a curious position for an academy backed by one of the richest countries in the world and adamant that Football Dreams was a humanitarian program meant to help grassroots soccer in Africa. Sam told Oteng the academy was willing to give him around $1,000 for Bernard's license, but the coach balked, convinced he was being cheated. To resolve the issue, Sam suggested Oteng bring Bernard's parents to a meeting at a hotel in an upscale neighborhood of Accra so they could discuss the matter face-to-face.

The Coconut Grove was Sam's turf. He often conducted Football Dreams business at wooden tables set up next to the pool in the hotel's courtyard. Traditional African masks stare out from the courtyard walls, and the pool's tile floor is decorated with an image of a large palm tree heavy with coconuts. It's far from the only palm tree in the joint. Hundreds more cover the shirts of hotel staff serving Star beer and Bacardi rum to guests by the pool. The atmosphere may have been a bit kitsch, but it was far nicer than the places Oteng spent his time in Teshie. This was no meeting of equals, and home field advantage put Sam even farther on the front foot.

To help level the playing field, Oteng arrived at the hotel with backup. The coach may have been a bit player in the country's soccer scene but managed to convince the chairman of the Ghana Football Association's Disciplinary Committee, Farouck Seidu, that he was being taken advantage of and persuaded him to come along. As they made their way through the lobby to the poolside table where Sam was sitting, Oteng was surprised to see the country director had brought his own backup. Seated next to him was Colomer, who knew plenty about hammering out deals for potential young stars. Colomer was in town for the latest Football Dreams tryouts, and Oteng believed he had come to press Aspire's case. (Aspire later denied that Colomer had attended the meeting at all, despite statements to the contrary by Oteng, Seidu, and Bernard's parents.)

Bernard's parents arrived at the meeting separately in one of Accra's battered black and yellow taxis and joined the others around the table. Bernard, the center of attention, was missing because he had already returned to Doha after the end of his summer vacation. Oteng spoke to him by phone beforehand and convinced him Sam wasn't to be trusted. Bernard agreed the coach shouldn't hand over his license unless the country director agreed in writing to his demands. Since Oteng wasn't sharing in the money Aspire sent to Bernard's parents, he wanted to make sure the coach properly benefited from the value of his license.

Sam did most of the talking in the meeting, and it was clear from the outset that Aspire didn't plan on changing its position. The country director told Oteng it was the best deal his little neighborhood soccer operation was going to get. "I asked them, 'How much money have you earned in the past five years? Is it anywhere near $1,000?'" said Sam. "If you don't want it, no problem, take it or leave it, we'll just put somebody [else] in there. If you don't take it, there are 10 other boys who are good enough." According to Oteng, Colomer didn't speak much, but it seemed clear that Sam had his support.

Oteng refused to budge on his demands and was backed by the lawyer Seidu, who felt $1,000 was peanuts for a player of Bernard's caliber. "I said, 'What? You are joking. You want to take the player and pay this amount? If you ask me as a lawyer, I would say no,'" said Seidu. Someone brought up Colomer's role in jump-starting Messi's career to convince Oteng and Seidu to change their minds. "They were trying to give us confidence that if this man has something to do with Messi, then we can be sure he can help Bernard," Seidu later said. "I said, 'Well, it's true, but not for peanuts.'"

The discussion around the table at the Coconut Grove was a far cry from the big money negotiations over superstars like Messi and Ronaldo, but to Oteng, the outcome was just as important. He suspected Sam requested the meeting with Bernard's parents under the assumption they would support Aspire to keep the player in the academy. It was clear that Aspire was light-years ahead of anything Bernard could find in Ghana, but Oteng thought he was talented enough that he would be able to find another way to Europe if he had to leave the academy.

The coach said Aspire's arm-twisting at the Coconut Grove failed because Bernard's parents supported him instead of the academy, thanks to the years he spent raising and training the player. But Bernard's father, Noah Appiah, tells a different story. He said he and his wife had no idea what the meeting was about when Oteng asked them to come to the Coconut Grove and weren't aware there was a conflict over Bernard's license. They stayed quiet as the argument played out at the hotel, but Bernard's father said he told Oteng after the meeting he should give Aspire the license so Bernard could stay in the academy. Noah Appiah had visited Aspire twice since his son went to Doha, so he knew exactly what was at stake. But he didn't push the issue when Oteng disagreed, especially since Bernard was supporting his coach.

Back in Doha, John Benson sensed something was wrong. He was in class with Bernard and made one of his regular jokes about the player's lousy English. "Before when I did this, he would laugh," said John. "But he wasn't laughing." John asked what was wrong, and Bernard said he might have to leave the academy and return home because of a dispute over his license.

It was the spring of 2010, several months after the showdown at the Coconut Grove. According to Oteng, Sam told him after the meeting Bernard would have to leave Aspire because the coach refused to hand over his license, but the player stayed at the academy for a few more months until his father signed a termination agreement and so he could finish out his school year. "Oteng called me and said this is what Andy Sam has done, so I have to come back home," said Bernard. "I was very sad. Everybody at Aspire was very sad."

Sam insisted Aspire never forced Bernard out, even though he clearly took a hard line in the meeting at the Coconut Grove. He said Bernard decided to leave himself over frustration that the academy wouldn't transfer him to Europe. "Bernard thought he had arrived even at that age," said Sam. "I used to tell Colomer he ought to be very careful the things he says to some of these kids. It goes to their head." In reality, it may have been a combination of both issues that led to Bernard's departure. The player was indeed frustrated that Aspire wouldn't send him to Europe, and the conflict over his license may have been the final straw, persuading Bernard and his coach they were better off trying their luck elsewhere than agreeing to the academy's demands. (Aspire officials in Doha confirmed that they didn't renew Bernard's scholarship but refused to provide details, citing legal reasons.)

Whatever the reason for Bernard's departure, he was on his way out. Less than three years after Colomer stood in the dirt at Star Park in Teshie watching a player who reminded him of Messi, the midfielder waited outside Aspire for a car to take him to Doha airport. Bernard had put on a brave face saying goodbye to his friends at the academy, but now his eyes welled with tears. Colomer had predicted Bernard would become a star, but he wasn't catching a flight to Barcelona or Manchester. One of the brightest diamonds discovered by Football Dreams was headed back to the mine where he was found. It wasn't the path anyone had imagined for Bernard when he arrived at Aspire. That first trip was filled with such hope, the fulfillment of a childhood dream that soccer would whisk him away from the life he knew in Ghana. He never anticipated it would be a round-trip and now faced the uncertainty of finding another way out.

Bernard's departure was a clear indication that Football Dreams was even more challenging than the organizers had imagined. Scouring the African continent for those few players who can blossom into future stars was hard enough, but that was just the beginning of the equation. Managing the players' hopes and frustrations along the way could be just as difficult, especially in an environment as foreign as Qatar with staff who knew plenty about professional soccer but relatively little about the nuance of dealing with players from Africa.

Not long after Bernard left Aspire, the academy abandoned its plan to host Football Dreams kids in Qatar altogether. Officials sent the players from the first two classes who had been placed in Doha to the academy run by Colomer in Senegal. That didn't go down well with Hamza, Adama, and John Felagha, who had become accustomed to the world-class facilities on offer at Aspire in Doha. They nicknamed the academy in Senegal "Baghdad" to express their displeasure with their newfound surroundings. Hamza was even sent home for several months at one point as punishment for being so difficult. "There were times when Colomer was so frustrated he wanted to kick him out of the academy," said Sam.

Aspire said it stopped hosting the Football Dreams kids in Qatar because they had little, if any, impact on improving the local play-ers, although some of the coaches in Doha, disagreed, including Michael Browne. Andreas Bleicher, the German who helped launch Football Dreams, also said the African players struggled with the country's language and culture and ended up getting homesick. He said it was difficult to integrate them into the academy's school given that some of them had problems with basic reading and writ-ing, meaning they had to craft individual programs for the boys. But the kids themselves said they were generally happy at the academy in Doha and were clearly upset when they had to move to Senegal. The difficulty of schooling the kids shouldn't have come as much of a surprise since Aspire had three African players at the academy before it launched Football Dreams.

In fact, Aspire kept two of those players, Serigne Abdou Thiam and Antoine Messi, in Doha even after it sent the Football Dreams kids to Senegal. The third, John Benson, had already graduated. Serigne Abdou ended up playing a key role on the Qatari national team that won the Under-19 AFC championship for the first time in 2014, although it's unclear how he joined the squad without violat-ing FIFA rules on naturalization.

Could it be that hosting the Football Dreams kids in Qatar made less sense after FIFA made it more difficult to naturalize them for the country's national team? Aspire denies that was a factor in its decision, but it's easy to see how placing the players off-limits could have made the hassle of keeping them in Doha seem less worth-while and help explain the radical decision to abandon the original aim of Football Dreams.

Regardless, the success or failure of Football Dreams now rested on Colomer's satellite academy in Senegal. Could he produce a superstar to help justify the millions spent on the project and cast glory on Qatar in the process? The loss of Bernard was clearly a blow, but Colomer was grooming a new star, Ibrahima Dramé, the towering striker found in the sleepy Senegalese town where he first came up with the idea for Football Dreams. The "serial killer," some called him, because his finishing was so deadly. Ibrahima was scoring goals by the bucketload, and in the currency of professional soccer, there's nothing more valuable than that.

CHAPTER 7

Brothers

Ibrahima was on a hat trick. Twice already, he had glided past Diawandou and put the ball in the back of the net. Now he was knocking on the door yet again. One of Ibrahima's teammates threaded a pass through the defense, and the ball was set up perfectly for him to run onto it and notch his third goal of the match. But Diawandou was fed up. Not only was Ibrahima the new guy in town, but they were also on Diawandou's turf. Colomer had set up his Football Dreams satellite operation on the grounds of Diawandou's old academy in Thiès. With its patchy grass fields and aging concrete buildings, it was a far cry from the academy in Doha but would have to do until Colomer could come up with a better solution. The Spanish scout brought Ibrahima and a handful of other players he found during the second year of Football Dreams to Thiès in the fall of 2008 so they could train for a few months before going to the final in Qatar.

Colomer wanted to see how they stacked up against the first class of kids he discovered, and Ibrahima quickly attracted the spotlight— a little too quickly, in Diawandou's mind. He figured now was the time to teach him a lesson, to remind him that the players around him were also among Africa's best and this wasn't going to be a cakewalk. As Ibrahima ran onto the ball, his long strides eating up the ground, Diawandou timed his tackle. He could have swept the ball away, but that wasn't his goal. That wouldn't have sent a strong enough message. He swung his foot in and took out Ibrahima's legs, sending him tumbling to the ground and injuring the striker's ankle in the process. He would be out for three weeks. Sprawled on the field, Ibrahima was outraged. "I screamed at Diawandou in Wolof, 'Why did you do this? We are the same! We are brothers!'"

Ibrahima was half right. They would become brothers, but they weren't the same. Both were from Senegal, but Ibrahima's childhood in Ziguinchor was a far cry from the comfortable middle-class upbringing Diawandou experienced in Thiès. Even though Ibrahima's brother Sekou dropped out of school at the age of 12 to work at Ziguinchor's port, the family was still struggling to make ends meet. That's what drove Sekou to consider taking a life-threatening journey across the ocean to Spain to find a better job. Ibrahima had persuaded him not to go, saying the family's life would change if he made it into the academy. That meant he had a serious weight on his shoulders as he took his first-ever flight to attend the final tryout in Doha at the beginning of 2009.

But Ibrahima was still brimming with his trademark confidence. His uncle and coach, Amadou Traoré, accompanied him to Qatar for the first week of the final, and when Traoré left to return to Senegal, Ibrahima told him, "Sleep well, I will succeed." Due to injury, the striker missed the most memorable game of the tryout, a 7-0 thrashing of one of AC Milan's youth teams. The result indicated the kind of talent Colomer had assembled in the second Football Dreams class. But even among this group, Ibrahima stood out once he recovered from his injury. "He was a player you would never forget," said Michael Browne, Aspire's head soccer coach. "You watch him at times and think, 'What's he doing?' and then all of a sudden he would get it and he would put it in the net from anywhere."

Ibrahima was desperate to be one of the few kids chosen to stay in Qatar. Having seen both the academy in Thiès and Aspire's facilities in Doha, there was no question in his mind about the best place for him to train to become a European star. But Browne wasn't just looking for the most talented players to stay in Doha. He was also focused on filling gaps in the academy team at Aspire. If a squad already had a promising Qatari striker, he didn't want to insert an even better African who would challenge the local for playing time. Unfortunately for Ibrahima, that meant he was headed to Senegal. "If you were selecting the best players, I would have taken him," said Browne.

Ibrahima didn't realize that and was upset about not making the cut. "I wanted to be among the best," said Ibrahima. "I wanted to be able to keep my head up." But not everyone thought it was a bad result. Over the course of the tryout, Ibrahima had grown close to a Senegalese doctor who worked with Football Dreams, Babacar Ngom. Even before the final was over, he told the striker he would actually be better off in Senegal. "He said, 'Qatar is nice, it's beautiful, but if you sit in Doha, you cannot improve your football,'" said Ibrahima. "'Because here in Doha you can eat, you can sleep, you can have everything, but you cannot fight because you don't have the boys who are good. You have to go to Senegal to fight for your future because all of the black boys are there at the academy.'" Ibrahima wasn't entirely convinced because Aspire was so spectacular, but he was certainly determined to fight wherever the academy put him.

Colomer wasn't satisfied with Diawandou's old academy in Thiès, either, and moved the Football Dreams kids to much nicer digs in the fall of 2009, a year after starting his satellite operation in Senegal. Aspire began renting half of Diambars, an

academy opened in the small coastal resort town of Saly in 2000
by several prominent Senegalese players, including Patrick Viera,
who became a legend at Arsenal and ended up winning the World
Cup with France in 1998. Diambars still fell far short of Aspire in
Doha, but as one of the nicest academies in West Africa, it was a
significant improvement over the facility in Thiès. As one Football
Dreams player put it, "Doha is five stars, Senegal three stars."

Diambars has six well-maintained fields, five of which are artificial turf and the sixth natural grass. The rest of the academy has the
feel of a no-frills resort located a few blocks from the ocean. Colorful wildflowers line the sidewalks, and sprinklers run constantly to
keep the grass a lush green under Senegal's baking sun. The players
are housed four to a room in two-story, cream-colored concrete villas topped with red tile roofs. The rooms are equipped with ceiling
fans, not air conditioning like Doha, so they can get extremely hot
in the often sweltering weather. The academy also has a cafeteria,
a nice gym, and even a pool where the kids can cool off. There are
also several rooms where the Diambars' players attend class, while
the Football Dreams kids travel by bus to an independent private
school in town.

The players are kept under much tighter lock and key than the
boys at Aspire in Doha. They're only let out of the academy to roam
around town one afternoon a week, perhaps a good thing since Saly
is conspicuously known as a sex tourism destination for French men
and women, and prostitutes abound in the town's bars and restau-
rants. Saly served as a Portuguese trading post long ago and first
started attracting large numbers of tourists in the mid-1980s, many
of them middle-class vacationers from France. Hotels and restau-
rants catering to foreigners have sprung up since then, places like
Le Petit Zing, a restaurant bar that serves pizza and steak frites to
sunburned tourists during the day and then plies them with Flag
beer and Western pop long into the night. Most of these spots are

located along the town's sandy beach, where fishermen push their long wooden boats out to sea in the morning and locals play pickup soccer in the late afternoon once the heat begins to abate.

Moving inland from the paved beach road, which buzzes with tourists on ATVs, Saly begins to look more familiar. This is the part of town where the locals actually live, and the dirt roads are lined with crudely built concrete houses topped with rusty metal roofs. Goats roam the streets looking for something to eat, and horses walk by pulling beaten-up wooden carts. Almost every male above the age of about 5 seems to be wearing a knockoff European jersey, just like the ones sold down on the beach road next to fake Ray-Bans and Rolexes. There's Messi adjusting the straps on a donkey, Ronaldo patching a fishing net in the shade of a tree.

Behind the high concrete walls that surround Diambars, Ibrahima, Diawandou, and the other Football Dreams players battled to become the next name emblazoned on jerseys sold around the world. The kids may not have had all the trappings of Aspire in Doha but did have Colomer and the experience he brought from Barcelona. They saw him as the link to that unknown world of high-end European soccer they so desperately wanted to join.

The kids meant plenty to Colomer as well. There was, of course, the tantalizing prospect that one of them could become the world's next superstar. Colomer was proud of the role he had played in jump-starting Messi's career, but he couldn't take credit for actually discovering him back in Argentina. Football Dreams was different. If one of the Africans ended up taking the soccer world by storm, nobody would get more credit than Colomer. An African Messi would be his Messi. A player like that would mark him as one of the world's greatest producers of talent, a reputation he had been looking to cement ever since he was a teenager searching for skilled young recruits for his soccer school back in his hometown of Vic.

But the kids weren't just a means to an end. Colomer genuinely

Colomer sharing a laugh with the Nigerian goalkeeper John Felagha at the Football Dreams academy in Senegal.

cared about them. "For them, this is a chance," he said, "for them, for their families, for their towns, for Africa." Colomer may have been relatively cut off from Bernard and the other Football Dreams players in Doha, but in Saly he could often be seen offering encouragement and a few words of wisdom to the boys after a match. He was especially close to the players in the first class and became a father figure to many of them. "I always think Colomer is a messenger from God because he came to Africa to pick talented players," said Anthony Bassey, a striker the Spanish scout found in Nigeria the first year. Colomer also got to know the kids' parents, who visited the academy once a year, and often intervened if he noticed a player had problems on the home front.

Out of all the boys, Colomer grew closest to Diawandou, the captain of the first class and a recognized leader among everyone. "Colomer is like my father," said Diawandou. "He never tells me something that I don't do." There were flashier and more physically imposing players at the academy and others who were more vocal off the field. But none commanded the kind of respect Diawandou did during the heat of a match or in a team meeting. "He was a born leader, a very strong character on and off the pitch," said Wendy Kinyeki, a Football Dreams staff member from Kenya. "He knows how to get people to listen to him. Even when there was discontent, when they lost a match, or the coach was being unfair, he was always bringing people together, acting as a mediator and buffer to make people see both sides, make sure nobody blew off their lid."

Over time, Colomer increasingly relied on Diawandou's leadership and often communicated messages to other boys at the academy through the Senegalese captain. "Colomer only had my number," said Diawandou. "Whenever he wanted to tell something to a player, he called me." Diawandou relished his close bond with Colomer, but it didn't go down well with everyone at the academy. "Some players got jealous," said Ibrahima. In such a competitive environment, kids started to worry that Colomer's close relationship with Diawandou and others in the first class meant the Spanish scout might do more to help them become top players in Europe. After all, not everyone was likely to make it. The stakes were so high and the margins so thin, everyone was looking for that edge that could mean the difference between success and failure.

The schedule at the academy was grueling. A typical day might begin with an hour and a half of training at 7 a.m., followed by breakfast and three and a half hours of school. The players would then return to the academy for lunch, have a rest, and do a second training session around 4:30 p.m. The boys would end the day with two more hours of school, dinner, and then it was off to bed. They followed this routine for four or five days a week and also had a game on the weekend. Much of the training mirrored what Colomer had used at Barcelona's academy. In fact, he told the BBC his goal was to build "the new La Masia for football talents from developing countries."

La Masia was the brainchild of the revered Dutch striker Johan Cruyff. He and his coach at Ajax, Rinus Michels, had revolutionized soccer in the late 1960s and early 1970s. Together, they created the beautiful, flowing blend of attacking soccer that came to be known as Total Football. Teams struggled to deal with Ajax's fluid system in which players constantly switched positions during matches, and the club won the European Cup three times on the trot in the early 1970s. Cruyff was so creative in his manipulation of space that he has been described as "Pythagoras in boots." The slender striker was also famous for his delightfully gnomic expressions, like "playing football is very simple, but playing simple football is the hardest thing there is."

Michels and Cruyff eventually brought their captivating brand of soccer to Barcelona, and the striker won the Ballon d'Or twice while he was at the club. Even more important, Cruyff suggested starting a youth academy modeled after the one at Ajax. The club's president agreed, and Barcelona started housing young players in 1979 at La Masia, a craggy old Catalan farmhouse near the team's Camp Nou stadium. Cruyff further strengthened the academy when he returned to Barcelona as coach in 1988 and ensured all youth teams played in the same fluid, attacking style. This system formed the bedrock of the success Barcelona had twenty years later under coach Pep Guardiola and Messi at his goal-scoring greatest.

Colomer wanted his academy teams to play the same kind of soccer that Barcelona executed so beautifully. Training methods had evolved since the time he spent at Clairefontaine in the 1990s. The repetitive exercises used by the French academy to build technique had fallen out of favor because they didn't improve game intelligence, one of the most important skills needed to become a professional. The coaches at La Masia, and many other academies, now use small-sided games instead because they train technique and game intelligence at the same time. Barcelona is also well known for honing its players' touch, vision, and passing in tight spaces by using games of keep-away, known as *rondos* or *toros* in Spanish.

Some coaches believe small-sided games are so useful for training because they replicate the kind of pickup soccer that researchers have proven is most useful in developing game intelligence. "They don't work on technique at Barcelona," a French national team coach, Erick Mombaerts, told *The Blizzard*. "They just play games on reduced pitches, adopting the same principles as the street football you see in Brazil and Africa. Even the 12-year-olds play matches all the time. For six years, they work solely on collective play, so it's little wonder they can pass to one another with their eyes closed."

But how does game intelligence work exactly? It's clear that the ability to analyze the situation on the field and execute the right decision almost instantly is the mark of a good player, both young and old. The colorful TV commentator Ray Hudson often talks about the game's stars having "kaleidoscope eyes." But how does street soccer actually help a player develop game intelligence? What's going on in a player's brain that gives him the ability to shoot through pockets of space that don't seem to exist and feed the ball into passing lanes that others can't see?

The Nobel Prize–winning psychologist Daniel Kahneman provided valuable insight into the inner workings of game intelligence in his best-selling book, *Thinking, Fast and Slow*, even though it wasn't primarily focused on sports and didn't mention soccer at all. For simplicity's sake, he described the brain as two different systems. System 1 operates quickly and automatically, with little or no effort. It can do things like detect one object is farther than another and answer the math problem $2 + 2 = ?$. System 2 is slower and more taxing but better at complex problem solving. It can park a car in a narrow space and fill out a tax form.

A soccer player dribbling at high speed and evaluating his next move as teammates and opponents shift around him needs to do System 2 thinking but execute at System 1 speed. That's where the thousands of hours of training come in. With enough practice, players can transform what would be System 2 thinking for a novice, like deciding whether to dribble, pass, or shoot in the face of an onrushing defender, into a System 1 process. It can even seem effortless, a state psychologists often refer to as flow, or more colloquially, as being in the zone.

Kahneman doesn't call this type of thinking game intelligence but labels it expert intuition. He gave the example of chess masters to show what System 1 can accomplish with the right training since they can often come up with a strong move only seconds after looking at a board. He cited the work of another Nobel laureate, Herbert Simon, who published a seminal study in 1973 with fellow psychologist William Chase, looking at how chess masters process the game so quickly. Their findings led to a pivotal theory applicable not just to chess but also to sports in general.

They proposed that chess masters perceive the board in chunks, clusters of positions they have seen before. That way they don't have to grapple with a large number of individual pieces, and a quick glance at a board is often all it takes to recognize a layout. Grandmasters have a mental database of millions of arrangements of pieces broken down into at least 300,000 chunks, allowing them to quickly process what they see and make a decision. "What was once accomplished by slow, conscious deductive reasoning is now arrived at by fast, unconscious perceptual processing," wrote Chase and Simon. "It is no mistake of language for the chess master to say that he 'sees' the right move."

Soccer is likely no different. Elite players have developed their game intelligence by building the same kind of mental database as chess masters through thousands of hours of training, except they're chunking midfielders and defenders, not knights and pawns. Training may even change the physical structure of a player's brain. One study of high-level athletes found that they had increased cortical thickness in certain areas of their brains compared to nonathletes and that it was correlated with training. One of these areas is associated with biological motion perception. In soccer, this would relate to the ability to anticipate an opponent's movements in a match, an absolutely essential skill.

Some of the top clubs in the world have started using innovative training methods off the field in an attempt to improve the cognitive skills that underpin game intelligence. Manchester United spent $80,000 to install a system called NeuroTracker that requires players to track digital yellow spheres as they bounce around a 3D screen, much like they would track teammates and opponents moving around the field. At Bayern Munich, they use a device called the SpeedCourt that can be set so that players have to run to different electronic sensors in the floor, following a sequence that flashes on a screen in front of them for a short time at the beginning of the test.

The rival German club Borussia Dortmund employs a system called the Footbonaut, which consists of a 150-square-foot artificial turf surface surrounded on four sides by 72 square panels. Machines send balls hurtling at a player standing in the middle of the turf from any of the four sides of the room. A beep alerts the player where the ball is coming from, and he must quickly turn, receive the ball, and pass it into whichever of the panels surrounding him lights up. These training methods have their supporters and critics, but none of them can substitute for the thousands of hours of training a player needs on the field to make it to the top.

Colomer certainly knew the importance of logging plenty of

training hours. In fact, he boasted that by having his players train in the morning and afternoon, they racked up twice as many hours as the kids back at Barcelona. Many academies have shied away from holding two training sessions a day for various reasons, including concern over physical wear and tear. But how many hours of training does a player actually need to make it in the world of professional soccer?

The youth development plan adopted by the Premier League in 2011 promoted the so-called 10,000-hour rule popularized by Malcolm Gladwell in his best-selling book *Outliers*. He called it "the magic number for true expertise," and many in the media have interpreted the idea as meaning 10,000 hours of practice is necessary and sufficient to make anyone an expert in anything. The concept is based on work done in the 1990s by K. Anders Ericsson and two other psychologists, who studied the amount of practice by violinists and pianists at the Music Academy of West Berlin. They found that aggregate practice time, not innate talent, determined a musician's skill level, and top violinists and pianists had accumulated an average of 10,000 hours of practice by the age of 20. They extended their conclusions to sports in a paper led by Ericsson, and he came to be known as the father of the 10,000-hour rule, although he never called it a rule himself. He said the genes necessary to be a pro athlete "are contained within all healthy individuals' DNA." They just need to practice.

But the reality is more complicated, as David Epstein outlined in *The Sports Gene*. He pointed to a subsequent study that looked at the number of hours required to become a chess master. It found that while the average was about 11,000, similar to what Ericsson predicted, the range was 3,000 to 23,000. That meant some people had to practice nearly eight times more to become a master. Others trained for 25,000 hours and never made it at all.

Studies now indicate that practice only accounts for a low to moderate amount of the difference in skill between athletes, musicians, and others. What accounts for the rest? At least part of it is genetic differences, said Epstein. Genes help to determine not only things like height and speed but also an athlete's response to training and willingness to work hard. An elite athlete therefore needs both the right genes and the right training, a combination of "innate hardware and learned software," according to Epstein. Nature and nurture.

Despite this complexity, the Premier League focused on the 10,000-hour rule in its youth development plan and encouraged English academies to increase the number of training hours to catch up to their European counterparts. But the truth is that players at major European academies get nowhere near 10,000 hours of training. The authors of the book *Youth Development in Football* surveyed six major European clubs, including Ajax, Barcelona, and Bayern Munich, to find out the number of training hours that kids get from the Under-9 level until they graduate at around the age of 18.

The highest number was 4,700 hours at the French club AJ Auxerre. They found the number to be about the same at Aspire in Doha, which ran training sessions twice a day like Colomer in Senegal. Of course, not every player needs 10,000 hours to make it. In general, though, the authors speculated that the number of hours of training at European academies meant many players aren't ready to represent top-level teams when they graduate and still need time to progress. But in the cutthroat world of professional soccer, they often don't get it, and many wash out of the game.

These figures don't take into account the number of hours spent playing matches and, more importantly for some kids, time spent training in more informal settings like the street. Rasmus Ankersen, the author of *The Gold Mine Effect*, found that it wasn't unusual for Brazilian kids to log 10,000 hours by the time they turn 13, taking into account the time they spent training at school, at their club, and on the street. In contrast, he estimated the average English player wouldn't reach that number of hours until he hit the age of 30, or perhaps a few years earlier if he got into an academy. This difference helps explain why Brazilian players have dominated the soccer world for so many years.

Like Brazilians, the African kids Colomer assembled in Senegal had spent thousands of hours playing in the street and elsewhere before they even made it to the academy, and the experience showed when they took the field. They played professional teams from Senegal's top leagues on the weekends and often crushed them. One of Diawandou's best memories was when his class destroyed one of the country's most successful clubs, Jeanne d'Arc, as Colomer proudly watched from the sidelines. "It was an amazing game," said Diawandou. "They were older than us, but we won 6-0." The Football Dreams players developed the reputation as the team to beat in Senegal, and opposing clubs celebrated like it was the World Cup on the rare occasions they won. Journalists even printed the results in local newspapers even though the games were only friendlies.

The Football Dreams players began to build a reputation in Europe as well. The second class of kids traveled to Italy in May 2010 to compete in the Ciociaria Cup, a tournament held at an area between Rome and Naples with 32 teams from around the world. They blew away most of the competition, outscoring their opponents 19-1. The team took home the trophy after beating a side from Paraguay, Club Nacional, 2-1 in the final, and Ibrahima was the tournament's top scorer, with twelve goals.

It was the first major tournament that any of the Football Dreams teams had won, and the kids were ecstatic. A photo of the players taken on the field after the victory shows them crowded around the tall metal trophy they won, wearing blue and white Aspire uniforms. Ibrahima stands at the back with a smile on his face and his arms around his teammates, while several of the other players scream in delight. The only disappointment was that the trophy ended up getting mangled on the way home when they were forced to put it through the X-ray machine at the airport in Rome, and it got stuck.

The Football Dreams players also traveled to Spain at least once a year to play tournaments and friendlies against the country's top youth teams. Once again, they almost always came out on top, even against Barcelona and Real Madrid. "Every time we play against Barcelona, we have to play against one year older than us because if we play the same age, we beat them," said Colomer.

On one occasion, the first class of kids took on one of Real Madrid's youth teams at the club's glamorous training facility, Ciudad Real Madrid. One of the strikers from the first class, the Nigerian Jasper Uwa, who scored against Neymar's Brazil in Doha, got injured before the match, so the coaches plucked Ibrahima from the second class to see if he could keep up his goal-scoring ways against older kids at one of the world's top clubs.

The answer was an emphatic yes. Ibrahima scored a hat trick and provided an assist to help the team bowl over Real Madrid 5-0. Lamine Savané, the Football Dreams country director in Senegal, was at the match and noticed several Real Madrid executives gathered at their office windows watching the carnage taking place on the field below. "The people at Real Madrid were pissed off," said Savané. "We beat them so badly. Since then, they have never accepted any friendly matches against them."

Playing together helped Ibrahima and Diawandou forge a strong friendship. Ibrahima may have been outraged when Diawandou hacked him down during their first encounter in Thiès, but he eventually forgave him and gained respect for him as a leader and role model. He was impressed by how focused Diawandou was on his quest to become a star, day in and day out. "It's very simple what he does," said Ibrahima. "He trains very hard, never gets injured, and plays all the games."

Unlike many of the Football Dreams players, Diawandou wasn't one to do a lot of socializing in the few moments of free time the kids could find between training and school. That was more Ibrahima's style. He loved to joke with his teammates, especially his close friend Fallou Niang, a Senegalese midfielder from Thiès who was about half the size of the big striker. Ibrahima would often playfully slap him around in training, prompting laughs from the others.

Diawandou was much more serious and would stay in his room or sit with Senegalese members of the staff when he didn't have somewhere to be. But Ibrahima would often seek him out for advice. "He knew I was his biggest brother," said Diawandou. "He always came to ask me, 'What are you going to do with the team? What are you going to do with the game tomorrow?'"

Ibrahima would share his thoughts as well, telling Diawandou what it was like to play in Italy and what to expect from Italian teams. But mostly he just listened and tried to follow Diawandou's example. Ibrahima could have turned to the captain of his own class, Yobou Thome, a powerful central defender from the Ivory Coast. He was clearly talented and would go on to captain his country's Under-17 national team. But they didn't share the same bond. After all, Ibrahima and Diawandou were from the same country. They spoke the same language. They were brothers.

CHAPTER 8

Glory and Shame

As fellow countrymen, Diawandou and Ibrahima both dreamed of becoming Lions. While winning European tournaments with their academy classmates and beating top clubs in friendlies were gratifying accomplishments, making Senegal's national team, the Lions of Teranga, meant even more. Getting a call-up was, of course, a matter of intense national pride. It also conferred special status at the academy. All the Football Dreams players considered themselves to be among Africa's elite, but those tapped to represent their countries could hold their heads up that much higher.

Most important, though, making the national team was one of the best ways to attract the attention of scouts from the best clubs across Europe. These scouts didn't usually spend their time traveling across Africa like Colomer looking for undiscovered talent. They preferred to skim off the top, and one of the ways they did that was by watching youth tournaments like the Under-17 World Cup that feature top national teams from across the globe. Within Africa, the premier tournament is the Africa Cup of Nations, which pits the continent's best teams against each other every two years. Future African stars like Michael Essien from Ghana and John Obi Mikel from Nigeria went on to top European clubs like Chelsea and Real Madrid after first shining for their youth national teams.

Diawandou and Ibrahima hoped to follow in their footsteps, and by the fall of 2010, they had taken a big step in that direction by becoming two of the most important players on Senegal's Under-17 national team. Diawandou was the captain, and Ibrahima was the team's leading goal scorer. There were plenty of other familiar faces around them as well, since the team contained nearly a dozen Football Dreams players, a remarkable number. That's the kind of impact top academies at places like Barcelona and Ajax have had on the national teams in their countries after decades of building their programs and producing some of Europe's biggest stars. A wave of Colomer's recruits had made the jump less than three years after he selected the first Football Dreams class.

But making the national team was only one step toward impressing scouts from Europe's top clubs at the Africa Cup of Nations. Senegal also had to qualify for the tournament, something the country's Under-17 national team had never done before. Standing in their way was one of Africa's traditional powerhouses, Ghana, which had won the tournament nearly two dozen times at the senior and junior levels. Senegal's tally was zero. After playing a series of qualifiers against other nations, the Lions of Teranga were scheduled to compete against Ghana's Black Starlets in a two-game playoff in November 2010. The winner would make it to the Under-17 Africa Cup of Nations in Rwanda the following January.

Diawandou and Ibrahima had their work cut out for them. Not only did Ghana have an impressive track record, but the team also had its own reserve of Football Dreams players. They included the squad's captain, Hamza Zakari, the temperamental defensive midfielder who was such close friends with Bernard in Doha. That meant it wasn't just national pride on the line but also bragging rights when the players got back to the academy. "If you play against your teammates, it's so difficult," said Ibrahima. "If they win, you're going to go back to the academy and have to keep quiet because they're going to talk!" Nobody wanted to end up second-best, and all of them were desperate to be the ones to showcase their skills for scouts in Rwanda come January. Their careers might depend on it.

Senegal's coach, Boucounta Cissé, got his first glimpse of the talent Aspire had to offer before he took over the national team and was coaching a club in Senegal's first division. Cissé was close friends with Babacar Ngom, the doctor who worked at Colomer's academy and once told Ibrahima he was better off training in Senegal than Doha. The doctor helped arrange games between Cissé's club and the academy teams, and he was blown away by the players' skill. "As a coach, it was amazing to see them play," said Cissé, who coached Senegal's Under-20 national team in the 1990s. "During the game, we were really suffering. That's how I knew there was a lot of quality on the team." After Cissé became coach of the Under-17 team at the end of 2009, he brought a squad to the academy that was crushed 5-0 by the Football Dreams players in a match in which Ibrahima scored a hat trick. "Afterward, I asked how old the kids were," said Cissé. "They told me they were under 17, and I said, 'perfect.'"

He scooped up nearly a dozen Football Dreams players for his team. The decision was criticized by other academies in the country that were jealous more of their players didn't make the cut. Cissé ignored the sniping and immediately appointed Diawandou captain. "Before I chose him as a player, when we played against Aspire, I saw that he was a leader on the field," said Cissé. "He's charismatic and has the character to lead the team." The coach was also impressed by his passing game and his ability to bring the ball forward from

Diawandou (top right) and Ibrahima (top, third from right) with other members of Senegal's Under-17 national team.

the back. "His only handicap is his size," said Cissé. "He's not very tall for a central defender." Diawandou topped out at around five feet, nine inches and had to compensate for his lack of height with superior defensive positioning and technical skill.

The coach definitely had no concerns about Ibrahima's size. He was well over six feet at that point and would eventually grow to six feet, four inches tall. Some of his teammates called him Adebayor, after the big Togolese striker voted African Footballer of the Year in 2008. Ibrahima was the leading goal scorer in the initial qualifying rounds, notching five goals in four games against Liberia and Guinea to set up the playoff with Ghana. "He scored a lot of quality goals, not just with his head, but his feet as well," said Cissé.

Ghana's coach, Frimpong Manso, also relied on Football Dreams for players but not to the same extent as Senegal. It was more difficult for him to see the talent Aspire had to offer since the academy wasn't based in Ghana. He first spotted Hamza when he took his Under-17 team to Aspire in Doha in the fall of 2009 to play against the kids there. "It was then that I realized Hamza was fantastic," said Manso, a former player for Ghana's national team. "I watched him and could see his sense of judgment, his understanding of the game, and his command on the field. His technical level was also very high." Manso also liked the way Hamza directed teammates around the pitch, so he appointed him captain.

Another key Football Dreams player for Ghana was Samuel Asamoah, a small midfield playmaker with exquisite touch and vision. "To be frank with you, he was able to do anything with the ball," said Manso. "His technical level was very, very high. He can control first touch, dribble, and the way he gives passes, I was surprised he could do a lot of things even the seniors couldn't do."

Samuel was one of Colomer's favorites as well but almost missed out making it into the academy in Senegal because he was accidentally left off the list for the final tryout in Accra the first year. Colomer realized the mistake a couple days into the tryout, and the organizers rushed to Samuel's home in one of Accra's neighborhoods. But there wasn't enough time left for him to participate. Colomer didn't give up and lobbied Aspire to give him a place at the academy. "I said, 'Look, I'm sure he's among the best, but it was just a mistake he was not there,'" said Colomer. Aspire eventually agreed, and the Spanish scout returned to Ghana months after the tryout to find the little midfielder. Colomer only needed to watch him play for a few minutes to confirm he was as good as he initially thought and personally escorted him to Senegal.

Some were surprised there was a name missing from Ghana's team: Bernard Appiah. In September 2010, several months after Bernard had returned from Doha for the last time, he heard his name announced over the radio as one of the players called into the national team camp to determine the Under-17 squad that would take on Senegal in November. Aspire said academy officials emailed the Ghana federation months earlier and recommended he be considered for the team. Bernard figured it was the best chance to bounce back from his departure from Aspire and attract attention from clubs in Europe.

Bernard's old coach, Justice Oteng, took him to the location in Accra where the camp was being held, and the player stayed for several days, battling for his chance at redemption. But it didn't come. Manso told Bernard he hadn't made the squad, so he would have to return home, a crushing blow. The verdict shocked the team's captain, Hamza, who was also at the camp training alongside his friend and former teammate. "I was very, very surprised because I know the quality of the players they were looking for, and Bernard had everything," said Hamza.

Even the Ghana federation official responsible for overseeing the Under-17 team, Jordan Anagblah, was surprised by the decision, said Youssif Chibsah, a midfielder who played with Ghana's senior team and tried to help Bernard after he returned home. Anagblah passed away in 2012, but Chibsah went to see him before that to speak about Bernard missing out on the national team. "He told me he was really surprised when the coach finally dropped him," said Chibsah. "But that was the coach's decision, and they didn't want to interfere."

Manso said he doesn't even remember Bernard, even though he was on the list of players called into camp. The coach also saw him play against Ghana's Under-17 team in Doha in 2009, when he said he first spotted Hamza. Bernard was sensational in the game and shredded the national team's defense, as caught on the highlight video recorded by Aspire.

Bernard and Oteng are convinced the Football Dreams country director in Ghana, Andy Sam, intervened to make sure the player didn't make the team because of the dispute with Aspire over his license. "I know Andy Sam influenced them because they are his people," said Oteng, a reference to the director's position on the federation's youth committee. "That's why Appiah was eliminated. He was far better than most of the players." Sam denied the accusation and insisted he never spoke to Manso about Bernard. "Bernard went to the camp, and when he didn't make the grade, he said I had convinced the president of the federation to kick him out," said Sam.

In reality, not speaking to anyone about Bernard may have been enough to keep him off the team. The national team selection process in Africa is seen as notoriously corrupt, especially at the youth level, because of routine allegations that choices are influenced by connections and bribes rather than simply merit. The stakes are so high because of the chance to attract attention from Europe while playing for the team. For a player like Bernard who lacked an influential supporter in his camp after he left Aspire, it could be difficult to make the cut. That was much less of a problem for the Football Dreams players who continued to have the academy's support. Qatar had amassed significant influence in the soccer world by that point, especially in Africa, through the millions of dollars it was spending on Football Dreams and its controversial quest to host the 2022 World Cup. The FIFA vote that produced Qatar's unlikely victory took place only about a month after Senegal and Ghana took the field for the start of their two-game playoff.

The first leg took place at El Wak, a small, tired stadium in Accra owned by the Ghanaian army. Spectators had the choice of sitting in long rows of faded yellow plastic seats that lined one side of the pitch or standing on concrete terraces that ran down the other. The stadium is located across a busy road from the runway at Accra's main airport, and passenger jets roar over the field when games are in progress.

Ghana was seen as the favorite, and the team's coach, Manso, tried to psych up his players and the team's fans by telling the media before the game he wanted Senegal "dead." "We know Senegal will be tough customers, and that's why we're guarding against any form of complacency," said Manso. "Hopefully we'll . . . raise the flag of the country high."

The first half was fairly even, akin to two boxers circling each other at the beginning of a prize fight, throwing the occasional jab and probing for a weakness. Ghana's midfield playmaker, Samuel, sprayed passes in every direction, looking for a way through, but Diawandou kept his back line tight and the ball out of the back of the net. At the other end, Ibrahima used his size and strength to bully Ghana's defenders in the box, but Hamza was just as effective in marshaling his troops to neutralize the big striker's attacks, sending the game to halftime with the score 0-0.

The second half started in much the same fashion, but Ghana's captain finally broke the stalemate in the 76th minute. Hamza stepped up and received a pass inside Senegal's penalty box, composed himself, and unleashed a powerful shot along the ground that beat Senegal's beanpole of a keeper, Babacar Niasse, also a Football Dreams player. Ghana's players exploded in celebration and mobbed Hamza to congratulate him. Minutes later, the team doubled its lead when one of Hamza's teammates smashed in a free kick. Senegal's players could only shake their heads in frustration and disappointment. The game ended 2-0, leaving Senegal with a mountain to climb in the second leg if they hoped to make history and qualify for the Africa Cup of Nations for the first time.

Diawandou and his teammates were crushed after the match. They couldn't even look their coach in the eye when they headed back to the locker room. With so many Football Dreams players on the team, they had been sure of success. None of them wanted to hear "I told you so" from the other academies in Senegal if they missed out on the tournament. They were supposed to be the best of the best.

The match had dented that belief, but they weren't ready to give up. By the time the team made it back to their hotel in Accra, Diawandou had composed himself and called the players together for a meeting to rally them for the second leg. He told them they could still qualify, but it was going to take sacrifice. The most important Muslim holiday of the year, Eid al-Adha, or Tabaski as it's known in Senegal, was approaching. Muslims around the world return home to spend time with their families and often slaughter a goat or sheep to honor Abraham's willingness to obey God and sacrifice his son.

But Diawandou told his teammates the only way they were going to make it to the tournament would be if they skipped the holiday and trained every day until the second game. "I said, "Gentlemen, we don't need to go to our homes,'" said Diawandou. "'We need to go straight to camp and train like crazy.'" That's exactly what they did when they returned to Dakar, while trying to block out the skeptics around them. "People said, 'You disgraced us. You went to Ghana and they beat you 2-0. Don't even think about qualification, you're already out,'" said Diawandou. "That kind of thing makes you more motivated."

The second leg took place a couple weeks later at Demba Diop, a large, weathered stadium in the middle of bustling downtown Dakar. It's surrounded by vendors hawking everything from tires to king-size beds on the crowded streets outside. Colomer was in the audience and looked on proudly as the Football Dreams players from both sides filed onto the stadium's worn artificial turf field in the afternoon sunlight. Ghana was dressed in red and yellow stripes, and Senegal was in mostly white. The rest of the academy players and staff sat beside Colomer on the stadium's hard concrete stands, having made the two-hour drive from Saly.

As usual, Diawandou set up in central defense to marshal his team from the back, a bright orange captain's armband wrapped around his left bicep, his head a nest of short, spiky dreadlocks. Ibrahima went for a more aerodynamic look, his head closely shaved. He took his place at the center of attack, ready to use his size and nose for goal to give the opposing keeper hell. The pressure was on. Since Ghana had won the first leg 2-0, Senegal needed to better that score to qualify, or at least match it to send the game to penalty kicks. Knowing the team needed goals, Senegal pushed forward aggressively from the first whistle, with a mix of quick passes in midfield and long balls from Diawandou looking for Ibrahima upfront. Time and again, Ghana swatted them back and looked dangerous on the counterattack, with Samuel and Hamza feeding balls through to their own strikers.

Senegal finally broke through midway into the first half with a clever assist from a little midfielder, Samba Ndiaye, the son of a poor fishmonger from Kaolack whom Colomer found on the first day of the Football Dreams tryouts in 2007. After executing a slick turn, Samba threaded a pass into the box for another Football Dreams player, Babacar Ndoye, who was discovered the second year just outside Dakar, where his father worked as a mechanic. The small, speedy winger took one touch to take him past the last defender and then slotted the ball under the keeper. Rather than celebrate wildly, Babacar and his teammates immediately ran back to their half to restart the match, knowing they needed at least one more goal to give themselves a chance. Babacar even placed his hands over his ears to block out the roar of the crowd as he stood at the halfway line waiting for the game to resume, so he could focus entirely on the mission at hand.

But Ghana's defenders proved stubbornly difficult to beat again, even though Senegal's coach poured players forward, and the score remained 1-0 deep into the second half. Cissé looked to the bench for options, and his eyes settled on Serigne Mbaye, a lanky Football

Dreams player known for his speed and creativity. This was his first game with the national team, but the coach wondered if he could be the key to unlocking Ghana's stingy defense. Cissé worked it over in his mind for a moment and then called the boy over. With little more than a quick wish good luck, he subbed him into the game on the right wing with about 20 minutes remaining. Perhaps Serigne Mbaye could help Senegal's team conjure up the miracle it needed to qualify for the tournament. After all, it was a miracle he was on the team at all.

Colomer had found Serigne Mbaye on the outskirts of Dakar only days after first discovering Diawandou in 2007. The tryout was held on a small dirt field used by Serigne Mbaye's local soccer school in Rufisque, a down-at-the-heels port city that spills out of the greater Dakar area. Serigne Mbaye caught Colomer's attention as soon as he took the field. He was wiry and quick and could glide by players almost effortlessly, even though he was wearing plastic sandals instead of proper soccer shoes. He was also one of the most inventive players Colomer spotted the first year and had a knack for pulling off the unexpected, whether it was a shot, cross, or dribble. That wasn't a coincidence. Serigne Mbaye had to be better at reading the field than the players around him.

After Serigne Mbaye finished his match, Colomer asked his assistant, Ndongo Diaw, to call him over so they could take his picture and get the information needed to invite him to the final country tryout in Dakar. "I asked Ndongo many times to call this boy over," said Colomer. "He didn't turn around, and we realized he couldn't hear."

Serigne Mbaye lost most of his hearing at the age of 6 after contracting malaria. His father, a customs official at the local port, died of the same disease only nine months later, compounding Serigne

Mbaye's misery. Sign language is almost nonexistent in Senegal, so Serigne Mbaye was largely cut off from others. His mother, Youanidou Lô, tried to send him to school, but they wouldn't accept him, so he turned to soccer to find solace. He played constantly in the street and at his soccer school, which was only a five-minute walk from his house. Immersed in the energy and tumult of the game, it was the one place he could forget his disability and stand as an equal with the other neighborhood boys. On the field, Serigne Mbaye wasn't the kid you should feel sorry for or tease. He was the cunning attacker you wanted on your team if you were going to win. He would sneak his mother's best glass cups out of the house to use as trophies in these neighborhood games.

Colomer was shocked to learn Serigne Mbaye was almost entirely deaf, but a good player was a good player. He wasn't going to deny Serigne Mbaye his shot at Football Dreams just because of his disability. Life had been cruel enough to the young boy already, but he had refused to fold. That was the kind of determination Colomer was looking for, so he went ahead and invited Serigne Mbaye to the final country tryout in Dakar.

The odds were certainly stacked against him, and not only because he had to compete against the best players chosen from more than 60,000 kids in Senegal. He showed up for the tryout in Dakar without ever having owned a pair of soccer shoes. Up to that point, he had always played barefoot or in cheap plastic sandals. One of the scouts at the final, Pere Gratacós, who once coached Messi at Barcelona, took pity on Serigne Mbaye and gave him his own cleats, a pair of black and white Adidas Copa Mundials. "The image of him giving Serigne Mbaye those shoes is amazing," said Savané. "In Africa, when you have a white coach acknowledge you are good, you are very proud." Like soccer itself, that was another legacy of colonialism.

The scouts were a bit hesitant at first to put Serigne Mbaye on the field since they had never dealt with a deaf player before and the competition was so high. But the boy quickly showed them they had nothing to worry about. "The second the ball is running and they are playing, you go from being nervous to saying, 'Just let the kid do what he does,'" said Savané. "He does this all the time playing with his friends. He has his bearings."

But Serigne Mbaye wasn't selected as one of the players headed to Doha for the final tryout. He picked up a knee injury on the final day of the test, and Colomer sent him to the hospital to get treated. That wasn't the only reason they didn't include him in the group going to Doha, though. Serigne Mbaye was certainly talented enough, but the Football Dreams staff was worried about what people at Aspire would think if they showed up with a deaf player. "He wasn't one of the three because of his disability," said Savané. "We were just starting the project and knew the frame of mind in Aspire."

They didn't plan on abandoning Serigne Mbaye altogether, though. "We told him to train and stay in shape," said Savané. "We said we would come back and help him." Serigne Mbaye took them at their word. As soon as his knee healed, he teamed up with his younger brother to train several times a day at his dusty neighborhood pitch. If Colomer did return, he wanted to be ready.

That day finally arrived when the Spanish scout launched his satellite academy in Thiès and invited Serigne Mbaye to join. But it was a rough transition. He barely spoke and mostly kept to himself when he first arrived because he was so scared and intimidated. At school, he would stare at the floor because he couldn't understand what the teachers were saying. The academy tried to find someone to teach him sign language but didn't have any luck.

Serigne Mbaye's mother eventually contacted Diawandou and

Serigne Mbaye training at the Football Dreams academy in Senegal.

implored him to help her son. "I called Diawandou, and I said, 'I give you this boy, you can help him,'" said Serigne Mbaye's mother. "In the beginning, Diawandou made decisions for him. Whenever they needed something, they spoke to Diawandou." The academy moved the two of them into the same room so it would be easier for Diawandou to help Serigne Mbaye with whatever he needed. They also bought the player a hearing aid, but he refused to wear it because he didn't like attracting attention to his disability. "The only place he wants to stand out is on the pitch," said Wendy Kinyeki.

The pitch was the one place he didn't need much help. "Serigne Mbaye is so very good," said Ibrahima. "If he dribbles against you one-on-one, he will finish you." He also had exceptionally good game intelligence, likely because of his disability. "He is good at reading the game," said one of his coaches, Jordi Rovira. "He knows where he needs to go each time. He knows the solution."

Whenever Rovira had trouble communicating with Serigne Mbaye on the field, he got assistance from Diawandou or one of the other Senegalese boys since they all spoke Wolof and could help the deaf player understand. Over time, the kids were able to pull Serigne Mbaye out of his shell off the pitch as well. Rovira's wife also took it upon herself to help Serigne Mbaye and began holding one-on-one classes with him. She taught him basic things like writing his name, which helped build his confidence. He learned to read lips as well and became much more talkative, even though it was still difficult for many to understand him. "That's how he learned to say people's names," said Kinyeki, who watched over Serigne Mbaye and the other boys like they were her own kids. "Someone would look at him and say a name and he would try to copy it. He couldn't exactly say 'Wendy,' but it would still come out."

One of Kinyeki's most cherished memories was the first time Serigne Mbaye said her own name. She had suffered a severe asthma attack and spent two days in her room at the academy recovering. Serigne Mbaye approached her when she finally emerged to get some food from the cafeteria. "Wendy, sorry," said Serigne Mbaye as well as he could manage and walked away. Kinyeki stood awestruck, her eyes welling with tears. "It was just two words," said Kinyeki, her eyes wet once again. "Serigne Mbaye will always hold a special place in my heart."

He eventually grew so comfortable at the academy he even developed a reputation as a bit of a joker and loved to needle his teammates and the staff to get a laugh. "He is the biggest clown," said Savané, the Senegal country director. "All the other kids would show me deference as the director. But Serigne Mbaye would walk right up to me, and the other kids would help explain he was making jokes, saying he needed new shoes or saying the other kids were crazy." Savané always walked away chuckling and marveled at Serigne Mbaye's strength and character. He wasn't alone.

"Serigne Mbaye is one of those people you meet who changes your life," said Kinyeki. "When you want to think about all the things you don't have, you think about Serigne Mbaye and his attitude to everything he's gone through. He still remains optimistic. He still remains strong. He still laughs. He's still cheerful. And he can't hear. The rest of us, we can hear, we can see, we can walk around, and we whine about everything that's wrong in our lives. And he doesn't. He just teaches the rest of us something. Just be grateful for everything you have because you never know."

Serigne Mbaye was clearly grateful when he found out he had been selected to join Senegal's national team. After the squad lost to Ghana, the coach, Boucounta Cissé, was forced to replace an injured player for the second leg in Dakar. He needed a winger, someone with speed and creativity who could trouble Ghana's defenders. A few weeks earlier, Cissé had taken the national team to play a warm-up match against the Football Dreams kids, and one player at the academy had stood out in his mind. "Serigne Mbaye played very well," said Cissé. Despite his disability, the coach thought he might be able to help the squad. Plus, Cissé liked the idea of being the first coach to select a deaf player for the national team.

He ran the idea past his good friend at Aspire, the doctor Babacar Ngom, who thought it was excellent. In fact, the doctor was the first one to tell Serigne Mbaye he had been selected. He called him into his room at the academy, and Serigne Mbaye lit up with a smile and gave him a huge hug when he found out. The rest of the staff and his teammates were just as excited. They knew how talented he was and could see how much making the squad meant to him. "Everybody on the team was happy," said Ibrahima. "It motivated us." But Serigne Mbaye wasn't content with simply being on the team. He told the academy staff that he wasn't going to Dakar just to ride the bench. He planned to play.

As Serigne Mbaye took the field with 20 minutes left in the match against Ghana, Colomer and the other members of the academy in the stands looked on in wonder. The fact that Serigne Mbaye made the team had been hard enough to believe. Now he was actually getting a chance to show what he could do. "The second he came in, the dynamics of the game changed," said Savané. "He brought energy, speed. He was relentless." His presence lifted the spirits of his teammates as well, but still the score remained 1-0.

With only minutes remaining, one of Senegal's defenders played a long ball out of the back. A teammate managed to get his head on it at the top of the box, and the ball skirted to the right of the goal, where Serigne Mbaye ran onto it with every bit of speed he could muster. He managed to reach it just before it went over the end line and chip it back in front of goal, where one of the team's strikers was running at full tilt. The keeper jumped up, and it looked like he was going to make the save. But he couldn't bring it fully under control, and the striker managed to knock it loose and tap it over the goal line, sparking delirious celebrations. "It was unbelievable!" said Savané. "It was like a Hollywood drama. The crowd went nuts and people started chanting Serigne Mbaye's name." He was the one person in the stadium who couldn't hear it as he danced around in happiness with his teammates.

But the game wasn't over. A penalty shoot-out now loomed to determine who would qualify for the tournament. Senegal's coach tasked Diawandou with deciding who would take the shots for the team. One of the players he turned to was Serigne Mbaye, who was still riding high after his last-minute heroism. That joy was now tinged with a healthy dose of nerves. He watched as Ghana's captain, Hamza, whacked his team's first penalty toward the bottom

left corner, only to have it saved by Senegal's keeper, sparking raucous cheers around the stadium. Showing no nerves, Diawandou
walked up to the spot next and calmly stroked Senegal's first penalty into the back of the net. He ran over to high-five his keeper and
then urged the crowd to cheer even louder.

The advantage had flipped by the time Serigne Mbaye stepped
up as Senegal's fourth shooter, and Ghana was one shot up. He
walked from the halfway line toward the penalty spot, his calm gait
belying the anxiety he felt inside. He flicked the ball into his hand
with a neat roll of his foot and held it for a moment before placing it
onto the turf, lining it up exactly and stamping the ground behind
it. He slowly walked back toward the 18-yard line and waited for
the referee to give his signal. He sprinted toward the ball and then
slowed at the last moment, cutting it toward the left corner. His ploy
tricked the keeper, who dove the other way. But agonizingly, the ball
bounced off the left post and rolled out of the box. Serigne Mbaye's
hands went to his head in anguish, and he looked around in a daze.

Watching from the halfway line, Ibrahima couldn't believe it
either. "I was surprised because I had never seen Serigne Mbaye
miss a penalty before," said the striker. Serigne Mbaye slowly walked
back to his teammates, shaking his head in disbelief. Diawandou
walked up to give him a pat on the back of the head and told him
not to worry. But the deed was done, and Ghana could win the
game with the next shot, knocking Senegal out of the tournament.

Everyone was forced to wait a few moments as the referee ran
over to confer with one of his linesmen. Ghana's next shooter, Abraham Anang, whom Colomer found in Accra during the second year
of Football Dreams, stamped his feet nervously as he stared down
Senegal's keeper. Serigne Mbaye had a bit more time to wonder how
his assist would be measured against his missed penalty kick if Senegal went on to lose the game. Finally, the referee blew his whistle
and Abraham jogged toward the ball, only to scoop it over the cross-

bar. The crowd cheered wildly, and nobody was more relieved than Serigne Mbaye.

Senegal would go on to win the game thanks to a goal by another Football Dreams player, kicking off wild celebrations that wouldn't have been out of place at the World Cup. Senegal's players sprinted across the field and jumped on top of their coach, as Ghana's team collapsed on the ground at the halfway line. At Serigne Mbaye's home on the outskirts of Dakar, his mother danced with joy in front of the TV, and then her phone started ringing off the hook as friends and family called to congratulate her. Back in the stadium, Serigne Mbaye capped off the celebration by running down the field carrying a large red, yellow, and green Senegalese flag he had gotten from a spectator, a moment of patriotism and personal triumph that meant everything to him.

The staff at the academy were overjoyed at the role Serigne Mbaye had played in the win over Ghana and could see how the experience had changed him when he returned to Saly after the match. "When they came back from the national team, now you saw a man," said Ndongo Diaw, a Football Dreams staff member. "He knew he was an important person, all of Senegal knew him. At the academy, everyone was greeting and congratulating him. In training, you could see he wanted to show that he was a big player."

But the joy was all too fleeting. It wasn't long before he glanced at the newspaper and discovered he wasn't one of the players selected to travel to the tournament. The coach said he appreciated everything Serigne Mbaye had done for the team in Dakar but wanted to stick with the group that had gotten them most of the way through the qualifiers. The player was devastated, and it would take him days to recover. "I don't think I ever saw Serigne Mbaye as sad as that," said Wendy Kinyeki. "You could see him trying to figure out, 'Did I do something wrong? Why wasn't I called back? I did such a great job. Why am I not being given another chance?' That really crushed him and made me sad." But Serigne Mbaye didn't let his disappointment get in the way of supporting the players who did travel to the tournament. He was always the first one to turn on the TV and gather the other Football Dreams kids whenever one of Senegal's games was broadcast. He wasn't on the team, but they were still his teammates.

Losing Serigne Mbaye was an emotional blow for many of the players headed to Rwanda, but the team suffered a much bigger setback just days before they were scheduled to leave for the tournament. They found out that their most important player wouldn't be making the trip. Rather than leading the team from his position in the back line, Diawandou would end up watching the tournament on TV, sitting next to Serigne Mbaye at the academy. He wasn't left out because the coach thought the team didn't need him. He wasn't hobbled by injury either. The reason Diawandou wasn't at the tournament was much more troubling, not just for him, but for the entire Football Dreams program.

It all started with a trip to a clinic in Dakar. It should have been little more than a formality. All the tournament organizers needed to do was check the boys' ages to confirm they weren't too old to play. Only players born on or after January 1, 1994, were allowed to participate, meaning they were no older than 17. That shouldn't have been a problem for any of the Football Dreams players since Colomer started the program in 2007 looking for 13-year-old kids born in 1994. The next year he was searching for kids from 1995, and so on. To check a boy's age, the tournament organizers used an MRI to examine the growth plate in his wrist. If an MRI shows a player's growth plate is fully fused, there's a 99 percent chance he's older than 17, according to FIFA. The world soccer body started using the test at the Under-17 World Cup in Nigeria in 2009, and the African federation introduced it for the first time at the tournament Diawandou and his teammates were headed to in Rwanda.

The test was badly needed because one of the biggest problems in youth soccer in Africa, and in many other parts of the developing world, has been age cheating, kids saying they're much younger than they are so they will have an advantage over other players. Imagine throwing a college-age player in with a bunch of middle schoolers, and you get the idea. Age cheating is so common in Africa that it's not unusual to hear coaches say things like, "The boy is 17, but his football age is 13," although not when they're worried about being overheard. Using birth certificates or passports to verify a player's age is often futile because they are so easily faked, or real ones are generated using false information.

Many soccer officials believe age cheating has been one of the biggest impediments to an African country winning the World Cup, as Pelé predicted would happen decades ago. Although several African nations, especially Nigeria and Ghana, have had great success at the Under-17 and Under-20 versions of the tournament, many of the players who participated were never heard from again because they were much older than advertised. They couldn't hack it when they tried to compete against world-class players their own age.

The problem continues to plague African soccer because players are so desperate to make it to Europe they will do anything it takes, including lie about their age to appear better than they are. Others who stand to benefit are usually onboard as well, like their coaches, families, and even federation officials who might make a bit of money from a transfer. Piercing this veil of lies can be difficult, especially when it comes to determining a player's exact age. But it's usually possible to deduce whether a player is significantly older than he says by asking him and those around him enough indirect questions that help peel back the lies. Still, it's a huge problem. "Age fraud is more serious than doping," one of the founders of Diambars academy, Saer Seck, told the media on the eve of the tournament to which Diawandou and his teammates were headed in Rwanda in January 2011.

A little over a week before the tournament was scheduled to start, the players traveled to a clinic in Dakar to get their ages checked. They left from Thiès, where the squad was preparing for the tournament at Diawandou's old academy. When the players arrived at the clinic, they waited their turn to file into the room where the MRI scanner was located and then all headed back to Thiès, making it in time for training in the afternoon. But Cissé had bad news for his captain. He had failed the test. This time it was the coach who had trouble looking Diawandou in the eyes. "I was very surprised," said Cissé. Diawandou was outraged and protested that the test was wrong. His coach backed him up but said there was nothing he could do. "He was really upset, but I comforted him," said Cissé. "I told him I didn't think the test was reliable and will always believe he is a good player."

Diawandou also sought guidance from his uncle, Cheikh Gueye, who had raised him since he was a young boy. Gueye told him he should trust in God and believe that even though the path to the tournament had been cut off, a better one might appear. Diawandou reluctantly agreed, even though he was still heartbroken. "I said, 'No problem, I will leave everything to God,'" said Diawandou. "Maybe I would have gone there and gotten injured anyway." He met his best friend Baye Laye at a restaurant in Thiès to talk over the ordeal, and Senegal's coach and the other players called him while they were there to cheer him up. But it didn't do much good.

The coach and the other players needed some cheering up themselves. They were seriously worried about heading to the tournament without Diawandou. "It really destabilized the team because he was their captain," said the coach. "We didn't have a player who was as good to replace him." Diawandou's absence was clearly felt when the team got to Rwanda, even though he called the players while they were there to rally them. Senegal lost 2-1 to Egypt in the opening game and then went down 3-2 to Burkina Faso. They managed to beat Rwanda 1-0 in their third match, but it wasn't enough to send them through to the next round. The players were disappointed and left wondering what would have happened if Diawandou had been there. "It handicapped our team," said Ibrahima. "If he had gone, we could have done very good things."

The entire episode was embarrassing for Football Dreams, especially since it had been such a triumph for Senegal to qualify for the Africa Cup of Nations for the first time with so many players from the program. When asked later about the incident, Aspire officials said they doubted the validity of the test conducted in Dakar and were comfortable with their own records that indicated Diawandou was younger than 17 at the time. Diawandou also insists the test was wrong, although it likely wasn't. Information from Diawandou's friends and former schoolteachers in Thiès indicates he was around 16 years old, not 13, when he first tried out for Football Dreams in 2007. That would have made him roughly 19 when he put his wrist in the MRI scanner in Dakar in December 2010. The scholarship agreement Diawandou signed with Aspire stated that he could be kicked out if he lied about his age. But the academy staff stuck by the Senegalese defender, and the bond between Diawandou and Colomer remained strong.

Publicly, Colomer and others involved in Football Dreams stayed quiet when Diawandou was kicked off the team, perhaps hoping the controversy would simply blow over with time. There were a few articles in local newspapers, but that was largely it. The practice of age cheating was so common in African soccer that few people were

shocked, but some had expected Aspire would do a better job polic-
ing players' ages given the resources at its disposal.

That was the more troubling implication of Diawandou being
kicked off the team. It raised the question of how many other
Football Dreams players were older than they said. In all likelihood, many of them were. Colomer was surprisingly blasé about
the issue when asked several years later how difficult it was to
determine if Football Dreams players were actually 13 when they
first tried out. "Zero difficult," he said in imperfect English. He
pointed out that Aspire required players to provide an original
birth certificate or ID card when they first tried out, but these
are easily faked for just a few dollars in many African countries.
Even if a player did lie about his age, Colomer didn't think it was a
huge problem. "They can change it, but in the end, is it important
if Eto'o is now 30 or 33?" said Colomer, referring to the famous
striker from Cameroon. "You look for excellent players. If he is 13
or if he is 15, we don't care because we aren't taking them to play
in an Under-13 league."

That was a recipe for potential failure. Many others involved
in African youth soccer say getting a player's age right is the most
important, and most difficult, thing a scout needs to do to determine whether a boy has what it takes to make it at the top level.
Even when a player's age is clear, the process is challenging because
a scout must assess future potential based on current performance,
an imperfect indicator. Recall that scouts often make the mistake of
choosing performance over potential by simply picking more physically mature players. That risk is even higher if a player is much
older than the scout believes, and it makes the link between current
performance and future potential even more tenuous. "Your assessment of performance has to be age-specific," said Joe Mulberry, the
director of recruitment at Right to Dream, one of the best academies in West Africa. "If the assessment is made on a player who is

not very close to the age you think he is, then your assessment of potential could be wrong."

Of course, African players have lied about their ages and made it at the highest levels in Europe. But many more have failed, and a scout's failure rate is going to be even higher if he gets a boy's initial age wrong, especially if he's way off. Diawandou was likely three years older than Colomer thought when he first spotted him in Thiès. That's a pretty big difference already, the equivalent of putting an 11th-grader up against 8th-graders. But other players found by the Spanish scout were even older. Yobou Thome, a defender from the Ivory Coast who became captain of both the second Football Dreams class and his country's Under-17 national team, was 21 years old when he first tried out, not 13, according to the date of birth recorded by his primary school when he first started class.

Yobou looks a little over five and a half feet tall in a photo taken of him at the final tryout in Abidjan in 2008. He doesn't necessarily look 21, but he doesn't look 13 either. One of the challenges for Colomer and many of the other European Football Dreams scouts was that they hadn't spent much time, if any, scouting in Africa before. In many instances, locals working with the program knew how old the kids actually were but had little incentive to tell the truth because they wanted to see their players make it into the academy and score a free trip to Doha in the process. It wasn't difficult for them to feed the foreign scouts myths, like saying African boys are bigger and stronger than Europeans of the same age. In fact, the opposite is often true because of poverty and malnutrition. Conversely, the scouts could also be tricked into thinking an African player was young because he was small, when in reality he might have just been small.

Eugene Komey, the head coordinator at the field where Colomer found Bernard Appiah, realized the player wasn't 13 years old when Football Dreams asked him to shoot video of the midfielder at his school after he was selected to go to Doha. The coaches of competing kids had complained to Komey at Bernard's first tryout in Teshie and at the final in Accra that the player was too old for the program. At the time, Komey brushed them off, saying he didn't have proof because Bernard's birth certificate said he was 13. But he discovered the coaches were right when they started shooting video of Bernard in what was supposed to be his class at school. "I realized the kids didn't know him," said Komey. "They didn't really interact with him because he wasn't in their class. Bernard had already completed school. They falsified all the documents."

Bernard was likely at least 17 years old when he tried out for Football Dreams in 2007, which helps explain why the player was so eager to leave the academy in Doha three years later. Aspire kept telling him he couldn't move to Europe until he was 18, but the reality was that he was already past that age but couldn't tell anyone. Bernard likely felt like he was wasting time at the academy, and the dispute over his license may have helped push him over the edge. By the time he left in 2010, he would have been around 20 years old, two years older than most players are when they graduate. Komey never told Colomer or other Football Dreams officials about Bernard's true age because he didn't want to prevent the player from making it to the academy. "Whatever it takes for him to go," said Komey, who subsequently quit working for the program.

What makes this all so surprising is that Aspire officials say they checked the ages of all the Football Dreams players who made it to the final tryout in Doha each year by conducting their own wrist examinations, using an X-ray machine for the first class and an MRI scanner for later classes. The reality that several of the players were apparently well above 13 years old when they tried out raises the question of how well these tests actually work in weeding out older players, especially from Africa. Aspire points out that the science behind the tests has not been specifically proven for African kids, whose bones might grow at different rates than children in the developed world.

Another question is how well the results from these tests are actually enforced, not just at Aspire but elsewhere. Yobou Thome captained Ivory Coast's team at the Under-17 Africa Cup of Nations in 2011 even though he was nearly 24 years old at the time. He was also captain later that year at the Under-17 World Cup in Mexico. Before both tournaments, FIFA used MRIs to check players' ages, but Yobou was allowed to play. This fact raises the possibility that other Football Dreams players on Senegal's team with Diawandou were also overage. The African confederation said they weren't. Others weren't so sure.

CHAPTER 9

The Milk Cup

The crowd in Northern Ireland was eager for the match to start. The small stadium only held a few thousand people, but the stands on both sides of the pitch were packed. The ground was normally home to Ballymena United FC, but the spectators who showed up that cloudy July evening in 2011 hoped to catch a glimpse of much bigger stars before they became household names. They were there to watch the Under-17 final of the Milk Cup, one of the biggest youth tournaments in the world. The competition, which began in 1983, was officially called the Northern Ireland Youth Soccer Tournament but came to be known as the Milk Cup because of sponsorship by the country's dairy council. Large billboards that said "Milk" ringed the field, along with advertisements for BBC Sport, which broadcast the 70-minute final live on TV. It was one of the biggest events of the year in Ballymena, a quaint town of only about 30,000 people perhaps best known as the birthplace of actor Liam Neeson.

Out on the emerald green field inside the stadium, Ibrahima faced down the devil, eleven of them actually, and still fancied his chances. The imposing frontman was back in Aspire's blue and white stripes and impatient for the referee to start the game. Six months had passed since Senegal was knocked out of the Africa Cup of Nations. The disappointment lingered, but Ibrahima knew a win by his academy team that evening would be a huge achievement that would attract even greater attention. It was the perfect opportunity for him to make his mark in front of scouts from some of Europe's top clubs. But it meant taking on those devils, Red Devils to be exact. That was no mean feat since Manchester United was one of the most successful clubs in history.

The English side had long dominated the Milk Cup, having won the tournament more times than any other team. Club legends like David Beckham, Ryan Giggs, and Paul Scholes had featured in the past, along with stars from other teams like Barcelona's Sergio Busquets; Radamel Falcao, when he was at River Plate; and Wayne Rooney during his first spell at Everton. The Manchester United squad up against Aspire contained several English internationals who would eventually make it to the club's first team, including defender Tyler Blackett and striker James Wilson.

Aspire's squad was one of the youngest in the tournament, at least on paper. It was composed of Football Dreams players found during the second and third years of the program, as well as a smattering of Qataris who didn't get much playing time. The absence of players from the first class meant that once again Ibrahima had to cope without Diawandou's leadership on the field. But this time, he wasn't concerned. He thought the Red Devils were the ones who should be worried, given the run of form he had been on over the last year.

The streak started in the spring of 2010 when Aspire won its first major tournament in Italy, thanks to a dozen goals by Ibrahima that earned him the award for top scorer. He followed that up in the fall by taking on the goal-scoring burden for Senegal as the country achieved its historic qualification for the Africa Cup of Nations. A few months later, Aspire traveled to Spain in the spring of 2011 for the Mediterranean International Cup, a big youth tournament started by Colomer over a decade earlier that attracted top teams from around the world. Once again, Ibrahima terrorized defenders and led the tournament in goals scored. Although his team lost 2-1 to Espanyol in the semifinals, the tournament's head scout called the big striker "a treasure" and identified him as one of the brightest lights in the competition. "He is a tall player, but coordinated and fast and . . . good with his head," the scout told a local radio station.

Ibrahima was on fire at the Milk Cup as well. He scored six goals in four games to help put Aspire in the final. Their opponent, Manchester United, made it to the last match with a 1-0 victory over the previous champions, Étoile Lusitana, an academy founded by José Mourinho in Dakar when he was the coach of Inter Milan. Aspire coasted into the final with a much more dramatic win against Desportivo Brasil, a team from São Paulo that would go on to win the tournament the next year. But in 2011, Aspire stopped them dead in their tracks with a 6-1 demolition that included a hat trick from Ibrahima, so it's no wonder he felt confident as he stared out at Manchester United's players in their iconic red and white uniforms, waiting for the final to kick off.

It didn't take long for Ibrahima to establish his authority once the referee blew his whistle. In the seventh minute, Cedric Tchoutou, a speedy winger from Cameroon's largest city, Douala, raced past Manchester United's left back a few yards outside the penalty box and whipped in a cross just before he reached the end line. Ibrahima sprinted between two defenders at the near post and powered a header into the far corner, leaving the keeper no chance. "Great finish from Dramé!" said the BBC announcer. The striker ran to give Cedric a hug and high-fived his teammates. But the look on his face was all business. The goal meant Ibrahima was tied for the golden boot award as the tournament's leading scorer, but sharing the prize wasn't in his game plan.

Fifteen minutes later, one of Aspire's defenders played a long ball across the field to Cedric, who controlled it with one touch and slid a pass into Ibrahima's path between two Manchester United players. The big striker ran onto the ball near the top right corner of the six-yard box and managed to blast it past the keeper at the near post, even though he had a defender on his heels lunging to make a tackle. "What a ball and what a finish!" the announcer exclaimed. Aspire's coaches were on their feet at the sideline, high-fiving and applauding along with the crowd. "It's a long way back for the Red Devils at this stage," the announcer said.

Not far enough for Ibrahima. Three minutes later, he made it a hat trick and allowed himself a quick smile for the first time. "Well, well, well, the scouts will be looking at this big fella," the announcer said. "He's a happy man." This time the cross came in from the left thanks to a Nigerian midfielder, Innocent Shoja. Ibrahima overpowered the defender marking him, and headed the ball with so much force from about six yards out that it whizzed just under the crossbar before the keeper could even get his arm up. "Good attacking of the ball by the big striker!" the announcer said. The keeper picked himself up off the ground with a dejected look on his face, and the announcer wondered just how much worse it could get for the Red Devils. "This could be embarrassing for Manchester United," the announcer said. "I think it's a long time since they have been in this sort of situation. We've still got ten minutes left in the first half, and already it's game, set, match."

The announcer was right. It would get worse. Twenty minutes into the second half, Ibrahima controlled a throw-in with his chest near the top of the penalty box and deftly pirouetted around a player on his back. He made it past a second defender with a lucky rebound off the player's leg and slid the ball to a teammate running onto goal. The keeper managed to block the first shot but couldn't keep out the second from Babacar Ndoye, the sprightly Senegalese winger who had scored in the playoff game against Ghana in Dakar. He sprinted toward the sideline in celebration, cupped his right ear, and leaned toward the crowd to get them to cheer even louder. Manchester United got a consolation goal a few minutes later, but there was enough time left for Aspire to add one more from close range thanks to a diminutive Cameroonian midfielder, Oumarou Kaina. "This is now a rout," said the announcer, as the game wound down with the score an astounding 5-1 in Aspire's favor.

Finally, much to Manchester United's relief, the referee blew the whistle, sparking wild celebrations by Ibrahima and his teammates. With gold medals dangling from their necks, the players danced around as young women working at the tournament poured plastic jugs of milk over their heads. The liquid glistened under the stadium floodlights as it flowed over their dark skin and jerseys. A couple players hammed it up for the camera, biting their medals as if to check they were real gold. A final photo shows the team on the pitch crowded around the large silver trophy they won. Ibrahima stands tall in the back, smiling broadly as milk drips from his face. Above his head, he holds the trophy he won as the tournament's top scorer, a white and gold cleat set on a wooden base. It was the third time in as many tournaments that Ibrahima had been the standout player, and his name was splashed across newspaper headlines the next day. "Dazzling Ibrahima Dramé is too hot for Manchester United's stunned young guns," said the *Belfast Telegraph*.

Although some people suspected Ibrahima and his teammates were quite a bit older than they said they were, that didn't stop scouts at the tournament from flocking to Aspire's head coach, Michael Browne, to find out how they could get their hands on the Senegalese striker and his teammates. "Clubs were approaching me saying, 'What is happening to these boys?'" said Browne. "I was saying, 'Look, they are not going anywhere. They are going to be part of the Aspire setup. You are wasting your time asking if you can take

The Football Dreams kids after winning the Milk Cup in 2011.

them on trial.'" The coach made sure the players knew the drill as well. "We said, 'Look, this is the reality. You cannot legitimately go and sign for a club until you are 18. People might be telling you all these stories, but at the end of the day, don't believe everything people tell you.'"

Bases covered, or so he thought. But promises of fame and fortune were difficult for the players to ignore, especially those who came from the most desperate backgrounds and knew success would radically transform the lives of their families back in Africa. That didn't mean they trusted every scout or agent who approached them. They knew Browne was right when he told them not to believe all the stories strangers were selling. But what if the salesman wasn't a stranger? Browne and others at Aspire never anticipated the threat from within.

One of the team's coaches at the Milk Cup was Arnold Rijsenburg, a former professional player from the tiny South American country of Suriname who had spent most of his career in Belgium. He stuck around after his playing career ended and worked as a youth coach at a couple of Belgium's top clubs, Anderlecht and Standard Liège, where he trained future stars like Romelu Lukaku and Marouane Fellaini before they moved on to bigger money in England's Premier League. Aspire sought to capitalize on this experience and recruited him to work as a coach in the fall of 2008.

Like all the staff who accompanied the Aspire kids to the Milk Cup, Rijsenburg was based in Doha, not Senegal. But the players knew him from regular trips to Qatar, and he had grown closer to them during the tournament, especially Ibrahima. With his dark complexion, Rijsenburg likely seemed a more familiar face to the Football Dreams kids than many of the Western European coaches working for Aspire. He also spoke French, so he could easily communicate with players like Ibrahima from Francophone West Africa, which further cemented the connection. But Rijsenburg didn't plan on staying at Aspire much longer. He had notified the academy shortly before the Milk Cup that he would not be renewing his contract.

A few hours after Ibrahima's triumphant tournament victory, he was relaxing in his hotel room with his good friend Fallou Niang when he heard a knock on the door and opened it to find Rijsenburg. Although he wasn't expecting the coach, he wasn't surprised to see him either. Ibrahima knew why he had come. Even before the tournament started, Rijsenburg had pulled Ibrahima aside and told him he should think about leaving the academy early to try his luck in Europe. Rijsenburg said he had the connections to help. Strikers who rack up goals are the sport's kings, after all, and attract the most interest from clubs. Rijsenburg again talked to Ibrahima about leaving after he scored a hat trick in the Milk Cup semifinal and was now at the player's door once more.

At least that's how Ibrahima tells the story. Rijsenburg provided a different version of events. He said it was actually Ibrahima and several other boys who approached him to find a way to Europe, not the other way around. He insisted he had no intention of trying to make money and simply wanted to help the players get to European clubs because he thought it would be better for their development, even though academy officials had made it clear that the African players were off-limits.

There's no disputing what happened next, though. Rijsenburg introduced Ibrahima to an agent at the tournament, Nenad Petrovic, who had expressed an interest in the big striker. Petrovic worked with a former Anderlecht player, Bertrand Crasson, and both of them were familiar with Football Dreams because they had traveled to Doha a few months earlier with Anderlecht's general manager, Herman Van Holsbeeck. While they were at Aspire, they met with Rijsenburg and Andreas Bleicher. Now they were in Ballymena, looking to pry away one of the program's most promising stars, as well as several of his teammates. "They said, 'We need you after the tournament,'" said Ibrahima. "'We can bring you to the big teams in Europe. You cannot sit in the academy and wait. Aspire cannot make all the players professionals. Now you need to leave to have a new life.'"

Ibrahima had been approached by scouts and agents before. Many of the Football Dreams players had. After powering his team to victory in Italy in 2010, several people representing Italian teams introduced themselves to Ibrahima as he wandered about town. One of the coaches from the academy in Senegal, Jordi Rovira, usually kept a close eye on the players and intervened whenever he saw one of the kids being targeted. But Rovira, Colomer, and the others from Senegal were absent from the Milk Cup.

One of the reasons the players were interested in leaving the academy was that they were increasingly jealous of Colomer's close relationship with the kids in the first class, especially Diawandou, and were worried he wouldn't do as much to help them strike it big in Europe. Nobody felt this more acutely than Ibrahima. The smile on his face as he raised the golden boot award at the Milk Cup disguised a deep malaise. Before the tournament, Ibrahima often complained to his teammates that no matter what they did, they never received the kind of praise and attention Colomer bestowed on the first class. That feeling only intensified after the win in Northern Ireland when the striker again failed to hear from the Spanish scout, a pattern that increasingly upset him after his accomplishments over the past year. "I went to Spain and took best player and scored so many goals, but Colomer didn't tell me congratulations," said Ibrahima. "He didn't say anything. In Italy, it was the same. In Ireland, the same."

Ibrahima was worried that the lack of attention meant Colomer didn't value him highly enough as a player. That concern deepened shortly before the Milk Cup when the Spanish scout gathered the entire academy for a meeting in one of the classrooms at Diambars and told them he was sending two Ghanaian players home, Adama Issah and Abraham Anang. They were the first players officially kicked out of the program, since Aspire maintained Bernard left on his own. Colomer said he was sending the pair home because Adama had suffered a string of persistent injuries and Abraham had disciplinary issues.

Ibrahima and his teammates were too shocked to say much during the meeting but left angry and upset, worried they might be sent home themselves at some point and find their dreams of becoming a European star dashed forever. "It was so bad for me, for all the boys, because I never thought Colomer would say that," said Ibrahima. "He sent them back to their country to start their life again. That's so difficult. They lost everything. I was thinking if it was me, what would happen? If it was me, he would do the same. I said OK, I need to leave Aspire because if I don't leave Aspire now, tomorrow I could go like that."

Ibrahima was thus inclined to take the agent, Petrovic, up on his offer at the Milk Cup. But he wanted to run the idea by his old coach in Ziguinchor, Amadou Traoré, so he borrowed a phone, grabbed his friend Fallou, who was also thinking of leaving, and dialed Traoré's number in Senegal. At first, his old coach was reluctant to endorse the idea since he figured Ibrahima had a good thing going at the academy. "He said, 'Cool down. Don't make any decision until you come back here,'" said Fallou. It was a sensitive issue for Traoré because Football Dreams was a family affair. The program's country director in Senegal, Lamine Savané, was his cousin.

But Ibrahima was insistent and told his old coach the situation at Aspire wasn't as good as it seemed. "He said the head of the academy had special boys he wanted to help," said Traoré. No matter how many goals he scored, Ibrahima was sure he would never have the kind of relationship with Colomer that Diawandou did. The players had become good friends, but that wasn't enough to stave off pangs of jealousy and concern about his place in the academy's pecking order. Ibrahima never shared these feelings with Diawandou or Colomer, an act that may have taken the big striker down a different path. Instead, he decided it was better to leave and try his luck with someone he felt fully appreciated him. Ibrahima knew he would be giving up the money Aspire was sending his family, but that wasn't going to last forever. This was the chance to earn much more and secure his family's future for good.

Rijsenburg called Traoré as well, and the Senegalese coach eventually told Ibrahima he agreed with his plan to leave the academy. "He said, 'OK, if you know it's good and they will take you to a team, then it's better for you to leave,'" said Ibrahima. Traoré likely had his own interests in mind as well. Like Bernard's coach in Ghana,

Traoré wasn't clear what kind of money he would get from Aspire if Ibrahima made it to Europe after graduating from the academy. "It's a big problem," the coach said. "If a player becomes a professional, the team the boy came from should benefit." Traoré appreciated the free Nike equipment Aspire handed out every year, which included roughly a dozen balls and two dozen training bibs at each of the fields where they held tryouts, but he didn't think it was enough to compensate him for giving up his best player.

Ibrahima kept in close touch with Rijsenburg and Petrovic after he returned to Ziguinchor for summer vacation at the beginning of August, and the Aspire coach told him Anderlecht was interested in signing him. It was an exciting prospect since Anderlecht is considered Belgium's top club and was the launching point for Romelu Lukaku, a Belgian striker of Congolese heritage who hit it big in England's Premier League. That was exactly the path Ibrahima dreamed of following. The two even had similar builds since Lukaku stood six feet, three inches tall, although Ibrahima had a bit more filling out to do to equal the Belgian striker's commanding presence on the field.

By this point, roughly half a dozen other Football Dreams players were planning on leaving, including Ibrahima's friend Fallou. But Fallou called only a week before Ibrahima was scheduled to travel to Belgium to tell him he wouldn't be going after all. His father had vetoed the plan and told him it was better to stay at the academy. Ibrahima was disappointed but remained committed to his decision to leave. He didn't get any resistance from his parents, who were nervous but put their faith in Traoré and let him figure out the best path for their son's career.

Traoré wanted to make a clean getaway without tipping off Aspire and told Ibrahima's mother to say she knew nothing if anyone from the academy contacted her. But Ibrahima didn't feel comfortable sneaking away, so he sent a text message to the country director, Savané, before he and Traoré boarded the overnight ferry to Dakar to catch their flight at the beginning of September. Ibrahima told Savané he was headed to Europe and wouldn't be returning to the academy. All hell broke loose as Aspire panicked about losing one of their best players. They grew even more alarmed when they realized Ibrahima wasn't the only one jumping ship. The day that he and Traoré traveled to Dakar was supposed to be the start of the academy's fall term, and several other kids were missing as well.

Savané called Traoré when the coach arrived in the capital and requested he and Ibrahima come to his office to talk things over. Traoré agreed out of respect for his cousin but had no intention of changing his mind. The two of them argued for over an hour as Ibrahima sat silently and stared at the framed soccer and basketball jerseys on the office walls. Traoré eventually cut off the conversation, saying they were sticking with their decision, and rushed with Ibrahima to the Belgian Embassy, arriving just in time to get their visas to fly to Brussels that evening. They headed to Traoré's sister's house in Dakar afterward to prepare for their flight. But Aspire hadn't given up. Savané showed up at the house with George Sagna, the Football Dreams sports director in Senegal, to make another push to get Ibrahima to stay.

Sagna was one of the first Senegalese to play professional soccer in Europe and wielded his experience in an attempt to change Traoré's mind. "George said to me, 'You don't understand what you are doing,'" said Traoré. "'Football in Europe is very difficult.'" Traoré said he wasn't worried because he believed in Ibrahima's talent, but they told him the striker was too young to sign with a club because he wasn't 18. Traoré countered by saying Lukaku had played at Anderlecht when he was only 16, Ibrahima's official age at the time. But they told him that was different because Lukaku was born in Belgium, not Africa. (In fact, according to information from friends and family back in Ziguinchor, Ibrahima was likely in his early 20s when this happened. But that wasn't a secret he or his coach could reveal without risking their entire mission, and to this day, Ibrahima maintains that he was 16 at the time.)

Even Traoré's sister scolded him for trying to whisk Ibrahima off to Europe. "My sister said, 'What are you doing?'" said Traoré. "'You know this boy is your player, he was in your football school, but he's not your son!'" Ibrahima was upstairs watching TV while the group argued in the living room beneath framed photos of family members on the walls. Eventually, Traoré's sister called him downstairs to ask him directly whether he wanted to go. "She said, 'If you're not sure, it's better you tell us,'" said Ibrahima. "I said, 'Yes, I want to go.'" Secretly, however, his brash confidence was fading, and he was starting to doubt leaving was the right decision. But he didn't say anything at the time. Traoré's sister finally told the others they weren't going to change her brother's mind, so they should just give up. Savané and Sagna reluctantly filed out of the house, and Traoré and Ibrahima headed to the airport.

While the two of them were waiting at the gate for their flight, Ibrahima had a true change of heart but didn't feel brave enough to tell Traoré since he had gotten them into this situation in the first place. Instead, he snuck into the terminal's cramped and smelly bathroom and sent texts to Savané and several others at the academy saying he was having second thoughts but felt pressured to go by his coach. It's unclear if this was the reality or Ibrahima's attempt to shift blame. Traoré insisted afterward that he would have turned right around if Ibrahima had told him he didn't want to go. "I think when he got to the airport, he had a crisis of conscience," said Wendy Kinyeki, the Football Dreams staff member who was close with Ibrahima. "These guys have been so good to me all this time, how do I just bail?"

Ibrahima started to have doubts when Colomer called him at Traoré's sister's house and pleaded with him to stay. Part of him resented the call because Colomer had waited until he was leaving to praise him, and he knew the Spanish scout must have contacted Diawandou to get his number. But he also realized that perhaps Colomer and others at the academy appreciated him more than he had known. Diawandou, who was in Doha at the time, also called Ibrahima at the airport and tried to convince him to stay, but the striker said it was too late. "I told Diawandou I didn't want to go, but it was no longer my decision. It was my coach's," said Ibrahima.

As this drama played out at the airport, Aspire made one last attempt to keep the striker from leaving. Savané contacted Ibrahima's mother to persuade her to join their side and even got Ziguinchor's chief of police to call her to see if she consented to her son's departure. But she told both of them she didn't know anything about soccer and put her full trust in Traoré. Still, it was an incredibly difficult time for her because she was worried whether her son was making the right decision. Aspire had done so much for Ibrahima and even paid for her to visit Doha. The money the academy sent her was even more important, and she used it for everything from buying food to paying her kids' school fees. She had no idea what would happen now that Ibrahima had abandoned the academy and was winging his way toward Belgium with Traoré. "I couldn't sleep the night he left," she said.

Colomer was outraged at Rijsenburg and the half dozen players he helped lure away from the Milk Cup. The tournament victory should have been one of Football Dreams' greatest triumphs, but it had morphed into a nightmare. The other players who left included a pair of Cameroonians who had excelled in the Milk Cup final: Cedric Tchoutou, the pacey winger who provided Ibrahima's first two assists; and Oumarou Kaina, the little midfielder who scored

Ibrahima's mother outside the one-room home in Ziguinchor where she raised her four children.

the final goal. "The story shows the danger of agents hovering around," said Savané, the Senegal country director. "That's the dark reality of the football business. At the end of the day, it's a crazy race looking for Eto'o, Drogba, so they can ride off into the sunset with big amounts of money."

The captain of the second Football Dreams class, Yobou Thome, also failed to return after the summer, but he wasn't at the Milk Cup. A German agent lured the defender away while he was captaining Ivory Coast's national team at the Under-17 World Cup in Mexico. Yobou decided to leave even though Aspire paid for him to have surgery to correct a potentially life-threatening heart defect discovered when he was in Doha for his final Football Dreams tryout. Yobou's age was likely a factor in his decision since he was actually 24 years old at the time and may have felt like he was wasting precious time at the academy. Ibrahima and the others who left may have had similar concerns because they too were likely older than they claimed.

Colomer assembled the entire academy inside one of the classrooms at Diambars to vent his frustration over the players who snuck away. He demanded to know why those at the Milk Cup didn't tell him about the secret exodus that was under way. "He was very angry!" said Babacar Ndoye, the Senegalese winger who also scored in the Milk Cup final. Like Fallou, Babacar wanted to leave after the tournament but was stopped by his father. Colomer warned the players against making the same mistake as those who left and assured them they were better off at the academy. "Colomer told the boys, 'We will not force you to stay,'" said Forewah Emmanuel, a Football Dreams staff member at the meeting. "He said, 'I am honest with you. I took you from your villages when you never knew I would come. We train you for five years, and you have confidence in me because what we promise you, we give you. If you meet someone you don't know, and the person says he will take you to Real Madrid and you believe that person, you are making a mistake. Are you going to believe in someone you know or someone you don't know?'"

Colomer said he would warn European clubs not to sign any of the boys who left because they were Aspire players and weren't yet 18 years old, according to several kids at the meeting. Ibrahima discovered this threat was real after landing in Brussels, where he was met by Rijsenburg and Petrovic at the airport. Ibrahima and Traoré said they soon found themselves in the office of Anderlecht's general manager, Herman Van Holsbeeck, and the big striker eagerly expected to sign a contract with the club. But Aspire had gotten to Van Holsbeeck first, they said, and warned him not to sign Ibrahima. The general manager peppered Traoré with questions as soon as he arrived. "He asked, 'Was Ibrahima at Aspire Academy before?'" said Traoré. "Did he have a contract?" Van Holsbeeck told Petrovic to clear up the situation before Anderlecht made any moves.

In the meantime, Ibrahima took to the training field at Anderlecht and did what he does best, scoring five goals in the first three matches he played. That seemed to produce a change of heart by the general manager. Traoré said Van Holsbeeck contacted him to propose they sign a contract directly, cutting out Petrovic because he was demanding too much money. Traoré was inclined to accept the offer, but Ibrahima didn't feel comfortable going around Petrovic's back since he was the one who facilitated his trip, so he torpedoed the deal. A few months later, Van Holsbeeck told the press that Anderlecht never had any intention of snatching Ibrahima away from Aspire because he wasn't old enough. "Only when a player is 18 can there be a transfer," he said. "But we will negotiate directly with Aspire without intermediaries."

Petrovic and his associates eventually gave up on Anderlecht and told Ibrahima they wanted to take him for a trial at AS Monaco. "They came one evening and said get your bags," said Ibrahima. Thus began a painful months-long odyssey as he traipsed across Europe looking for a team that would take him. After Monaco, he went to several clubs in Italy, including Novara and Udinese, before finally ending up in Bulgaria at CSKA Sofia. At times, he intersected with the other players Petrovic had lured away from the academy, but a deal proved elusive. There were issues with his age, his lack of a European passport, the threat of retribution from Aspire, and the amount of cash Petrovic wanted for the big striker. "I was so tired of it!" said Ibrahima. "Everywhere I went I did my best, but they said no because the agent asked for a lot of money."

Ibrahima's mother was having a rough time back in Ziguinchor as well. Petrovic sent a little money while her son was searching for a club, but it was less than she had been getting from Aspire. She struggled to make ends meet and would soon find it even more difficult as the money from Petrovic dried up as well. After months of traveling, Ibrahima finally reached his breaking point in Bulgaria.

"They wanted to sign us, but I took my bags and returned to Senegal," said Ibrahima. "I didn't want to sign for a club in Bulgaria. That's no football country. I decided to go back."

It was a steep fall for the big man. In 2012, months after dazzling the soccer world at the Milk Cup, Ibrahima was back to square one in Ziguinchor, with no club, no academy, and no clear way forward. The best that can be said is that at least he had a ticket to fly home at all and didn't end up stuck in Europe like thousands of other African players. But like Bernard, he now faced the daunting prospect of forging his own path out of Africa without the money and connections he once had at Aspire. In fact, he thought many people at the academy would be happy to see him fail.

Colomer was determined to prevent any more players from leaving but also wasn't quite sure what to do with the ones who remained. Even before the Milk Cup debacle, he and others at Aspire had been debating the best way to funnel the boys to clubs in Europe when they reached the end of their time at the academy. In the fall of 2010, Colomer chose a group of players from the first two classes to train with Barcelona's reserve squad, known as the B team, while they were on one of their regular trips to Spain.

One of the Spanish scout's closest friends, Sandro Rosell, had recently been elected the club's president, and it seemed like the perfect opportunity to showcase the Football Dreams players for Barcelona's coaches. Rosell, a smooth-talking Catalan businessman, was the one who brought Colomer on as Barcelona's youth director years earlier. He was also closely tied to Football Dreams since a company he owned, Bonus Sports Marketing, provided the operational backbone for the talent search. Given these connections, perhaps Barcelona would pick up some of the boys, which would help validate the talent Colomer had discovered and provide Football Dreams the perfect outlet for the best players after they graduated from the academy.

The group Colomer selected included the captains of both classes, Diawandou and Yobou, the slick Ghanaian playmaker Samuel Asamoah, and half a dozen others. A photo shows them with their arms around each other in the Barcelona locker room, wearing pink training jerseys bearing the club's iconic crest. One notable absence from the group was Ibrahima, and his exclusion added to the list of the striker's grievances against the Spanish scout. The boys trained for several days with a Barcelona squad that included future first team players like Thiago Alcántara and Cristian Tello, whom Colomer first signed for the club years earlier. The B team's coach was Luis Enrique, who would later win a historic treble with a senior side that included the deadly attacking trident of Messi, Neymar, and Suárez.

Barcelona was reportedly interested in several of the players, but none ended up transferring to the club. It's unclear why exactly. They weren't officially 18 years old yet, but Barcelona had taken players younger than that from outside Europe, including from Africa, since the club had a deal with Samuel Eto'o's foundation that funneled Cameroonian kids into its academy. Barcelona's recruitment of minors would get it into trouble with FIFA several years later when the club was hit with a yearlong transfer ban, but it wasn't yet an issue at the time.

It's possible club politics got in the way. A few days before his election as president in June 2010, Rosell caused an uproar by telling a Spanish newspaper there were too many Africans in Barcelona's academy already because they were taking spots from the locals. He said everyone knew most of them were older than they claimed. That meant they had trouble competing when the other kids caught up physically and often faced the grim reality of having to return home. He spoke the truth, but it was quite a statement for someone who owned a company recruiting African players for Aspire on an unprecedented scale. Rosell always praised Football Dreams, but the program faced exactly these same difficulties. About six months later, after Rosell brokered a controversial 150 million euro deal for Qatar to sponsor Barcelona, he made it clear in a TV interview that the club wouldn't take Football Dreams players into its academy at all. He clearly thought he had enough African kids on his hands already.

The avenue to Barcelona was clearly more complicated than Aspire had anticipated. Instead, Colomer sent the boys from the first class to Doha in the fall of 2011 as they officially neared the age of 18. He paired them with Bartolome "Tintin" Marquez, a veteran Spanish coach with a no-nonsense demeanor who was tasked with preparing the players for their eventual transition to Europe, no matter which club ended up taking them. He had played midfield for one of Spain's biggest clubs, Espanyol, for years before eventually becoming the team's head coach. Tintin picked up his nickname as a young player because one of his teammates thought he had the same spiky hair as the famous Belgian cartoon character. The name stuck even as he approached his 50s and was now almost completely bald.

Tintin said the initial plan was for the first class to form a team to play in Qatar's second division so they could get professional experience before moving to clubs in Europe. The boys trained with their coach for about a month to get ready for the competition, but they said Aspire called off the entire plan only a week before the start of the season with little explanation. Academy officials later explained that they abandoned the idea because Qatar's second division wasn't competitive enough for the kids and they faced problems with local federation regulations. They also wanted to avoid fueling suspicion that the goal was to naturalize the boys and have them play for Qatar's national team, since that had been such a flashpoint for criticism. According to FIFA, the players would have to live in Qatar for five years after they turned 18 for that to happen, a real possibility if they were playing in the country's league. Qatar has continued to naturalize plenty of foreign players over the years, just not from the Football Dreams program.

After Aspire jettisoned the plan to play in Qatar's second division, Colomer and the others debated a new way forward. Should they turn the players loose to agents, try to find them teams themselves, or buy a club of their own? They eventually rejected the first two options out of concern the boys might be taken advantage of or end up on teams where they spent most of their time on the bench. "The gap between 18 and 21 is the most decisive in a professional career," said Andreas Bleicher. "I'm sure there are so many talents who should play in top clubs who don't make it because in these years they don't get the chance to play." Aspire didn't want to see that happen with the Football Dreams kids, so they decided the best solution was to buy a club to ensure the players got the professional experience they needed to move on to the biggest teams in the world. That required even more money for a program that had already cost tens of millions of dollars, but Qatar certainly wasn't short on cash.

Colomer relied on Diawandou to keep his class in line until Aspire could purchase a club. He was worried some of them might follow the lead of Ibrahima and others who left the academy early, so he called Diawandou and instructed him to make sure it didn't happen. The Senegalese captain gathered his teammates for a meeting inside his room at Aspire. "I told them we are near to being professionals," said Diawandou. "We need to be patient. Everything will go its own way and come at the right time. If you rush, your life will go the wrong way." Diawandou was lucky because he came from a fairly comfortable background, so he was less tempted by the riches agents often dangled in front of the Football Dreams players to get them to leave. He even shut down his Facebook account because too many agents were contacting him when he was at the academy in Senegal.

But others had more trouble shutting out the agents whispering in their ears. They may have been back in the lap of luxury in Doha with Aspire's world-class facilities and colossal air-conditioned dome, but as the months dragged on, some grew restless. After years of hard work, they were desperate to make it to Europe and worried any holdup might put the dream at risk. They questioned whether sticking around Qatar was really their best bet or if they should follow those who left with Rijsenburg and were already in Europe. "They were phoning and Skyping with their families," said Stefan Wetzel, a social worker who assisted the boys. "The families were saying, 'You have been playing four years with Aspire. They promised you would play professionally. Where's the money? We're suffering here.'"

These calls weighed on the boys' minds as they trekked back and forth to training every day. "Some players were worried," said the Nigerian goalkeeper John Felagha. "But Colomer said he was fighting to get a club, and I believed him." Many others did as well since Colomer's bond with the first class was so strong. They also had faith in Diawandou, who kept them united with the kind of leadership that was absent in the classes that had splintered. He urged the players to maintain their trust in Aspire because of everything the academy had done for them so far. "If they say be patient, we need to be patient because they gave us money, they changed our lives, they changed the lives of our families," said Diawandou.

Finally, in the spring of 2012, just before the players were scheduled to return home for the summer, Colomer and Bleicher called the entire class together for a meeting at Aspire. They had good news and bad news. The good news was Aspire had finally bought a club and almost all the players would be headed to Europe to fulfill their dream of becoming professionals. The bad news was they didn't have room for everyone, so several boys didn't make the cut, including Serigne Mbaye, the deaf player who had achieved glory helping Senegal qualify for the Africa Cup of Nations for the first time. Nobody had doubts about Serigne Mbaye's talent, but his disability once again held him back. "He's a very good player," said Tintin, who would continue managing the kids in Europe. "But it's difficult to coach him. If he doesn't see it on a blackboard, he doesn't understand."

In fact, Serigne Mbaye didn't fully understand what Colomer and Bleicher were saying in the meeting, and it was only when they pulled him aside afterward he realized he wouldn't be part of the team. It was a crushing blow, just like when he was left off the squad that traveled to the Africa Cup of Nations. Aspire promised they would find a way to help him once he returned to Senegal, but that didn't do much to ease the pain for him or his teammates, who had grown to become his family. "It was very difficult," said Diawandou, who had done more than anyone to help Serigne Mbaye. "You spend five years training at the academy, and then they tell you that you are not going to be a part of the project. It's not easy, but football is like this."

Serigne Mbaye had to head home, but Aspire allowed him to take up residence once again at the academy as they tried to figure out what to do with him. The staff dreamed of helping him to achieve his goal of playing in Europe and sent him for trials at a first division club in Norway. Once again, he impressed the coaches, but the club didn't feel like it could take on the burden of a deaf player in its ranks. A couple more years passed as Serigne Mbaye drifted back and forth from the academy to his family's home on the outskirts of Dakar. He put on a brave face, but it wasn't easy living in limbo.

Finally, he caught a break toward the end of 2014. It wasn't Europe, but it was still an impressive achievement for someone facing Serigne Mbaye's odds.

Aspire connected him with a team in Senegal's top division, Mbour Petit Côte, run by a relative of one of the academy coaches. The club also had the advantage of being based down the road from the academy, so Serigne Mbaye could continue living with the Aspire staff if he could convince the team's coach he was good enough to make the squad. That didn't end up being a problem. "After seeing him, I realized he's a genius," said the coach, Abdulkarim Mane. "He plays very well and is very intelligent on the pitch." Serigne Mbaye made good on the coach's belief in him, scoring a few goals and providing several assists in his first season. He impressed his teammates as well, not just with his play on the field but also with his carefree attitude off the field. "He's always joking," said one of his closest friends on the team, midfielder Siddy Saar. "He would be in Europe if he didn't have the problem with his hearing. He's got the talent, and we all pray for him." Serigne Mbaye may not have made it to Europe, but he was likely one of the few deaf players ever to compete in the first division of any league.

Back in Doha, Diawandou and the others who were headed to Europe were ecstatic. All their hard work had paid off. After all those anxious calls from family members back home, the boys could finally hold their heads high and say proudly that they would soon be professionals. They had been dreaming about this moment their whole lives, and success meant they had beaten almost impossible odds. There are roughly 175 million African men between the ages of 18 and 34, prime soccer-playing years, and many of them grew up fantasizing about playing as a professional in Europe. But the number of those who succeed is minuscule. Only a few thousand Africans play for European teams in any given year. No wonder the Football Dreams kids were thrilled. "It was like a party," said Forewah Emmanuel, a staff member from Cameroon who was in Doha watching over the boys.

It didn't even matter that they had never actually heard of the club where they were headed or the little Belgian town it was named after. Forget Barcelona and Manchester United, at least for now. They were about to become proud members of the Eupen Pandas. It wasn't exactly what they had dreamed of growing up in Africa, but it was a start.

PART THREE
PROS

CHAPTER 10

Battle of Belgium

Eupen is a quaint town of 20,000 people nestled next to the German border in southeastern Belgium. It's so small that the entire downtown area, with its stately old buildings, imposing stone churches, and charming bakeries, can be explored on foot in about 15 minutes. Apart from a few passing cars and residents chatting over glasses of Eupener beer at tables set up in the town's main plaza, there's usually so little noise that robins can be heard chirping in the trees. It gets even more serene just outside town, where country roads wind pass rolling green pastures dotted with sheep, ancient stone houses, and the occasional abbey brewing the strong beer for which Belgium is so well known.

Eupen wasn't always so peaceful. The town, which dates back to the early thirteenth century, has a turbulent history in which it was repeatedly passed back and forth between kingdoms, empires, and countries, before finally being returned to Belgian control after World War II. Soldiers in that conflict fought some of their fiercest battles near Eupen, including the Battle of the Bulge, the last major German offensive of the war. It started with a surprise attack through the densely forested Ardennes region that inflicted heavy casualties on American troops. But they fought back, and the battle played a key role in depleting Germany's forces and eventually winning the war for the Allies. Eupen's oldest residents still remember the day American tanks arrived to liberate them from the Nazis. U.S. troops also introduced them to chewing gum for the first time. Eupen itself was largely spared destruction during the war and has been pretty quiet ever since, but reminders of the war's brutality lurk nearby. A cemetery filled with the graves of thousands of fallen U.S. soldiers is only a ten-minute drive away.

Even in Belgium Eupen is viewed as existing on the fringes, both for reasons of geography and because it's a German-speaking region in a country dominated by French and Flemish. Eupen is the seat of government for Belgium's German-speaking community, which numbers only about 75,000 people. The biggest excitement in Eupen every year usually revolves around the town's annual Carnival parade, especially the choice of the festival's prince and his two female pages, all of whom dress up in black, white, and gold medieval costumes complete with tights, puffed sleeves, and ceremonial caps. The sleepy town certainly wasn't prepared for Aspire's surprise announcement at a press conference in June 2012 that it had purchased the local soccer club, KAS Eupen, on behalf of Qatar.

Arab sheikhs and Russian oligarchs have been scooping up some of the biggest clubs in the world for hundreds of millions of dollars, including Chelsea, Manchester City, and Paris Saint-Germain. But Aspire's purchase of KAS Eupen was a far cry from those high-profile deals. Instead of a brand-name team in a top league in a major European city, Qatar was now the proud owner of a relatively unknown second division club in a small town that struggled to attract more than a couple thousand spectators to its home games. Hardly a gem by conventional standards. But

Colomer and other Aspire officials considered Eupen to be perfect precisely because their needs were so unconventional.

They had been looking for a club they could control and fill with a steady flow of young African players. These criteria ruled out many of Europe's top soccer nations because they either had restrictive rules about how many non-Europeans could play on a team or prohibited outside investors from owning the majority of a club. Aspire was basically left with teams in Portugal and Belgium but crossed the former off the list because none of the players spoke Portuguese. Even though Eupen is officially a German-speaking town, most of the residents also speak French, as do many of the Football Dreams players. Aspire was also worried about the boys getting into trouble once they were on their own outside the academy, so they specifically looked for clubs in small towns outside of Belgium's capital, Brussels. They figured smaller towns would offer fewer distractions that could tempt the players away from the focus and hard work needed to become a top professional.

Another reason Aspire was interested in KAS Eupen was that it was effectively bankrupt but had the potential to grow. The team, which was formed in 1945 in the aftermath of World War II, spent most of its history as an amateur side dwelling in Belgium's lower divisions. The players mostly came from Eupen or surrounding towns. They earned a living by working at bars, sandwich shops, and other local businesses during the day, trained a few nights a week, and played games on the weekends, for which they might be paid a couple hundred euros a month. After the matches, they stayed up all night drinking with fans at local bars around town. All that changed in 2009 when an Italian investor arrived on the scene, bringing both money and professional players from Italy and Switzerland. The team managed to make it to Belgium's top division for the first time in its history, forcing the local government and the club to kick in millions of euros to upgrade the stadium to hold 8,000 people per the federation's regulations.

The team only lasted a year in the first division, and the money from the Italian eventually dried up. As unpaid bills multiplied, a German investor arrived in 2011 as a replacement, but he was arrested back home after a few months for allegedly running an investment pyramid scheme similar to Bernie Madoff's. The situation was so dire before Qatar arrived that the players had the electricity and water cut off in their apartments and their cars repossessed because the club couldn't pay the bills. "It was the same for me," said Michael Radermacher, Eupen's team manager. "I had a car from the club. One day at noon, I had to take my children to school. I went to the parking lot, and the car was gone."

The team had to rely on private individuals to pay for the players' salaries, and some staff members at the club weren't being paid at all. In early 2012, the Belgian federation refused to issue Eupen a license for the next season because the club was basically insolvent. Given this situation, it's perhaps no surprise that the local *Grenz Echo* newspaper greeted Qatar's purchase of the team by comparing it to a fairy tale in which a knight shows up on a white horse, frees the princess, and rides off with her to live happily ever after.

Some in town agreed, especially former players who said the team would have been forced to start over in Belgium's lowest division if Qatar hadn't arrived on the scene with its checkbook. During the negotiations, one of Aspire's representatives reportedly laughed when the club said the academy would have to assume a few million euros in debt as part of the purchase. That was chump change for Qatar. It all was. Aspire reportedly paid about 4 million euros for the club, brought in an entirely new coaching staff, and injected much-needed cash into the team. Almost overnight, the club went from scrounging around for 100 euros to pay the local baker to being flush with cash.

Word quickly spread through town that the local team, known as the Pandas, was now owned by a mysterious Arab country and would soon be filled with African teenagers, a reality some found unsettling. Questions, rumors, and speculation bounced down Eupen's normally quiet streets. "You had some supporters hoping the emir of Qatar was like the prince from *Aladdin* and would come with millions of dollars," said Thomas Evers, the lead soccer writer for the *Grenz Echo*. "They were dreaming that in three years we would be playing in the Champions League because you have the emir and he will bring superstars like Paris Saint-Germain. And then they saw fifteen African players who are 18 years old and had never played a professional game. People said, 'What will happen?'"

Radermacher couldn't wait to meet the players. Eupen's affable team manager was on his way to the biggest hotel in town, the 28-room Ambassador, to greet the Football Dreams contingent when they first arrived in July 2012. He was excited about the prospect of welcoming what he understood to be an elite group of African players and had visions of Didier Drogba and Yaya Touré dancing in his head. But he was in for a shock when he first spotted them in the lobby. "I came into the hotel, and I saw children!" said Radermacher, laughing at the memory.

Unlike the strapping players people often expect from Africa, few in the first Football Dreams class came anywhere close to six feet tall. That's in part because Colomer came from Barcelona and had a penchant for the small technical players the club often produced. It was also likely because many of the boys were older than 13 when they first tried out and therefore didn't grow as expected over the years. At five feet, nine inches, Diawandou was actually one of the tallest players in the class.

Radermacher turned to Eupen's general manager, Christoph Henkel, to confirm the players he was staring at really were the ones he was supposed to be welcoming, although the likelihood of somehow coming across over a dozen other Africans in the lobby of the Ambassador Hotel was pretty much zero. "I said to Christoph, 'These are the players?' and he said, 'Yeah, very young.' I knew they were 18 years old, but in my head a professional player would be different." Many in town also questioned their size and harbored doubts about how they would perform in Belgium's rough-and-tumble second division. But those were far from the only concerns the people of Eupen had after Qatar swooped in from nowhere to buy their little local club.

One of the club's two supporter groups, the Zebras, made up of younger "ultra" fans, boycotted the team's games because they didn't agree with Qatar's purchase. They saw it as an attempt to hijack the club's tradition and culture and turn it into a business benefiting the new owner. "Football is for you and me and not for fucking industry," said one of the group's members, Peter Schuller. They were angry that Aspire had changed Eupen's jerseys from red and yellow, the city's traditional colors, to blue and white to match the academy. Eupen also played in black and white, a practice that generated the team's long-standing nickname, the Pandas.

Some of the criticism around town had a racist tinge to it. A local slurping down beer at one of Eupen's small bars blurted out, "The al Qataris are terrorists!" when asked what he thought, "and the Saudi Arabians, too!" At least he knew the identity of the country that bought the team. Another local said it was either "sheikhs from Bhutan or Oman." He couldn't remember which. A few of the town's older residents said they didn't agree with having African or Arab players on the team at all. Eupen is almost lily white, and the only other black people wandering around town mostly come from an asylum center for refugees located near the team's stadium.

But most critics said they simply didn't like the fact that the team was no longer made up of local players they knew and could go drinking with after games. The Football Dreams players rarely went out at all and were completely focused on climbing the professional ladder. But Aspire understood the importance of the connection between the town and the club. The team's general manager, Christoph Henkel, joked that perhaps he should hire a player whose only job would be to drink with fans after matches. "I thought maybe an Irish guy," he said. "He never plays, but after each match, he's the king of the bar here."

Fans also complained that Eupen's new coach, Tintin, didn't interact with them much or speak German, so they couldn't impart what they insisted would be useful advice to help manage the team. "People here know the players, know who is good," said Manfred Schumacher, a grizzled bartender serving pints of beer at the cozy Columbus Cafe near the town's main plaza. "When the coach pulls out a player, the people are not happy." But Tintin was quite happy to miss out on this advice and said he wasn't going to explain to the locals why he played certain players and not others. "I come from a very different world, a professional world," said the coach.

Aspire wasn't the first to use a Belgian team as a platform for launching African players or to spark opposition doing it. In 2001, French coach Jean-Marc Guillou led a consortium to buy a financially troubled first division club in northern Belgium called KSK Beveren. Guillou became the team's manager and began importing players from an academy he ran at ASEC Mimosas in the Ivory Coast, taking advantage of the lax rules on how many Africans could turn out for a club in Belgium.

Beveren reached the final of the Belgian Cup in 2004, and the club managed to sell many of the Ivorian players to bigger teams elsewhere in Europe, including Yaya Touré, Gervinho, and Emmanuel Eboué. Many ended up at Arsenal, and it later came to light in the media that the British club provided a loan to help Guillou's group acquire Beveren. The two were connected because Arsenal's coach, Arsene Wenger, used to be Guillou's assistant in France. Although Beveren proved successful in feeding players to big clubs, some in Belgium criticized Guillou's system because he would often field teams composed entirely of African players, and the coach eventually left the club in 2006.

The purchase of Eupen sparked comparisons with Guillou's operation, but Aspire officials sought to differentiate what they were doing by saying they were focused on developing players rather than making money. They also pointed out that even though Eupen contained over a dozen Africans, only a few of them usually started. The coach, Tintin, knew the academy wanted him to help the Football Dreams players to progress, but he also needed to win games. That meant he often relied on a core of more experienced players augmented by a few regular Football Dreams starters, including Diawandou, who was made co-captain, the smooth Ghanaian playmaker Samuel Asamoah, and Anthony Bassey, a lightning-fast striker from Nigeria. The coach sprinkled in the other Football Dreams players where needed, and some got very little playing time. Aspire also sent a few Qatari kids to Eupen, part of the country's effort to improve its national team ahead of the 2022 World Cup, but most trained with the reserve squad since they weren't good enough for the first team. Many in town suspected they would see the African boys playing for Qatar in the World Cup as well and thought that was the whole point of Football Dreams.

Eupen won the first game of the season, beating Dessel Sport from Antwerp 1-0 in front of their home supporters. But the Football Dreams players had a tough time adjusting to the physicality, tactics, and bad fields of the Belgian second division, and the team only won once more in the next 10 games. The players not only had to get used to opponents hacking them down but also to fans whistling at them when the team wasn't performing. It was the first time the Football Dreams players had experienced the constant pressure of competing in a league. While they had played in tournaments and friendlies against some of the biggest teams in the world, they had never battled for league points week in and week out. Unlike the academy, they knew if their performance didn't cut it, they were always at risk of being sent home. "The pressure is much higher," said Diawandou. "Here you are playing for money. People are playing to help their family."

Colomer, who sits on the team's board, often flew all the way from Senegal to watch the boys play, giving them a hug and a few words of encouragement before they stepped on the field. Eupen would often dominate possession because the players were schooled in Barcelona's quick passing game. But they struggled to score goals against teams that made up for their lack of technique with a combination of experience and brute force. Referees often weren't much help since they let players get away with so much more than you would see on televised matches from Europe's top leagues.

A game in the Belgian second division often looks like a thinly veiled wrestling match as the players grab at each other in their fight for the ball. When things really get out of hand, as they frequently do, the ref often tries to reestablish control with a flurry of yellow cards and the occasional red. But it never seems to do much good. "Most of the matches we had 70 to 80 percent ball possession, but no goals even though we had unbelievable chances," said Henkel, the general manager. "We would lose 1-0, 1-0, 1-0, 2-1 because the other teams came two or three times at the goal and scored." The Football Dreams players clearly still had a lot to learn.

They were also grappling with a new world off the field as they faced the challenge of living on their own for the first time. The Football Dreams players had spent the last five years in a completely sheltered environment that catered to their every need, and the

African towns where they grew up before bore little resemblance to Eupen. They spent the first few weeks living at the Ambassador Hotel as the club found them apartments where they could live in groups of two or three. But there was plenty of confusion when Radermacher, the team manager, dropped them off at their apartments for the first time. "The players asked, 'We stay here alone?'" said Radermacher. That was the plan, he told them. They also learned they would have to buy and cook their own food.

"Normally I say, 'This is the apartment, here are the keys, see you tomorrow,'" said Radermacher. But he agreed to take them to the supermarket the next day. Unfortunately, that proved equally confusing. The players kept trying to pay the cashier for individual items, as you might in an African market. "I told them, 'You have to take it all and then go to the cashier,'" said Radermacher. "But it was just this one time. They aren't stupid."

Cooking wasn't any easier than shopping for the players once they returned to their apartments. Radermacher dropped by to check on a couple of the boys one day, and the Nigerian goalkeeper John Felagha said he had a problem and wanted the team manager's help. "He said, 'Hey, I put my chicken in the oven, but it never finished,'" said Radermacher. He agreed to have a look, but John didn't lead him to the oven. Instead, he walked over to the dishwasher, opened it up and showed the team manager his uncooked chicken. "You have to put dishes inside, not food!" said Radermacher, trying to hold back his laughter. John complied and began filling the dishwasher with clean dishes. "No, not the clean ones!" The club eventually arranged a cooking course for the kids to show them how to make things like fish and salad, but they mostly ended up subsisting on a diet of pasta and rice because they were easier to make. At least they got breakfast and lunch at the club before and after training.

In general, the locals were pleasantly surprised by how well mannered the Football Dreams players were. Even those who didn't

Football Dreams players at a café in the center of Eupen.

agree with Qatar buying Eupen's team praised the players for always offering a handshake whenever they met in the street. The boys were lucky that many of Eupen's residents were just as well intentioned. Evers, the writer for the *Grenz Echo*, said he once spotted a few players struggling to get cash out of an ATM in the center of town. "They asked me for help and wanted to give me their PIN code," said Evers. He helped them out but told them they really shouldn't be handing out their PIN to people on the street.

Struggling with ATMs was just one problem the boys faced as they figured out how to manage having significant amounts of cash for the first time. Each Football Dreams player earned at least 77,000 euros a year, the Belgian-mandated salary for non-Europeans. Many spent freely on iPhones, expensive watches, and stylish new clothes from designers like Gucci and Wati B, bringing a distinctive flair to Eupen's normally conservative, buttoned-down streets and cafes.

But the boys also faced constant demands on their newfound

wealth from family and friends in Africa. They felt an intense responsibility to help those less fortunate and wired significant amounts of
money back home. "I do that almost every month because I know
how it feels to live without something," said Anthony Bassey, who
used to juggle a soccer ball on street corners in the Nigerian city of
Uyo to help his family make ends meet. "I always send money for
my siblings, for my mother to put them in school because that is the
most important thing for now. Also to buy some food and keep some
money for themselves whenever they need it."

But some of the players had little ability to gauge how much
they could afford to send back and showed up at the club toward
the end of the month several times to say they had run out of cash.
Still, the demands from home were relentless. Anthony had to
change his cell number at one point because he was getting too
many calls. He also grappled with a relative stealing money that
was meant for his mom and siblings. "There was a time when I was
having lots of problems with my family," Anthony said. "There was
too much pressure. I couldn't concentrate, so I decided to change
my phone line."

Diawandou faced fewer demands from his family since they were
already doing pretty well even before he went to the academy. But he
received plenty of attention from friends and acquaintances, especially when he returned to Senegal for vacation. He often stayed
holed up in his house to avoid the hassle. "I cannot go out," said
Diawandou. "People are always asking you for things; 'give me juice,
give me money.'"

He largely stayed at home in Eupen as well when he wasn't training and played video games or watched movies with the two Senegalese players he lived with, Samba Ndiaye and Ibrahima Diedhiou.
The three of them created a home away from home in their small
wooden house near Eupen's stadium. They drank Senegalese coffee
and put dark brown Maggi sauce on everything they ate, just like

they would back home. They even found a couple of local Senegalese friends who approached them after they heard the players speaking Wolof on the field. The new friends helped out by doing much of the cooking and cleaning at the house, making it even easier for the players to settle in. "Now we have a family," said Diawandou.

As the Football Dreams players adjusted to life off the field in Eupen, they also gained more confidence on it, even though they faced a new nemesis: the cold. Their arrival coincided with one of the most brutal winters in years, bringing snow and frigid temperatures from November through March, a huge change for kids who had spent almost their entire lives in the heat of Africa and the Middle East. Many of the players had never even seen snow before arriving in Eupen. Now they were forced to train in it day in and day out. Never had the sizzling temperatures in Senegal or the weather-insulated dome in Qatar looked so good.

Despite the polar vortex, the team's performance gradually improved over the rest of the season, although never hitting the heights that perhaps some in the club and town had hoped. The team benefited from adding a few older players from Spain in the middle of the season, which injected even more experience into the young squad. "The players needed half a year to find their place on the field," said Henkel, the general manager. "After that, they learned from match to match to be clever, to be professional, and to play to win the game."

The Belgian season was divided into three different sections of 10 games each, and Eupen managed to finish fourth in the second portion of the season. By the end, the team was in eighth place overall, safely above the relegation zone but far away from clubs battling for promotion. Aspire's goal was to make it to the first division because that would give the Football Dreams players even stiffer competition and a higher-profile platform to advertise their talent to bigger European clubs.

According to fans, the standout Football Dreams players that first season were Anthony Bassey and Samuel Asamoah. They loved how Anthony used his speed to menace defenders on the right wing even though he was only a little over five and a half feet tall. Samuel was even smaller but dominated the midfield against opponents who seemed twice his size. Even the coach, Tintin, thought Samuel had the best chance of making it to a top club out of all the Football Dreams players. "He's very fast, has great endurance, control, passing, and vision of play," said Tintin. "If we put Asamoah in Barcelona, he would play."

But Samuel wasn't the player Barcelona came looking for that season. It was the captain, Diawandou, who led the team from his position in central defense. While attacking players usually attract more attention, defenders can actually be more vital to a team's success. Keeping a clean sheet is over two and a half times more valuable than scoring a goal in terms of a team winning points, according to the book *The Numbers Game*. But a defender's skill is often more difficult to see because his biggest contribution is preventing goals, not scoring them. A defender doesn't always do that with scything tackles that draw cheers from the crowd. In fact, the best tackle is the one a defender never has to make because superior positioning breaks up a play before it can even get started. But defensive positioning isn't what usually stands out in the minds of fans and coaches. They're focused on goals.

Diawandou was a little short compared to central defenders at many of Europe's top clubs, but Barcelona had shown a willingness to buck that trend with players like Javier Mascherano, whose nickname is *Jefecito*, "the little boss." Like Diawandou, Mascherano was a converted midfielder who only stood about five feet, nine inches tall. But the Argentine star possessed the technical skill, vision, and grit to hold off opposing strikers and could start Barcelona's attack by bringing the ball forward out of the back. Diawandou sought to emulate Mascherano, and Barcelona clearly had similar ideas. The club contacted the Senegalese defender through Colomer to say they wanted him for their reserve squad, Barcelona B, which could serve as a launching point for the senior team.

That was an absolute dream for Diawandou. Barcelona was, of course, one of the biggest clubs in the world and home to Messi. It also happened to be Diawandou's favorite team, and he had been schooled for years to play in the style of the Catalonian giants. But Diawandou didn't jump on the next plane to Barcelona. Instead, he turned the club down. Colomer told him it wasn't the right time. He still needed more experience, and Aspire was relying on him to help Eupen make the jump to the first division next season. It was a testament to his trust in the Spanish scout that he agreed. Imagine how many players in his position would have been tempted to brush Colomer aside, although Eupen did improve his contract to persuade him to stay.

"I didn't want to let the project down," said Diawandou. "Everything I have gotten until now is because of Aspire. If they tell me to stay, I'm going to stay because they have taken me far." He also took Colomer's guidance to heart that he needed more experience before making the jump to a top club, advice other players at the academy had ignored. "If you're going to Barcelona, you need to be ready. I was not ready. I knew at Eupen I would play all the games. If you play, you get more confidence. But in Barcelona I would be in the second team, and who knows if I would play or not."

Many other Football Dreams players at Eupen fared much worse than Diawandou did. At the end of the season, the club told over half a dozen of them that they were surplus to requirements and either needed to find another European team or head back home to Africa. One of them was the Nigerian goalkeeper John Felagha, who struggled with a persistent knee injury and lacked the size

Diawandou dribbling the ball during one of Eupen's away games in Belgium.

to compete with Eupen's starting keeper from Germany. "He just couldn't make it at this level," said Tintin. "He has good qualities but not as good as the goalkeepers we had." John failed to find another club in Europe that would take him and was forced to make the difficult journey back to his hometown in the Niger Delta. But he didn't give up hope. "I spoke with Colomer and Lamine, and they said I should be patient," said John. "They will look for something for me. I'm among the pioneers of the project. I want to succeed so the other goalkeepers can see they can do it." They never ended up finding John another club but did invite him to join the Football Dreams staff to help with tryouts across the world, leaving some of his classmates quite envious.

Eupen's coach also cast off Hamza Zakari, the Ghanaian midfielder who captained his national team in the Africa Cup of Nations playoff against Senegal. Tintin had no doubts about Hamza's talent but barely played him because the two frequently clashed. "He has excellent qualities," said Tintin. "He is fast, plays well. But the mentality is not there. There are football players like this whose mentality doesn't allow them to compete." Tintin wasn't the first to grow frustrated with Hamza's sometimes prickly attitude. Even at the academy, he developed a reputation as someone who was difficult to coach. "Hamza is a player who if he wants can be unbelievable," said academy coach Jordi Rovira. "But do you want to be the best, or is the pressure too much?"

Tintin first had issues with Hamza when he started coaching the Football Dreams players in Doha and the Ghanaian constantly refused to train, saying he was injured. The coach was dubious and figured much of it was in his head. Tintin finally reached his breaking point in Eupen during a friendly match before the season even started. Hamza refused to come out of the locker room at halftime, leaving only 10 players on the field and the coach apoplectic. Hamza said he felt sick and couldn't play, but Tintin didn't want to hear any more excuses. "Tintin was very angry with him," said Forewah Emmanuel, one of the Football Dreams staff members. "He told Hamza, 'When I am talking to you, look at me!' But Hamza was not looking at him. Tintin said, 'Fine, you will not play.' Hamza was nervous, but the coach didn't understand his problem." For his part, Hamza insists he really was sick and believes Tintin simply didn't like him from the beginning.

The coach eventually gave up trying to understand Hamza's problems and simply told him he needed to find another team. Luckily for the Ghanaian, he was able to find a club playing in Norway's top division, Tromso IL, that would take him on loan. But he continued to be plagued by various ailments, real or imagined, and soon found himself transferred to a second division club in the tiny Icelandic town of Selfoss. That didn't work out either, and before long, Hamza was back in Ghana wondering what to do next. "We are still trying with Hamza," said Lamine Savané, the Football Dreams country director in Senegal. "We are trying to push him to understand. A professional coach just doesn't have the time. If you're difficult, I have someone who is easy, so why bother?"

Many of the other Football Dreams players who left also ended up playing for clubs in third- or fourth-tier soccer nations like Latvia or Estonia or had to make the tough trek back to Africa to regroup. Although they may have thrived at the academy, they struggled to succeed once they were up against opponents in Europe likely closer to their own age. For instance, Jasper Uwa, the zippy little Nigerian striker who scored against Neymar's Brazil in Doha and continued to rain in goals during his time in Senegal, couldn't replicate that form at Eupen. "Many times a player will score many goals in one category but not when they move up," said Tintin. Like Jasper, many of the players lacked the talent necessary to make up for their size in a league that often prized brute force over technique.

There were opportunities to play in Africa as well, but the players often had no interest because they would earn a pittance compared to Eupen. It would also be a blow to their pride after everyone thought they were going to be big stars in Europe. They cultivated this image online while they were at the academy by posting pictures of their travels around the world and their meet and greets with famous players like Messi. "It's very difficult for them to go back after it doesn't work out, especially because of the life they project on Facebook," said a Nigerian Football Dreams staff member, Godwin Malu.

Unfortunately, they had little to fall back on if professional soccer didn't work out. Despite Aspire's message that education was just as important as training while they were at the academy, only one of the Football Dreams players from the first class actually received a high school diploma. The number was zero in the second class. The situation didn't improve much in future years either, as only 10 percent of the kids ended up getting a diploma while they were at the academy. Aspire officials said they struggled with the fact that the boys arrived with varying levels of education and sometimes lacked the motivation to study. Some of the boys admitted as much, saying they used school as a chance to catch up on sleep since they were exhausted from training twice a day and didn't think class really mattered. That attitude continued when the players reached Eupen, even though Aspire brought in a social worker who offered to help them continue their education. "The offer is there for all the players," said Stefan Wetzel. "They have a lot of time and could do something, but it's tough to motivate them."

Some of the older players at Eupen also tried to convince the boys to think about their future if soccer didn't work out, including Manel Exposito, whom Colomer lured to Belgium years after coaching him at his local soccer school in Vic and then signing him at Barcelona. "My advice as well is to study," said Exposito. "It's good to grow as a football player, but maybe one day you will get injured and your career stops, and later what do you do?" But most of them ignored his advice, even after they watched many of their Football Dreams classmates forced out of the club. They were convinced they were the ones who would succeed.

The second season started with much more promise. Eupen leaped to first place in the league after the first 10 games, a position that would automatically mean promotion to the first division if the team could hold on to it until the end of the season. Anything less would lead to a difficult four-way playoff. Eupen's rising fortunes improved the town's attitude toward Aspire and the Football Dreams players, and more people started coming to the matches. The bump was limited, though. The largest crowds still maxed out at around 3,000 people since the team had to compete for attention with big German clubs across the border, like FC Cologne and FC Schalke 04.

Perhaps most important, the Zebras returned. The supporter group still opposed Qatar's purchase of the club, but its members grew bored whiling away nights they used to spend at the stadium cheering on their team. "After many months, the guys were sitting in the bar and were thinking, 'Fuck, what are we doing? Saturday night, Jesus Christ, we have nothing to do,'" said the 23-year-old president of the Zebras, Raphael Pelzer. After a heated debate beneath the Eupen banners that hung from the ceiling of their local watering hole, A Ge Pompke, many of the supporters agreed to return. "We said, 'OK, we will do it for our hometown because the club represents the city and the German region,'" said Pelzer.

The club also encouraged their return by once again using red and yellow jerseys at times to match the town's traditional colors, just like the Zebras had demanded. The supporters appreciated the gesture and marched back into the stadium to take up their customary position behind goal. They hung their large red and yellow Zebras banner over the railing and picked up where they left off, banging drums and leading the crowd in raucous chants. The ringleader, a bearded guy with a beer gut, carried a megaphone and used it to great effect. It was the kind of atmosphere that had been missing since the Zebras' boycott, and the team was glad to have them back. There was a second supporter group in town, the Pandas, but it was mostly composed of older fans who spent games slurping down beers and steaming cups of mulled wine. They left the drumming and chanting to the youngsters. The players showed their appreciation by filing over to the Zebras' end after matches to sign autographs and high-five the fans.

Colomer was also happy with how the team was doing and once again flew from Senegal on many weekends to watch the Football Dreams players compete. "We are maybe the youngest team in

Europe for the first and second divisions; we play good football and many people come see us," said Colomer, sitting on the sideline of one of Eupen's games that season in the small town of Tubize. "I think we are on our way, but when you work with youth, it takes time. You have to be patient, and people need to trust you."

Excitement grew in Eupen as the end of the season approached and, with it, the chance of promotion to the first division. The team entered the last week of the season in second place but still had one more chance of regaining the top spot and automatically moving up. As it turned out, the final match, on April 27, 2014, was against KVC Westerlo, a club from a small town near Antwerp that sat in first place, one point above Eupen. If the Pandas could win the game, they would slide into the top spot and be promoted. Eupen had beaten Westerlo 1-0 back in November, but that was at home. Now they had to play in Westerlo's stadium, no easy task. Westerlo had spent 15 years in the first division before being relegated to the second division a few seasons earlier and was desperate to move back up.

As the match approached, a war of words broke out between the coaches of both teams. Westerlo's manager, Dennis Van Wijk, told the press, "Which do you prefer? Seeing a team with 99 percent Belgians move up to D1 or seeing a club with 99 percent foreigners become champion?" Tintin fired back by saying Van Wijk was no Belgian himself since he came from the Netherlands. "They call me Tintin," said Eupen's coach. "I'm more Belgian than he is!" Tintin also pointed out that both of Eupen's leading scorers were Belgian, while Westerlo relied on a pair of strikers from the Ivory Coast and the Netherlands.

This kind of attack was nothing new for Eupen. They had been hearing the same thing ever since the Football Dreams players showed up. "Everyone in Belgium was saying Eupen has too many foreigners," said Diawandou. But Tintin urged them to block out the criticism and only focus on beating Westerlo. "He said, 'This is your time,'" said Diawandou. "You are young. If you go to the first division, you will write your own story because you are the youngest team in Belgium." The Senegalese captain also gathered the other Football Dreams players together to rally them for the match. "I told them this is our opportunity," said Diawandou. "Promotion to the first division at 19 years old would be great."

Eupen's fans showed up en masse on street corners throughout town as the team's bus left for the two-hour drive to Westerlo. To fire up the players, the coach asked the bus driver to circle around and pass the fans several times as they cheered and held up banners. As the bus finally pulled away, Diawandou donned his headphones to listen to the Quranic music that had soothed his mind on game day ever since he was a young boy in Thiès. Other players also hit play on their iPhones or took out something to read, whatever they needed to steady their nerves.

Westerlo's fans were certainly looking to rattle them as soon as they arrived at the stadium, which was bathed in yellow and blue, Westerlo's team colors. Known as the Small Tank, the stadium could hold about 8,000 people, and nearly every one of them waved a Westerlo flag or scarf as they cheered on their side. They also wore yellow and blue wigs, as well as face paint and, of course, team jerseys. Over a thousand Eupen fans, including Colomer and several other senior Aspire executives, also made the trip, but they were drowned out by their rivals. Those who hadn't come watched the match on a huge screen set up in the center of Eupen, with beers in hand and black and white team scarves around their necks.

Diawandou was excited for the match and undaunted by the roar of Westerlo's fans around the stadium. "I love this kind of pressure," said the Senegalese captain. He led his side onto the field wearing a red captain's armband around the sleeve of his black and white striped jersey. Aspire's logo featured prominently in the middle of his chest. Eupen got a lucky break in the opening minutes of the match when a Westerlo midfielder was sent off for throwing an elbow into the face of one of Eupen's players, sending him tumbling to the ground. But the Pandas were unable to capitalize on being a man up before making their own mistake. The team's keeper, Jonas Deumeland, let an easy save slip through his legs about fifteen minutes later and was forced to drag down a Westerlo player inside the penalty box to prevent him from scoring. The referee sent him off, and his replacement, Hendrik Van Crombrugge, had the unenviable task of positioning himself in goal as Westerlo's Ivorian striker lined up for a penalty kick.

A goal would make Eupen's task significantly more difficult. A draw wasn't enough for the Pandas. Only a win would put them in the top spot, so if Westerlo scored, that would mean they needed two goals against one of the league's best defenses. But Van Crombrugge came up big. He dove to the right and parried the striker's shot away from danger, prompting cheers from his teammates on the edge of the box. Eupen knew they still needed a goal, so they poured players forward, leaving them exposed to a possible counterattack. That threat turned into a reality in the 31st minute. Diawandou and several of his teammates sprinted back to stop a Westerlo fast break, but a clever through ball sliced them open from left to right. One of Westerlo's midfielders ran onto it at the top of the penalty box and, despite a heavy first touch, was able to nudge the ball past the onrushing keeper. It slowly rolled into the far left corner as Westerlo's supporters erupted with joy.

Diawandou could only grimace in frustration and knew the team would have to produce something special to climb out of the hole they were in. Tintin threw on even more attacking players, but Westerlo's defense held firm and the team continued to look threatening on the counterattack. Eupen just couldn't find a way through, and their chance at automatic promotion faded as the minutes clicked by on the clock. Finally, the referee blew his whistle to signal the end of the match, and Westerlo's coach jumped up and down on the sideline in glee. He may not have won the war of words with Tintin before the game, but his team was back in the first division after a two-year hiatus.

Eupen now faced a difficult four-way playoff against a pair of teams from the second division and one from the first. They would all play each other twice over a period of less than three weeks, and only the team that came out on top would move up. Winning against Westerlo would have been so much easier, but Diawandou told the team they needed to put that out of their minds. "I said, 'We need to forget about this and just focus on the playoffs,'" said the Senegalese captain.

Eupen had an up and down experience during the playoffs. They only lost once in their first five matches, but twice they gave up a two-goal lead and let their opponents come back and level the score. If they had won those games, they would have gained promotion before the playoffs were even over. Instead, it once again came down to an away match on the last day. This one was against OH Leuven, the only first division team in the mix and the only side that had beaten Eupen so far in the playoffs, a 3-0 drubbing at home. Eupen now needed a tie or a win to move up, depending on what happened in the other game being played that day. Leuven was already out of contention, but both of the other teams in the playoffs still had a chance at promotion.

In many ways, Eupen's final match day was a reprise of the one against Westerlo a few weeks earlier. Eupen supporters cheered on street corners as the team bus left town, Diawandou switched on his Quranic music to relax during the one-hour trip to Leuven, and the team entered the stadium to the roar of rival fans, who happened to be waving green and white flags rather than yellow and blue. Diawandou once again led his teammates onto the field for the start of the match in their black and white stripes, but this time it was Eupen who jumped ahead to take the lead off a corner in the seventh minute. Florian Taulemesse, a French striker who joined Eupen after playing in Spain, outjumped the defender marking him and headed the ball into the back of the net, sparking wild cheers from his teammates and their traveling fans. If Eupen could hold on to the lead, they were headed to the first division for only the second time in the team's history.

But once again the Pandas let their opponents back into the game. Leuven equalized only five minutes later when one of its midfielders, who happened to be from Cameroon, turned in a rebound after a save from Eupen's keeper. Even though a tie might still see Eupen go through, the team needed to score once more to guarantee promotion. Tintin again poured players forward looking for that key goal, and it finally came in the 79th minute. But it wasn't Eupen that scored. This time it was one of Leuven's strikers who managed to get his head on the ball and put it into the net.

Despite Eupen's players putting everything they had into leveling the score in the game's dying minutes, they couldn't find a way to pierce Leuven's defense for a second time. As it turned out, a tie wouldn't have been enough to get them promoted anyway. One of the other teams playing that day, Royal Mouscron-Péruwelz, won their final match 4-2 and moved into the first division. Eupen's players were crushed after having three different chances to gain promotion over the course of three weeks and coming up short each time. Tintin thought the Pandas had simply been the victim of bad luck. "If Eupen had any luck, it would be in the first division," he said. "They were the best team that season, and it was the best season in Eupen's history. But they still didn't move up."

As the season finally came to a close, the question loomed of how many Football Dreams players would stay in Eupen. Before the playoffs, the head of Aspire, Ivan Bravo, said if the team didn't get promoted, some of the players might need to move to bigger clubs to experience a higher level of competition. But would the clubs come knocking? Diawandou had already turned down Barcelona once. The club's scouts had been back in the stands in Eupen to monitor his progress, but had his performance been good enough for Barcelona to make a second offer?

Tintin had been experimenting with playing Diawandou in center midfield and at right back in case the club didn't return. Barcelona was open to taking smaller central defenders, but many of the other big clubs were not. "It's very difficult at a top European club unless you are very special," said Tintin. "The central defenders tend to be bigger and faster." By playing somewhere else on the field, Diawandou might expand the number of big clubs that would consider taking him. But his heart was set on Barcelona. All he could do was return to Senegal for summer break and wait to see what happened.

CHAPTER 11

Miracle Land

Bernard Appiah watched Messi hypnotize the ball with his magical left foot and scurry past yet another helpless defender. He spent a lot of time watching Messi these days, looking for inspiration, looking for hope. Both were in short supply. Bernard may have once reminded Colomer of Barcelona's superstar, but he was now as far from emulating Messi's success as he had ever been. The midfielder sat on a bare pink mattress on the floor of a dingy concrete room he shared with three other players in Accra. The indigo blue walls were scarred by water damage and patches of peeling paint. Sunlight filtered in through a single window, illuminating a deflated soccer ball on the ground and a couple of tattered Bibles stacked on a broken wooden chair. Bernard stared at a video of Messi on the two-inch screen of his battered cell phone. It was hard to believe he met the Argentine sensation seven years earlier. Those days had been filled with such promise. A good day now was when he could scrounge up enough money to buy something to eat after training.

It hadn't always been so grim since Bernard had returned from Aspire in May 2010. He had been sad to leave the academy, and the dispute over his license and Aspire's refusal to transfer him to

Europe continued to sting. But when he first flew back to Ghana, he had plenty of confidence he could find another way to Europe. He moved back in with the pastors of his church, Rev. James Mensah and his wife, Agnes, and slept in a spare bedroom of their small wooden home. He swept the floors and cleaned the kitchen in the morning before going to train, just like he had done before he left for Aspire. The pastors were disappointed things hadn't worked out for Bernard in Doha but were glad to have him back. "He knows I love him," said Rev. Mensah's wife. "God should have mercy on him."

The pastors' house was located next to their simple wooden church, Miracle Temple, with its gently sloping gable roof and fading light blue paint job. Bernard had been sweeping the floor of the church years earlier when his old coach, Justice Oteng, came to tell him a foreign scout was expected in the neighborhood to hold tryouts. When Bernard returned from Aspire, the pastors pinned a photo of him with Messi to a bulletin board at the back of the church, a reminder of what he had achieved and a symbol of the success that hopefully still lay ahead.

Missing out on making Ghana's Under-17 national team for the playoff against Senegal in the fall of 2010 was certainly a blow, especially since Bernard and Oteng suspected the Football Dreams country director, Andy Sam, engineered the player's exclusion. But Bernard didn't have to wait much longer to catch the break he was looking for. A few months later, he was playing with his old team, Unique FC, on the rough dirt field at Star Park in Teshie where Colomer first spotted him in 2007. Standing on the sideline was Youssif Chibsah, a former midfielder for Ghana's national team who now played for a club in Sweden and was home on holiday. Just like Colomer, Chibsah was blown away by Bernard's skill. "He is an exceptional player, very, very talented," said Chibsah. "If you have eyes for football and for talent, you can see immediately that he has the talent."

Chibsah was reminded of one of Ghana's most famous players, Abedi Pele, a left-footed attacking midfielder who captained the country's national team for a good chunk of the 1990s and happened to get his start playing in Qatar before moving to Europe. "Abedi Pele was Africa's best during his day," said Chibsah. "He could single-handedly change games when things weren't going well. I thought Bernard had the same qualities and, with the proper guidance, structure, and good training, could become a player like that."

Chibsah spoke with Oteng and offered to introduce Bernard to a friend, Wilhelm Myrer, who had connections with clubs in Norway and Sweden. Oteng agreed after negotiating what he could never get from Aspire, a percentage of the proceeds if Bernard became a star. Chibsah spoke with Bernard as well and liked what he heard. "He was full of confidence," said Chibsah. "There was no doubt that this was someone I wanted to help." Bernard was reenergized and hoped this was the ticket to Europe that eluded him at the academy. Nothing would be sweeter than making the jump after everyone at Aspire told him it was impossible until he turned 18. "When I came back, I did not give up," said Bernard. "I was praying to God that God would give me another chance. I came back, and God was good."

Chibsah's friend Myrer worked for a Norwegian mining company in Liberia, and he ended up buying a club there, Monrovia FC, with the hope of grooming players and sending them to Scandinavian teams. Myrer invited Bernard and two other players from Unique to Monrovia, where they spent a few weeks playing with his club. Oteng tagged along to make sure they would be okay. Myrer certainly liked what he saw in Bernard. "He was very, very skillful," he said. "If you go to Africa, you can see a lot of players who are very physical but not very well trained. But he was trained. All the coaches and the guys in Liberia loved Bernard and the way he played. We could see that he had good talent." Myrer even arranged for them to play a friendly match against Liberia's Under-20 national team, and Bernard once again dazzled in his playmaker role. "When you do that, you play against adults that are twice your size, and he was really tough and did very well."

Myrer arranged for Bernard and one of the other Unique players to travel to one of Norway's top clubs, Lillestrom SK, in the summer of 2011. They trained with the club's Under-16 side for a few weeks and then traveled to Sweden to compete in one of Europe's biggest youth tournaments, the Gothia Cup. The team didn't do so well, losing two games and drawing one, but Bernard and his Ghanaian teammate were the standouts at the tournament. "I talked to the guy who was the youth coach who took them there, and he said they were the best two on the team," said Myrer. But Lillestrom said they couldn't sign Bernard until he turned 18. Bernard was almost certainly older than that, but like Ibrahima, revealing his true age would have raised a whole host of issues. Chibsah suspected Bernard's height may have also been an issue for Lillestrom given the physicality of Norwegian soccer. He was still only a little over five feet tall at the time and wasn't going to get any taller.

Bernard switched gears and returned to Sweden because a fourth division club there, Säffle FF, expressed an interest in signing him after seeing him play in the Gothia Cup. It was a far cry from the clubs like Lazio and Valencia that had targeted Bernard when he was at Aspire. But he was growing desperate and figured any foothold in Europe was better than returning to Ghana empty-handed. He had to head home before anything was finalized because he had overstayed his visa and couldn't get an extension. Still, he hoped they could come to an agreement and he would soon find himself winging his way back to Sweden.

While Bernard waited for word from Säffle, he got a call from a Football Dreams staff member in the fall of 2011 saying Colomer was in Accra and wanted to meet him. It would be the first time Bernard had seen the Spanish scout since he had left Aspire. He caught a ride to El Wak, the stadium where Ghana and Senegal faced off about a year earlier in the Africa Cup of Nations playoff. Colomer was holding the final Football Dreams tryout in Ghana there that year and wanted to reconnect with the player from the first class who had left such an impression on him. Bernard brought along a photo of him playing with Säffle in Sweden, an attempt to show Colomer his career was still on track even though he left the academy.

"When he saw me, he was very sad because Colomer always liked me so much," said Bernard. The Spanish scout gave him a hug and asked the midfielder to sit next to him until he finished scouting for the day so they could talk. As the two sat silently side by side, Bernard had time to stare out at the latest batch of Ghanaian Football Dreams prospects and wonder how their fortunes would compare with his. Finally, Colomer turned to Bernard to find out what had become of the player who once held so much promise for him. "He said, 'Oh, my son, what is going on now?'" said Bernard. "I told him I went to Sweden and showed him the crowd I went to train with, and he said it was very good. He wanted me again and said he would call me."

That may have been wishful thinking on Bernard's part. He never heard from Colomer again. The Spanish scout was in his fifth year of recruiting for Football Dreams at that point and had an entire stable of potential stars back at his academy in Senegal. That wasn't all Colomer had in Saly, either. He also opened a five-star hotel in town called the Rhino Resort that attracted soccer celebrities like Messi. Colomer may have compared Bernard to the Argentine at the beginning of the program and predicted he would become a star. But that was years earlier, and the Ghanaian had apparently proven more trouble than he was worth. A few years later, Colomer even said Bernard wasn't a true Football Dreams player because he trained in Doha rather than at the Spanish scout's academy in Saly. Whatever bond had existed between the two was well and truly broken.

Bernard also got bad news from Säffle. Like Lillestrom, the club said they couldn't sign him since he wasn't yet 18. It was a painful blow, and not just for Bernard. The number of people counting on him making it to Europe had expanded in recent months. Bernard got a text message from his girlfriend while he was in Liberia saying she had given birth to a baby girl, quite a shock since he didn't even know she was pregnant. He not only needed to find a way to support them but also had to look for a new place to live. Not surprisingly, Bernard's pastors disapproved of him fathering a child out of wedlock, and he no longer felt welcome living in their home.

Moving in with his parents wasn't really an option. His father had lost his job as a security guard around the same time, and without the money that had been coming from Aspire, he could no longer afford the rent for their house in Teshie. He and his wife were forced to move outside Accra to an unfinished home they had started building when Bernard was at the academy but couldn't complete when the money from Qatar dried up. As Bernard looked around for help, he discovered how few people he could actually count on. "When I had money, I had a lot of friends," said Bernard. "When I was in Ghana, people would say, 'Appiah, Appiah' when I walked down the street. I thought they liked me, but when I came back to Ghana and didn't have money, I realized they didn't. Sometimes they will see me in the street and just pass." Bernard eventually found another set of pastors to take him and his younger brother into their cramped two-room home. But it was unclear if they acted out of charity or because they saw the player as a potential path to riches if he could ever make his way to Europe.

In any case, Europe was out of the question for now. Bernard needed to make money and explored playing in Ghana for the first time since he returned. It wasn't a very appealing option since he would earn peanuts compared to what players make in Europe. It was also a blow to his pride since everyone in Teshie figured he was on his way to becoming a big European star once he got into Aspire. But Bernard didn't have much choice. His coach Oteng reached out to two of the biggest clubs in Ghana, Hearts of Oak and Asante Kotoko, but they wanted to take Bernard for their junior teams since they often relied on older, more experienced players for their senior sides. Oteng thought he was too good for this and refused to release him.

Instead, Bernard ended up making his way to a club in Ghana's second highest league, King Solomon, after playing a friendly match against them toward the end of 2012. Bernard's team, Unique, lost 2-1, but he scored his side's only goal and wowed King Solomon's coach. "He plays like Lionel Messi," said the coach, Thomas Duah. "He's very fast with the ball, and I liked his technique, his control." Bernard only earned about $50 a month, but the club promised him much more in winning bonuses, especially if he could help the team qualify for Ghana's top division. Bernard scored a bucketload of goals and carried King Solomon to a final playoff match to get promoted, but the team ended up losing 1-0. The loss wasn't the most painful part of the season for Bernard, though. He repeatedly clashed with the club's management because they only paid him a fraction of the winning bonuses they promised. He was so angry that he quit the team and vowed never to play in Ghana again.

In fact, he was thinking about giving up soccer altogether when he met Arenton Ofoe Chiri, a buttoned-down IT specialist in his early 30s who worked for a major bank in Accra and owned a team in Ghana's third highest league on the side. He played a bit of soccer himself in primary school but admitted he wasn't very good and abandoned the game as he continued his education. Years later, when he was back home visiting his parents, he ran into an old schoolmate who had been a wizard on the field but hadn't been able to make it because he got injured and had no money to pay for his recovery. Chiri decided to use his savings to help his old friend and ended up doing the same for other promising players who had fallen on hard times. "I started looking for talents who are going to waste, to help them achieve their dreams," said Chiri. This eventually led him to starting his own team, Miracle Land, which he funded himself for about $5,000 a season. Without the support of someone like Chiri, many talented players in Africa would end up abandoning soccer because they need to earn a living and take care of their families.

That was where Bernard was headed when he crossed paths with Chiri in 2013. "When I met him, psychologically he was down," said Chiri. "Around that time, he didn't even want to play football anymore. He had a lot of frustration because he knew that when he was at Aspire he was a star. But now nothing was happening because he lacked someone taking responsibility for his life and pushing him to the next level." Bernard's name filtered down to Chiri after he was named one of the best players at a tournament organized at a sports complex in Accra owned by Marcel Desailly, a defender born in Ghana who became a star in Europe and won the World Cup with France in 1998. Chiri took Bernard under his wing and even invited him over to his house to have his wife cook for him. He persuaded Bernard not to give up on his talent and promised to help him achieve his dream of making it to Europe. "I talked to him to make him feel like he's going to be somebody," he said. "I told him I want to see him play in the Champions League because he's got the potential."

Of course, Chiri could earn a bit of money himself if he was successful in reviving Bernard's career, since he negotiated a deal to split any proceeds with Oteng, but he insisted that wasn't his motivation. Bernard agreed to play for Chiri's team, Miracle Land, while they looked for a way to get him to Europe, even though he would once again only earn about $50 a month. Chiri also found him a new place to live, although like his salary, the dingy concrete room was

Bernard dribbling through a pack of his Miracle Land teammates during training in Accra.

no great shakes. Bernard was originally supposed to share it with just one other player, but four of them ended up cramming into the 12-by-12-foot room. One of the players was six feet, six inches tall, so space was definitely tight. But at least Bernard wasn't sleeping on the couch at his pastors' house, and Chiri occasionally ponied up money to buy him a new pair of cleats. "He started to gain that confidence again," said Chiri. "It was timely that I met him."

But getting Bernard to Europe proved more difficult than Chiri had anticipated. He connected with an agent in Sweden interested in bringing Bernard over for trials, but Chiri couldn't get him a visa since the player had overstayed his visa the last time he was in the country. Chiri also failed to get Bernard a visa for Belgium when an agent invited him for a trial with one of the country's top clubs, KRC Genk. Looking for any route out of Ghana, Chiri even flew

Bernard to Singapore for trials there since Ghanaians don't need a visa. But airport officials wouldn't let him enter the country because he wasn't carrying enough cash, and he had to return home without ever stepping on the field. As the years passed without progress, even Chiri began to worry Bernard might never achieve his dream of making it to Europe. "Appiah does not have time on his side, so I need to accelerate things because at the end of the day if I'm not able to do that, I have really disappointed him and I have disappointed myself too because he has the talent."

Bernard tried to remain optimistic, but it became increasingly difficult as the failed attempts to leave Ghana piled up. It was impossible to ignore just how far he had fallen. Every morning, Bernard willed himself to rise from his bare mattress and jogged along the highway for a half hour to an anonymous red dirt pitch tucked away in one of Accra's crowded neighborhoods. He and his Miracle Land teammates placed yellow and blue cones in the dust and trained for a couple hours to the shrieking sound of saw against metal coming from an auto repair yard next door. The years had taken their toll, and Bernard had lost much of the weight he gained when he was at Aspire, making him seem even smaller on the field. His game had grown rusty as well, although there were still flashes of brilliance, a sudden change of direction leaving a defender stranded as Bernard sailed by with the ball glued to his left foot, the kind of move that had caught Colomer's attention all those years ago. But now nobody was watching. Bernard had become just another African player hoping against the odds to be discovered. He was back in a crowd of millions, and talent wasn't always enough to escape. What Bernard needed was another miracle, but they were in short supply.

So was food. Bernard decided whether to run home from training each day depending on whether he had enough money to buy lunch. When he didn't, he walked to conserve his energy. The money from Chiri began to dry up as Bernard's chances of making it to Europe dimmed. At times, even a bowl of rice and beans from a roadside stand was out of reach, and he was forced to scrounge food from his neighbors or look to his pastors for help. He also needed a new pair of cleats. One of his white and blue Adidas Predators had a gash in the side, and he didn't have the money to replace it. Turning to his parents had become even less of an option because his mother suffered a stroke in 2015, and his father needed all the money he could get to care for her. Still, Bernard didn't give up on his dream. He not only made it to training every morning, but also ran up and down a highway overpass in the evenings to keep up his fitness. "When God brings you down, you can't give up," said Bernard. "You have to keep working hard. I'm praying to God that God should help me and let me stand on my feet again."

To cope with his fading fortune, Bernard leaned heavily on the memories of his time at Aspire, when he was seen as one of the chosen few marked for greatness. Even on warm days, Bernard often ran to training in a full blue and gray Aspire track suit that he brought back from the academy and tried to keep meticulously clean. The large wings printed on the back looked conspicuously out of place in an environment better suited to grounding Bernard's dreams than helping them take flight. But the track suit helped him stand out in a way that nothing else in his life could at that point. Strangers sometimes stopped him in the street to ask if he was part of Aspire, and he proudly said yes.

He could even show them the photos he kept on his phone. There was one that showed Bernard dribbling away from Coutinho when his academy team beat Neymar and the rest of the Brazilian squad in 2008. Another showed Bernard lined up with Diawandou and other members of his class after they played Valencia under Aspire's massive dome. Bernard had even more photos he kept in a plastic bag at home along with other mementos from his time at Aspire, including banners from many of the European teams he played, the

Bernard leaving Miracle Land training wearing the track suit he brought back with him from Aspire.

contract he signed with the academy, and even the itinerary of his last flight out of Doha.

Looking back, Bernard wished he had pressed his coach Oteng to give his license to Aspire, regardless of the price, so he could have stayed at the academy. "I would be a big boy now," said Bernard. "I would be playing my football in Europe." But Oteng stuck to his guns. He said he regretted Bernard hadn't been able to find another way out of Ghana but still didn't think he should have handed over the player's license without getting a percentage of the future profit. "Our football men in this town, they are wicked people," said Oteng. "They are greedy also." But some thought Oteng was also being greedy and should have given up the license for Bernard's sake. "He saw Bernard as an opportunity to make money," said Eugene Komey, the coordinator at the field where Colomer first spotted the little Ghanaian. "It's easier for me to let my players go. I can give you the card if you can assure me that the kid is going to play. But they wanted to hold on to the boy to make money at all cost."

Bernard wished he could reach out to Colomer one last time to beg for help but had no idea how to get in touch with him. "If you talk to him, tell him I need him," said Bernard. "It's very difficult for me now. I can't stay here." Time was certainly running out for the midfielder. He was already in his mid-20s, the prime playing age for professionals. If he had to wait much longer, he would miss his window entirely, if he hadn't already.

It seemed a lifetime ago that Colomer stood at Star Park and selected Bernard for a journey that took him tantalizingly close to the world of his dreams before he was cast back into the soccer wilderness. But his dreams weren't completely dashed. He still had hope of staging a miraculous comeback, one that would allow him to stop looking at the past as the brightest period in his young life. "I know I'm not done yet," said Bernard. "I have very far to go. One day I will look back and tell my story, and it will be a happy story because I pray to God and work very hard."

CHAPTER 12

Only the Beginning

The jerseys, framed in glass, leaned against the wall of Diawandou's living room, ready to be hung. They told the story of his remarkable journey over the years in a parade of colors. To commemorate his time at Eupen, Diawandou chose a blue and white jersey, eschewing the club's traditional colors for those of Aspire. There was also a green jersey with yellow Puma logos on the sleeves. That was the one Diawandou wore during his first match for Senegal's senior national team. He played the full 90 minutes in a 2-2 draw with Colombia in May 2014, becoming the first Football Dreams player to debut for his nation's top side. It was the first time he had made it back to the Lions of Teranga since being kicked off the Under-17 squad ahead of the Africa Cup of Nations several years earlier.

But there was an even newer jersey resting against the wall, a blue and red one with D. Diagne printed on the back in gold. Turn the jersey around, and you could be standing in Messi's living room. Diawandou had stared in awe at Barcelona's superstar years earlier when he came to visit the first Football Dreams class in Doha. Now the two players shared the same uniform, the same iconic crest. Diawandou had achieved his unlikely dream, one shared by millions of kids living all over the world, except perhaps Madrid. He had joined the Blaugrana, the blue and red; he had joined Barcelona.

Diawandou was driving to a friend's house during his summer holiday in Thiès when Colomer called to say Barcelona had made another offer for him to join its B team. The first time the club came for Diawandou, the Spanish scout had told him the timing wasn't right. But after two seasons at Eupen, his message had changed. "Colomer thought I was ready to go," said Diawandou. "He said, 'If you go now, you are definitely going to play. You don't need to do anything more at Eupen.'" Colomer thought the Senegalese defender was exactly the kind of player Barcelona needed. "He is a leader. Such teams need strong personalities," the Spanish scout told Aspire's magazine. "Physically, he may not be one of the biggest defenders, but he makes up for it in speed and demonstrates outstanding technique, important qualities when you're playing for FC Barcelona."

Colomer's call put Diawandou over the moon, but he kept the information from everyone except his close family because he didn't want to draw attention to himself while he was still in Senegal. On the day of his departure, he had a celebratory meal with his mother at home and quietly slipped away to Dakar airport's small international terminal. Over a half dozen years had passed since he first walked through the terminal doors, scared and excited about taking his first flight to a far-off Arab city he knew nothing about. There were butterflies this time as well but certainly not from fear of boarding the plane. That was old hat to Diawandou. He had flown all over the world with Football Dreams. One of his academy classmates even kept all his boarding passes and could shuffle them like playing cards. But Diawandou was the only one from his class making a one-way trip to Barcelona.

He was in good hands when he landed at Barcelona's airport, where he was met by his new agent, Ramón Sostres, who also rep-

Diawandou holding his Barcelona jersey on his first day with the club.

resented one of the club's biggest stars, Andrés Iniesta. It was a whirlwind first day for Diawandou. He went directly to the club's glamorous training facility for a tour and to complete his medical. He was then met by Barcelona's sporting director, Andoni Zubizarreta, and the board member responsible for the club's B team to sign his three-year contract, which had a release clause of 12 million euros. A photo taken after the signing shows Diawandou standing between the two of them as they hold up his first Barcelona jersey, a traditional blue and red one with D. Diagne printed on the back. It was an incredible moment. When Diawandou was at the academy, he always used to ask Colomer to bring Barcelona uniforms back from Spain. Now he had one of his own. "It felt good to hold a jersey with my name on it," said Diawandou. "My dream was always to play for Barça."

Back in Thiès, friends and family flocked to Diawandou's house to congratulate his mother after local newspapers reported he had signed with Barcelona. "There was a big crowd," she said. "People were calling to congratulate me as well." She had returned from the Ivory Coast a few years earlier and lived in a new three-story, six-bedroom house that Diawandou had built with the money he had made at Eupen. Painted red and white and accented with light blue doors, the house lent an air of refinement to an otherwise unremarkable area of the city dominated by dirt roads and half-finished concrete compounds. It rivaled the size of the family home where Diawandou grew up but wasn't crowded with dozens of other relatives. Parts of the house were still under construction, and much of it was sparsely furnished. But Diawandou took special care over the next few months to set up the main living room on the ground floor. That was where he planned to hang his jerseys from Eupen, Senegal's national team, and Barcelona.

There was one other uniform resting against the living room wall ready to be hung, a red and white one. But it didn't have Diawandou's name on the back. Below the number fifteen, the letters spelled out Dramé. Despite the big striker's defiant departure from the academy after the Milk Cup in 2011, the two players had remained close, and Ibrahima called Diawandou a few months after he joined Barcelona to ask if he could have one of his jerseys. Diawandou agreed on the condition that Ibrahima send him one as well. He thought his fellow countryman had made a terrible mistake leaving Aspire early but understood why given his family's tough background in Ziguinchor. "He was rushing to sign a contract to help his family, to help his mother," said Diawandou. "At the time, he was a great player, he was doing well in the tournaments and everyone wanted him, but he made the wrong decision."

Ibrahima had similar thoughts back in 2012 when he returned to Senegal after months of fruitlessly searching for a club in Europe. Like Bernard, he found himself back where he started, competing with millions of other young players to attract the attention of scouts who might pluck him out of Africa. He moved back into the crumbling concrete home in Ziguinchor where he grew up with his mother. She still cooked meals on a coal stove outside, looking over the dirt courtyard where Ibrahima first learned to dribble around plastic laundry tubs under lines filled with drying clothes. When Ibrahima needed a bit of space from his family, he stayed at a friend's house, but that meant sleeping on a thin mattress in a room that flooded in the rainy season.

Ibrahima left Aspire because he didn't feel like he was appreciated enough, especially by Colomer, and worried what that meant for his future. But members of the academy staff were devastated by his departure. "Of all the kids I lost, Dramé was the saddest because you see all that talent wasted," said Wendy Kinyeki. "In my opinion, he was going places. Seeing a kid lose an opportunity like this breaks my heart because of what could have been." The Football Dreams sports director in Senegal, George Sagna, visited Ibrahima's mother in Ziguinchor, hoping to lure the striker back to the academy. But even after Ibrahima returned from Europe, he resisted the notion of going back. "It was his personality, his pride," said his old coach, Amadou Traoré. "He told me, 'I will try to succeed, but I will not return. If I return to the academy, everyone will say you left but you came back.'"

Ibrahima also resisted Traoré's suggestion that he play for Ziguinchor's local club, Casa Sport, which competed in Senegal's top league, because he thought it would look like failure. "The people from Aspire would think I went to Europe, didn't have anything, and now I'm back in Africa," said Ibrahima. But with help from the player's former national team coach, Boucounta Cissé, Traoré eventually convinced Ibrahima to reconsider and join the club. They told him it was the only way to keep up his form so he could eventually make it in Europe. Casa Sport was certainly glad to have him since the striker scored a bunch of goals for the club, including one that helped the team win the Senegal Cup at Demba Diop stadium in Dakar in August 2013. It was the same stadium where Ibrahima and his teammates beat Ghana in dramatic fashion a few years earlier to qualify for the Under-17 Africa Cup of Nations for the first time.

Playing for the national team had been one of the high points for Ibrahima at the academy, but his biggest triumph was the 5-1 victory over Manchester United in the Milk Cup final in 2011. The win was clouded by the turmoil that followed when he left Aspire, but it ended up being his saving grace after he returned to Senegal. Late one winter night in 2012, Rolf Magne Walstad, the sports administrator for a club in Norway's top division, SK Brann, sat at his desk in Bergen, a beautiful city on the country's western coast built on a fjord and surrounded by mountains. Walstad decided to take a break from his work and Google his favorite English team, Manchester United, according to an article in a local Bergen newspaper. Up popped a story that said a squad from Aspire had thrashed the Red Devils the previous summer in Northern Ireland, thanks to a big Senegalese striker who scored a hat trick in the final and won the tournament's golden boot award.

Walstad was intrigued, made contact with Ibrahima through a Senegalese agent, and invited him for trials at Brann. Given the striker's previous experience in Europe, it could have seemed like a bad case of déjà vu. But Ibrahima impressed Brann's coaches, and the club quickly said they wanted to sign a four-year contract with the big man when he turned 18 and would send him a bit of money in the interim to help his family. Ibrahima agreed, wrapped up his stint with Casa Sport, and moved to Bergen at the beginning of 2014 to join his new club. The transfer felt like much-needed redemption years after leaving Aspire, and Ibrahima proudly sent Diawandou one of his red and white Brann uniforms to hang in his living room. It wasn't Barcelona, but it was a big step in getting his career back on track.

Most important, the contract with Brann enabled Ibrahima to build a new house for his mother, something that had long been his dream. Ever since their mud home collapsed in a rainstorm when Ibrahima was a child, his mother and siblings had all lived in a single room of his grandmother's ramshackle house. That was about to change. Soon after Ibrahima arrived in Norway, he wired money back to his family to begin building a new home on the same spot where the old one had collapsed, and less than a year later it was finished. The one-story, three-bedroom house, located off a dirt road next to a ditch filled with trash, was much less grand than the one Diawandou built in Thiès, but it transformed the life of Ibrahima's family in a much more profound way.

Rather than seeking shelter from the sun under a few rusty sheets of metal propped up by a wooden pole, Ibrahima's mother could sit on one of the new floral-patterned couches in her living room under the cool breeze of the ceiling fan, sipping a cold drink from the refrigerator and watching the flat-screen TV on the wall. There was even Wi-Fi that Ibrahima used to browse Facebook on his iPhone. When asked about the new house, his mother simply said, "Thank you God, thank you Ibrahima." The question brought tears to her eyes, partly from joy and partly from the painful memory of trying to raise four kids with no money and no house of her own after she had split up with her husband years earlier. "When she thinks about how difficult it was, she always starts crying," said Ibrahima's older brother, Sekou. "I always say, 'Momma, stop, that's over. You must be happy now and forget everything else.'"

Making the jump to Norway transformed Ibrahima into something of a local celebrity in Ziguinchor. His mother always knew when he returned home for holiday because she could hear the young boys outside shouting, "Ibrahima is coming!" When he walked

Ziguinchor's red dirt streets, locals flocked to him to say hi, and he often offered a fist bump or a high-five in return. After a challenging few years, Ibrahima seemed back to his old self, gregarious and brimming with confidence. But life in Norway was more difficult than he let on, and not only because he faced the prospect of pickled herring at mealtime. Ibrahima wasn't getting the playing time at Brann he had expected. He played plenty for the club's reserve side and was among the squad's top scorers. But he only logged a few minutes with the senior team during his entire first season and failed to score a single goal.

The coach told him he needed to be patient since he was still young, but Ibrahima disagreed and the two often clashed. "I don't want to sit on the bench," said Ibrahima. "I know I'm better than the players who are playing ahead of me." He eventually grew so disillusioned he left Brann after a single season and followed the sports administrator who brought him there, Walstad, to a team in Norway's second highest league, Honefoss BK. It was a step in the wrong direction, but Ibrahima was desperate to register the playing time and goals that would allow him to move to a much bigger club, one that met not only his expectations but also those of everyone who watched him tear apart Manchester United on that cool summer evening in Ballymena a few years earlier.

Looking back, Ibrahima wished he had never left Aspire after the Milk Cup. He still bristled at what he perceived as a lack of attention from Colomer but thought he would be in a much better position today if he had remained, and his coach Traoré agreed. "I'm sure if Ibrahima had stayed at the academy it would have been better for him," he said. "He was the best player and would have found a great club because he has the talent." Like Diawandou, perhaps Ibrahima would have received a call from Colomer one day saying a top club had come for him. He would never know, and the pain of what might have been lingered. But despite everything

Ibrahima outside his coach's home in Ziguinchor with the medals and trophies he won while at Aspire.

that happened, Ibrahima was still glad Colomer selected him out of millions to join Aspire and knew any success he had in the future would largely be due to the training and attention he received at the academy. "I still have good feelings toward Aspire," said Ibrahima. "Anything I am now and anything I will be tomorrow is because of Aspire."

Ironically, some of the players who stayed at the academy after the Milk Cup wished years later they had left like Ibrahima. They didn't see the pain the big striker went through after his departure, only that he ended up playing at a good level in

Norway. Many in Ibrahima's class appreciated the training, exposure, and financial support they received from the academy but
failed to find much success after they finished and felt like they
didn't get enough help from Aspire. They even began calling the
second Football Dreams class "Generation Sacrifice." Like Ibrahima, they accused Colomer of favoring the first class and felt the
problem got even worse after the Milk Cup, since the Spanish scout
was so outraged at the players who left and demanded to know why
none of those who stayed told him the secret exodus was under way.

Only four players from the second class were selected to join
Eupen, and those left out were upset that so many more from the
first year got to go. Aspire said there simply wasn't room for everyone,
but that didn't make the situation any easier. The number of spots
would dwindle even further in future years as Aspire sought to add
more Qatari players to the Belgian team in preparation for the 2022
World Cup. Academy officials said they were doing everything they
could to help the players, but finding them all European teams was
a huge challenge. "We are running around like crazy to find some
clubs, Norway second division, Iceland, Denmark, wherever, to try
to find further opportunities for these players," said Andreas Bleicher. The one place they weren't looking was Qatar, even though
some of the boys said they would be happy there, because they
were concerned people would accuse them of trying to naturalize
the players.

Aspire considered offering academy graduates the chance to use
the Football Dreams country director in Senegal, Lamine Savané,
as an agent, but some complained there was no way he could manage so many players at once. Bleicher said they also looked into the
possibility of setting up a separate agency to better assist the boys
but didn't follow through because they were worried people would
accuse them of trying to profit from Football Dreams. The decision
may have helped them defend against such accusations, but they

ended up with a cadre of unhappy players who viewed returning home to play in Africa as unacceptable failure. After all, weren't they supposed to be the best young talent the continent had to offer?

A Ghanaian goalkeeper from the second class even threatened to sue Aspire because the academy didn't find him a European team after he graduated. One of his fellow countrymen was so depressed when he returned home that he spent most of his time alone in his room despite attempts by his family to lure him out. Even John Benson, the first African player Aspire recruited before Football Dreams started, thought the academy should do more to help the program's graduates. "Most of the players are home now, and they are struggling," said John, who has enjoyed a successful career in Qatar's top league. "You showed them how to play football. You showed them how to live a luxury life. All of a sudden you said, 'OK, now we stop,' and then they had to come back home. This is not right."

At the same time, the players may have had unrealistic expectations of what Aspire should have done for them after they graduated. Creating a culture of dependency has long been a risk for foreign aid organizations operating in Africa. But how well did Aspire prepare the players for the reality that not all of them were going to make it? Academy officials said they tried to make clear that not all the players would succeed but couldn't control whether they absorbed the message or not. Part of the problem may have been that Colomer expressed such confidence in his ability to pick kids who could make it. Only a tiny percentage of players at European academies become professionals, and a much smaller sliver go on to top clubs. Colomer believed he could do much better because of his experience and the vast talent pool he had to choose from. He even predicted more than half the first class would become professionals, many at top clubs. But that wasn't how it played out. Despite over a dozen players from the first two classes turning out for their youth national teams, Diawandou was the only graduate from that period to make it to a major European club. Many of the others ended up playing at low levels in Europe, returning to Africa, or washing out of the game altogether.

Other academies in Africa expressed surprise that Football Dreams hadn't produced more high-profile players. "It doesn't make sense," said Joe Mulberry, the head of recruitment at Right to Dream in Ghana, during a visit to the academy in 2015. "There should be more successful outputs than there currently are." Many suspected the biggest problem was Aspire's failure to verify kids were 13 years old when they first tried out. They also pointed to the difficulties other foreign academies have had with the complexities of developing players in Africa. "A lot of academies have failed in Ghana because they have been European teams implementing European models," said Mulberry. "How well do they understand the subtleties and nuances of an African child?"

He also suspected that exposing the Football Dreams kids to the opulence of Aspire could create a sense of entitlement and dampen the drive needed to make it. "One of the key benefits of African players is they are extremely hungry to succeed for obvious reasons," said Mulberry. "As they enter the Aspire system, do they and could they ever maintain their hunger because they live in air-conditioned rooms and fly all over the world? It's an extremely difficult mental transition to take a lad potentially sharing a one-bedroom home with his parents and five brothers and sisters to go live in Aspire."

Aspire, on the other hand, maintains that critics of Football Dreams shouldn't rush to judgment on the players selected by the program since the oldest graduates so far are only in their early 20s, at least officially, and many have yet to finish the academy. Aspire officials also point out that the first few years of such an ambitious talent search are bound to be the most challenging, and results may improve over time.

These are fair points, but the failure of the program to produce more successful players could also be chalked up to the inherent difficulty of identifying future stars at a young age, even with a pool of millions and seemingly unlimited resources. In fact, the numbers are a little deceptive. Aspire may have scouted over 5 million boys, but they reduced their chances of picking the right kids because they only took about twenty into the academy each year and mostly kept them until they graduated, regardless of their performance. That was better for the boys than the norm at most academies, where they cast off players along the way who don't make the grade and replace them with more promising recruits. But it meant Aspire was stuck with its initial choices even if they didn't seem to be panning out.

Diawandou's success actually serves as evidence of just how challenging it can be to choose which player will make it to the big time. The Senegalese defender wasn't the biggest, strongest, fastest, or flashiest player Colomer selected. He didn't have Bernard's technique, Ibrahima's nose for goal, Anthony Bassey's speed, or Samuel Asamoah's game intelligence. He was certainly gifted with an impressive combination of many of these things, but the qualities that put him over the top were much harder to spot in a match or training session: his judgment, strength of character, self-discipline, and motivation. These attributes made him a great leader. They also helped him make smart decisions off the field that proved just as important as those on it.

Also, in what was supposed to be a rags-to-riches story of poor African kids desperate to succeed, Diawandou actually benefited from the fact that he came from a more comfortable background. That helped him resist agents and coaches dangling the promise of overnight wealth if he left the academy early, a temptation that tripped up both Bernard and Ibrahima, who initially seemed like they had more potential. Their fates showed how managing players' hopes and fears can be just as challenging and important as picking the right recruits in the first place. The likelihood that Bernard and Ibrahima were much older than they said also fueled their impatience to make it to Europe. Even though Diawandou was kicked off his national team for lying about his age, he may have actually been one of the younger players in the first few classes. That allowed him to be more patient. It also meant his development potential was likely closer to what Colomer expected when the scout first spotted him at his old academy in Thiès.

Technology offers the possibility of more efficient youth scouting going forward, as the kind of data-driven analysis made famous by the book *Moneyball* becomes more common in soccer and also more sophisticated. One limitation of much of the analysis done so far, even with more advanced statistics like expected goals and expected assists, has been that it has largely focused on actions involving the ball rather than movement that takes place elsewhere on the field. That's a big problem since 99 percent of what happens in a match occurs off the ball. This limitation has made the analysis much less useful, especially for assessing game intelligence. It's difficult to evaluate whether a midfielder is making the most efficient passes or whether a defender is lining up in the right spots to thwart potential attacks without factoring in the other players on the pitch.

But that's now possible as well. One of the leading soccer analytics companies, Prozone, introduced game intelligence modeling in 2015 that uses player tracking data to analyze action on the entire field. The data come from cameras around the pitch that track the players and the ball every tenth of a second, producing around 6 million pieces of data every match. To understand the complex interactions between players, the models interpreting the data employ the same principles scientists use to evaluate dynamic systems like schools of fish or flocks of birds. "The whole idea is if we look at football, particularly when it's speeded up, we get the same types of swarming patterns as we get in nature," said Paul Power, a former coach who helped design the models at Prozone before the company was acquired by STATS LLC. The models measure player intelligence through actions that alter the stability of the system, or match, much like a shark might scatter a school of tuna. Instability is key to creating attacking opportunities, while stability helps thwart them.

"A great example is a 1 v 1," said Power. "It might be Lionel Messi vs. Jerome Boateng. At first, you have a stable relationship. If Messi goes left, Boateng goes right, and so forth. But suddenly you add in Luis Suárez who makes another run, and this then perturbs the system," perhaps by freeing up space for Messi to dribble or giving him a passing option. Traditional metrics would never give Suárez credit for making the run since he never touched the ball. But the game intelligence models can calculate how much space he created for Messi and the amount he increased the chance of a goal. More broadly, they can show which players are particularly good at pulling defenders out of position to create attacking opportunities and, conversely, which defenders are best at shutting them down. Think how many defenders typically converge on Messi in an attempt to stop him every time he begins a run with the ball. "He soaks up the defenders just like a paper towel soaks up milk," the TV commentator Ray Hudson once said of Messi.

The game intelligence models can also reveal how effective players are when dealing with this type of defensive pressure. "When players are pressed, are they forced into errors, into taking safe options, or will they complete the high risk but high reward options?" said Power. The models can figure out the best dribbling,

passing, or shooting options based on player positions and evaluate
the wisdom of a particular choice. "Using this type of data, we are
then able to provide simple scores on intelligence and decision making, which is obviously what people want. We can see how a player
compares to the rest of the population and his age group as well."
This is potentially a huge leap forward, and the models are bound to
increase in sophistication over time. Think how much more effective they are at capturing game intelligence than showing players
clips of match footage, asking them to play brain games in a lab, or
simply relying on a scout's subjective judgment.

Since the technology is so new and represents a significant leap
in sophistication, it's not yet being widely used. "People don't really
know what to make of it," said Chris Anderson, the author of *The
Numbers Game*. He believes much of the data analysis employed in
soccer is still no more sophisticated than the use of leeches in medicine. "I think it's still relatively early in terms of providing actionable
intelligence, but it's clear if we really truly want to understand the
game, it has to be the next step. But it's incredibly data intensive, so
the amount of time you have to spend processing the data in order to
then use it and analyze it is really intense. Clubs generally have no
infrastructure and no interest in doing that, which is why companies
like Prozone are well positioned to take that off the clubs' hands. But
I don't think there has been enough acceptance of it within clubs to
pay for that because they are still barely beyond the leeches."

Most club youth operations are even farther behind the curve
in terms of using data, partly because robust statistics still aren't
available for many young players. It would cost serious money to
collect the data. The biggest innovation at many clubs in the last
decade is the development of databases to track young players of
note anywhere in the world. "So, if somebody says, 'I saw this really
great 14-year-old in Montenegro last week,' somebody can type it in,
find the name, and find the kid," said Anderson. "They will have the

basics like what position they play, how many minutes they played, and if they scored a goal. But it's not much more than that."

That may be the status today, but it's easy to imagine how much more refined youth scouting operations could become once tracking data of young players is more widely available and scouts have access to technology like game intelligence modeling or even more powerful tools. This is likely to happen as the hardware and software needed become cheaper and more ubiquitous. That doesn't mean it will be a silver bullet since predicting the future always entails uncertainty. Simply producing Messi by algorithm will remain a dream. But youth scouting, like soccer more broadly, is poised for a potentially dramatic shift in the balance between art and science, especially at the biggest clubs in the world.

Diawandou was riding high at Barcelona. Life got even better only a few days after he arrived when the club's sporting director, Zubizarreta, came to see him at the hotel where he was staying. He was scheduled to begin training in a few days, but the sporting director told him he wouldn't be starting with the B team. The club wanted him and a few others from the reserve squad to train with the senior team, since so many players were still on vacation after the 2014 World Cup, including many of Barcelona's biggest stars like Messi and Neymar. Gerard Piqué was absent as well, so Diawandou lined up in central defense beside La Masia graduate Marc Bartra and impressed coach Luis Enrique enough that he kept the Senegalese defender with the first team even after the entire squad returned.

It was almost too much for Diawandou to believe. The stuff of dreams. He would share the training pitch with some of the biggest names in international soccer, an achievement millions of players around the world could only fantasize about. It was the kind of thing Diawandou himself had imagined as a child when he was playing pickup soccer in the dirt street in front of his house in Thiès. "I said to myself this dream is coming true because I'm training with the best players in the world," said Diawandou. "People travel from all over the world to see Messi play or get an autograph, and I was sharing the same changing room with Messi. It was an amazing time for me."

Barcelona's captain and mesmerizing playmaker, Xavi, welcomed Diawandou to the group with a few words of wisdom. "Xavi is the master of the team," said Diawandou. "He said, 'Just play how you normally play. If you're at Barcelona, a hundred percent it means you're a good player.'" Diawandou took up his position in the locker room next to fellow defender Jordi Alba. There was Xavi slipping on his captain's armband, Iniesta lacing up his boots. Diawandou had actually moved into Iniesta's old apartment, thanks to the agent they both shared. The Senegalese defender quickly discovered that the Brazilians were the life of the party in the locker room, especially Neymar and Dani Alves. "They were always joking in the changing room, always dancing," said Diawandou. Not Messi. He may have dominated play on the field, but in the locker room he rarely spoke.

It was actually a reunion of sorts since Diawandou had met Messi over half a dozen years ago inside Aspire's massive dome in Doha. Someone even posted a photo of them from that day online. The Argentine star smiled easily into the camera, as his shoulder-length brown hair spilled onto his white dress shirt. Diawandou, skinny and baby-faced, looked a little tentative standing next to Messi in his blue and white Nike training jersey. It was also a chance to reunite with Neymar, whom Diawandou defeated on one of Aspire's outdoor fields only a couple months after the picture with Messi was taken. None of them had any idea back then that they would all meet again at Barcelona's hallowed training ground one day.

There was a downside to all this, though. It was no mystery why Messi, Neymar, and Suárez invoked fear in the hearts of defenders. They were outrageously difficult to mark, and now it was Diawandou's job to do just that in training. "To take the ball from them you need to kill yourself!" said Diawandou. Suárez was as strong as an ox and would do anything to win, including bite his opponents. For Neymar, simply beating defenders wasn't enough. Sometimes he sought to humiliate them by rainbowing the ball over their heads as they stood rooted to the ground.

But there was no doubt which of the three presented the greatest threat. Imagine having to face Messi dribbling at you at full speed, or standing still with his foot on the ball, daring you to come get it, knowing that with one flick of his hips, he could make you look like a fool, a mere spectator to his brilliance. "With Messi, sometimes you just want to watch him play because the things he can do are so amazing," said Diawandou. "You cannot stop him." Diawandou clearly held his own, though, because he was one of only two B team players to make Luis Enrique's squad for the group stage of the Champions League that year. He also started nearly every game for the B team once he finally joined the squad two months after arriving at the club.

When Barcelona first signed Diawandou, some supporters suspected it was simply done as a favor to Colomer because of his history with the club and Qatar's multimillion-dollar sponsorship of the team. "People weren't very happy with that signature because a lot of fans thought he wasn't a player prepared to play in the second team of Barcelona," said Ángel Iturriaga Barco, who has written several books about the club's history. "But at the beginning of the campaign, he started to play very well and convinced people." Even Colomer was impressed by how much playing time Diawandou got so quickly with the B team. "He knows it's very difficult to play at Barcelona," said Diawandou. "There are so many good

Diawandou during a match with Barcelona's B team.

players. He told me he didn't think I would play all the games I was playing."

They were clearly heady days for Diawandou, but the biggest thrill during his first year at Barcelona was finally being called up for a match with the club's senior team. Although he had made Luis Enrique's 25-player squad for the Champions League, he never dressed for a match in the tournament. Instead, he first donned a blue and red Barcelona jersey and walked into the Camp Nou with the rest of the senior team for the second leg of a Copa del Rey play-off against a lower league side, SD Huesca.

For most fans, it was a night like any other night. As they streamed toward the stadium, they passed booths selling all manner of Barcelona souvenirs: striped blue and red flags bearing the club's crest, colorful scarves stitched with the team's motto, "Més que un club," and jerseys emblazoned with the names of stars like Messi, Neymar, Xavi, and Iniesta. Some fans lingered over beer and tapas at bars outside the Camp Nou or stopped to snap photos in front of the stadium. But for Diawandou, the night was anything but routine. He had been dreaming of this moment his whole life.

The match itself didn't hold much drama, since Barcelona was already up 4-0 after the first leg, and the coach decided to rest several of the club's stars, including Messi. But that didn't dent the thrill Diawandou felt as he warmed up with the rest of the squad under the stadium's lights, pinging the ball back and forth with his Barcelona teammates, just like he had done with friends back in Thiès all those years ago. As a reminder of the amazing journey he had taken, all Diawandou needed to do was look up at the stands to see the name of the club's sponsor spelled out in gold, Qatar Airways.

It was undoubtedly a special moment for Colomer as well. Over a decade earlier, the Spanish scout had been the one to tell a shaggy-haired, 16-year-old Messi he was getting his debut with Barcelona's first team. Now he proudly watched as Diawandou followed in his footsteps. Of course, the players were in no way equal. In fact, Diawandou never even made it off the bench that night against Huesca and failed to fully break into the senior team over the remainder of the season. He would eventually end up back in Belgium the following year, where he finally helped Eupen get promoted to the first division.

There was certainly no shame in that. Given where Diawandou started and the odds of ever making it as a professional in Europe, his success was striking. But he wasn't that once-in-a-generation player Colomer hoped to find when he first set off across Africa nearly a decade earlier. The Spanish scout wasn't disheartened, though. The fact that Diawandou had made it to Barcelona at all fueled his belief that Football Dreams was working. Despite the ups and downs, Colomer was still convinced his wildly ambitious search could produce a player of superstar status someday and was determined to keep looking. "What Diawandou has achieved is only the beginning," he said.

Epilogue

Diawandou's jump to Barcelona may have felt like the beginning of Football Dreams' success, but in reality, it may have been closer to the end. At the close of 2016, two years after Diawandou walked into the Camp Nou with the rest of Barcelona's senior team, Aspire decided to halt the Football Dreams search a decade after it first began.

Ironically, financial concerns may have helped drive the decision. It turned out there were limits to Qatar's wealth after all. Like many countries in the Gulf, Qatar was buffeted by a severe drop in oil and gas prices that started in 2014 and ultimately led to a decline of roughly 70 percent in both markets. Prices eventually rebounded to some extent but were still far below their highs by the end of 2016. The plunge erased hundreds of billions of dollars from Qatar's wealth and led to drastic cuts in government spending across the country, including at Aspire. That meant the academy needed to figure out what to put on the chopping block, and Football Dreams offered the possibility of significant savings.

Aspire has always been quite secretive about how much it spent on the program, as it has been about many aspects of Football Dreams. But one academy official estimated at the beginning of

2016 that Aspire had spent well over $100 million on the project, and possibly as much as $200 million. That's significantly more than Real Madrid paid to acquire Cristiano Ronaldo from Manchester United, a much easier way to get your hands on a star player.

The amount spent by Aspire was, of course, next to nothing relative to Qatar's overall wealth, but the country obviously had to consider the return on its investment in such a radical soccer experiment. The original goal of Football Dreams, to help build the kind of world-class Qatari national team envisioned by Sheikh Jassim, clearly didn't pan out since Aspire only hosted the African kids in Doha for a few years and the country is still ranked toward the bottom of FIFA's top 100. Qatar once again failed to qualify for the 2018 World Cup in Russia, so the country will make its debut in 2022 when it gets an automatic spot for hosting the tournament.

Aspire has also trumpeted Football Dreams as a humanitarian project, but its merits in this respect are mixed. There's no doubt it changed lives. Without Football Dreams, there's little chance Diawandou would have ever made it to Barcelona or Serigne Mbaye would have become the first deaf player in Senegal's first division. Ibrahima might never have built a home for his mother. The program also benefited the countries involved by giving away millions of dollars of soccer equipment at fields where the scouts held tryouts and by handing out thousands of mosquito nets with Messi's image on them to prevent malaria.

But Football Dreams would likely get poor marks as a humanitarian program if judged by its transparency and cost-effectiveness. Much of the money spent benefited a small number of kids, the roughly twenty they chose every year to join Aspire, as well as their families. Only a minority of the boys could be expected to achieve their dream of becoming a professional in Europe given the challenge of choosing the right players, and that's exactly what happened. Although many of the kids in the first class got to go to Eupen, subsequent classes weren't so lucky, and a fair number of the boys ended up unhappy in the end, a curious result for an expensive humanitarian project. It didn't help that so few players received high school diplomas while they were at the academy that could have aided them if professional soccer didn't work out.

None of this is meant to imply, though, that the officials running Football Dreams had anything but the best intentions for the kids. They may have made some mistakes along the way, but so did the boys, and there's no doubt the academy staff wanted to see them succeed. The fundamental problem is that youth soccer at the highest levels is difficult to pair with humanitarian goals. There are simply too many broken dreams. Remember, only around 1 percent of the 10,000 kids in the entire English academy system end up making a living in the game. That means for every Diawandou, there are 99 others who end up more like Bernard and watch their dreams of becoming a star slip away. Technology may make the scouting process more efficient going forward, but there will still be plenty of broken dreams.

Even so, the supply line of young dreamers will continue, especially from many places in Africa where making it to Europe can seem like the only way up and the only way out. It may be a nearly impossible dream, but for many of them, the away game seems like only game worth playing. They don't focus on the 99 percent chance of failure. They see the 1 percent chance of success.

These young dreamers from Africa and elsewhere form the foundation of the entire multibillion-dollar professional soccer industry. But the dreams that play out on TV every weekend in the Premier League, La Liga, and every other major league around the world make up an infinitesimally small percentage of the total. They are the dreams of those who made it. Fans rarely see the disappointment of boys like Bernard who didn't. They often struggle in obscurity to let go of their dreams and figure out a new way forward.

Scouts are dreamers too. They face equally daunting odds of discovering a kid who can become a star. If only 1 percent of kids in the English academy system make a living in soccer, imagine what Colomer's odds were of finding the next Messi in Africa. With Football Dreams, he and the Qataris were playing their own improbable away game, one that offered the possibility of international acclaim if they could produce a true superstar.

After a decade of searching for talent, the final verdict on their scouting efforts is still out. By 2017, nearly four dozen Football Dreams players found by Colomer had represented their national teams in official matches, mostly at levels below the senior squad, according to Aspire. Over two dozen had signed professional contracts with Eupen, and others were playing at lower levels in Europe or back in Africa. Those would be impressive statistics for a normal academy operation, but Football Dreams was far from normal, and Colomer had set the bar much higher for himself when he first started.

A Football Dreams superstar could still be in the cards, though. One player found in Nigeria during the fourth year of the search, Henry Onyekuru, has shown great initial promise. The swift 19-year-old winger scored 22 goals during Eupen's first year in Belgium's top division, making him joint top scorer in the league. After the season finished, Everton swooped in to buy Onyekuru for a reported 7 million pounds, beating out Arsenal and several other Premier League clubs. But England's top league presents a far greater challenge than the one in Belgium, and it remains to be seen whether Onyekuru can continue pouring in goals at the same rate. Everton loaned the winger to the Belgian club Anderlecht for the 2017/18 season, so Onyekuru's day of reckoning is still to come.

If the Nigerian fails to make the grade, Colomer will have to hope one of the other Football Dreams kids he discovered turns out to be that gem of a player he was seeking. Aspire said it has no plans to shutter the academy in Senegal while the boys Colomer found are still training there. Aspire also said it hasn't decided whether its move to stop the Football Dreams search is permanent and will make a final decision after reviewing the program's results over its first ten years. That means Colomer will have to wait to see whether he'll get another chance to scour Africa for that future superstar he may not yet have found. If he does, Clemente Konboye, now an ex-Nigerian militant, is once again ready to escort the Spanish scout to Ogulagha to give the local kids another look. Fair warning, though: the field there is still a swampy bog, and ducks are bathing in the goalmouths.

Acknowledgments

Many of the people who worked on Football Dreams were generous with their time and provided critical insight into the program. I would like to offer particular thanks to the head of Aspire, Ivan Bravo, for his early enthusiasm and assistance, and to Ndongo Diaw, who patiently escorted me around Senegal during my first trip to the country and helped me make contact with the families, friends, and former coaches of the Football Dreams kids. These individuals were incredibly helpful in providing details about the boys, not only in Senegal but also elsewhere in West Africa. This was especially true of Bernard Appiah's old coach, Justice Oteng; Diawandou Diagne's uncle, Cheikh Gucye; and Ibrahima Dramé's old coach, Amadou Traoré.

But most importantly I would like to thank the Football Dreams kids themselves for the hours they spent speaking with me, especially the boys who make up the heart of the book: Bernard, Diawandou, and Ibrahima. Their stories were as gripping as they were heartfelt, and they didn't hold back. One of the hardest parts about the reporting process was hearing stories from boys like Bernard who hadn't been able to achieve the life in soccer they had dreamed about and were desperately looking for anyone who could help them find a team in Europe. They often turned to me as well, and it was with a heavy heart that I had to tell them I was only a journalist.

I received assistance from many others along the way who are too numerous to mention individually. They're spread out across West Africa, Qatar, Belgium, Spain, and many other places. They include scouts, coaches, players, fans, federation officials, academic researchers, translators, drivers, and friends who hosted me as I tried to keep my expenses to a minimum. Without their help, I would never have been able to get where I needed to go, connect with the people I needed to interview, or hoover up the vast amount of information needed to tell the story.

There are a few people who must be thanked by name, though, because the book never would have happened without their help. I would like to start with my agents, Will Lippincott and Ethan Bassoff. They saw the potential in my idea, even when it was only vaguely formed, and were vital in helping me craft the book proposal.

That was only the beginning of the process. I would never have been able to produce the finished product without the incredible help and support from my editor at W. W. Norton & Company, Matt Weiland, and many of his colleagues. Matt was masterful in helping me mold the book's structure so that the various components blended together in a smoothly flowing narrative. Plus, we played pickup soccer in Brooklyn together on the weekends, so I challenge anyone to come up with a better editor than that.

Finally, I owe the biggest thanks to my family. I would never have taken on such a project if my parents, Marjorie and Steve Abbot, hadn't raised me to have the self-confidence to take risks in life and exposed me to the wonders the rest of the world offered when I was still a child. My parents also schlepped me to countless soccer practices and games when I was growing up, so I'm indebted to them for my love of the sport as well.

But there is one person who stands above everyone else in helping me through the entire book process. That's my amazing wife, Elizabeth Radin. She was the one who encouraged me that it wasn't a crazy idea to quit my job to write a book about Football Dreams. She was with me every step of the way as I experienced the myriad sources of stress that came along with writing a book and read every draft I produced. She even served as my French translator in Senegal and Belgium and is now more fluent in soccer vocabulary than she ever wanted to be. I truly couldn't have done this without her love and support carrying me across the finish line.

A Note on Sources

This is a work of nonfiction, based on interviews;
travel through West Africa, Qatar, Belgium, and Spain; historical
photos and video; and secondary sources, including books, articles,
and academic papers. The research and writing were largely carried
out over a period of three and a half years, from 2014 to 2017.

Many of the people who worked on Football Dreams were
extremely helpful in informing me about the program and the kids
who were involved. I held interviews with everyone from top officials, like Josep Colomer and Andreas Bleicher, all the way down
to volunteers on the ground in Africa who made the tryouts happen. Michael Browne, who was Aspire's head soccer coach until
2014, was very helpful in outlining his experience with the Football
Dreams kids at the academy in Doha, as were several other coaches
who worked there, including Arnold Rijsenburg.

A handful of people who worked closely with Sheikh Jassim to set
up Aspire proved especially helpful in learning about the academy's
history. These include Vincent Chaudel, a French sports consultant;
Zohair Ammar, an Egyptian who advised the academy's founding
committee; and Mohana Rao, Aspire's first marketing director.

The group that worked at the academy in Senegal was also incredibly helpful, including country director Lamine Savané, head coach Jordi Rovira, and members of the staff who watched closely over the boys, such as Wendy Kinyeki, Ndongo Diaw, Forewah Emmanuel, Lamine Thiare, and Dr. Babacar Ngom. All of them provided touching stories about the kids and often didn't sugarcoat the challenges the program faced. I would also like to thank the Football Dreams country directors in Ghana and Nigeria, Capt. Andy Sam and Col. Sam Ahmedu, for the hours they spent speaking with me. Ahmedu also connected me with Austin Bekewei, who was incredibly helpful in organizing a trip to Ogulagha in 2015 so I could experience firsthand what it was like for Colomer to visit years earlier. I even traveled with the same militant, Clemente Konboye, who accompanied Colomer in 2007. In total, I held interviews with more than 200 people inside and outside of Football Dreams over the course of my research.

Most important were the hours I spent interviewing the boys at the center of the book: Bernard, Diawandou, and Ibrahima. Input from their family members, friends, and former coaches was also vital. For Bernard, this was especially true of his father, Noah Appiah; his old coach, Justice Oteng; the local Football Dreams coordinator, Eugene Komey; and the lawyer who tried to help Oteng, Farouck Seidu. Youssif Chibsah, the former Ghana national team player who helped Bernard after he left the academy; Wilhelm Myrer, who tried to find him a club in Scandinavia; and Arenton Ofoe Chiri, who also tried to get him to Europe, were all instrumental in understanding the challenges Bernard faced when he returned home.

Diawandou's background in Thiès was outlined in detail by his mother, Khadidiatou Gueye; his uncle, Cheikh Gueye; and his former coach, Bousso Ndiaye. For Ibrahima, his mother, Oumou; his brother, Sekou; and his old coach, Amadou Traoré, all provided invaluable assistance in learning about the big striker's childhood growing up in Ziguinchor and his experience once he made it to the academy and ultimately decided to leave. Many of these people not only shared their stories but also physically guided me to key locations from the boys' pasts, like where they lived growing up, where they learned how to play soccer, and where they tried out for Football Dreams. The boys who play a secondary role in the story, such as Serigne Mbaye, Hamza Zakari, John Felagha, Samuel Asamoah, and John Benson, provided important insight to fill out the stories of the main characters, as well as their own. In total, I interviewed over two dozen Football Dreams kids from the first two classes, as well as a smattering of others.

One of the most enjoyable parts of the reporting process was spending time in the charming town of Eupen, Belgium. With my then-girlfriend, now-wife providing French translation, we had a lovely time canvassing the town's cafes and bars to get public sentiment on Aspire's decision to buy the local team. Officials at the club were helpful as well, including the general manager, Christoph Henkel; the team manager, Michael Radermacher; and the coach, Bartolome "Tintin" Marquez. The lead soccer writer of the *Grenz Echo* newspaper in Eupen, Thomas Evers, was also incredibly helpful in learning about the club and understanding the town's response to Aspire. Sadly, Evers was killed in a car accident in May 2015, not long after I met him.

I relied on articles from a wide array of news outlets throughout the writing of this book, including the BBC, the *New York Times*, the *Guardian*, the *Financial Times*, the *Observer*, *Le Monde*, *Marca*, *AS*, *La Vanguardia*, *El Periódico de Catalunya*, *Grenz Echo*, the *Belfast Telegraph*, the *Qatar Tribune*, *Bergensavisen*, GhanaSoccerNet. com, and VoetbalNieuws.be. I found the soccer magazine *The Blizzard* to be filled with a wealth of useful information, including the history of France's top academy, Clairefontaine, and the story of Diego Maradona apologizing to Jorge Valdano for not passing him the ball when he scored his legendary goal against England in the 1986 World Cup. I relied on Aspire's magazine for several quotes from Colomer about Diawandou's jump to Barcelona, including the one that ends the book's last chapter.

Though I have played soccer nearly my whole life, I knew I needed to beef up my knowledge of the sport, especially in Africa. I read David Goldblatt's masterful tome, *The Ball Is Round: A Global History of Soccer*, and then followed that up with several Africa-focused books, including *The Feet of the Chameleon: The Story of African Football* by Ian Hawkey, *Africa United: Passion, Politics, and the First World Cup in Africa* by Steve Bloomfield, *African Soccerscapes: How a Continent Changed the World's Game* by Peter Alegi, and *The Lost Boys: Inside Football's Slave Trade* by Ed Hawkins. I supplemented my knowledge of this last topic, the illicit trade in underage African soccer players, by holding interviews with Jean-Claude Mbvoumin, the founder of the NGO Foot Solidaire.

I also visited several of the top soccer academies in Africa, including Right to Dream and the West African Football Academy in Ghana, ASEC Mimosas in the Ivory Coast, and Diambars and Generation Foot in Senegal. A host of officials at these academies were extremely generous with their time and walked me through their experiences scouting and training young players in Africa. They included Tom Vernon, Gareth Henderby, and Joe Mulberry at Right to Dream; Karel Brokken at the West African Football Academy; Benoit You and Julien Chevalier at ASEC Mimosas; Moussa Kamara at Diambars; and Olivier Perrin at Generation Foot. I also interviewed a variety of officials at national soccer federations across West Africa.

To learn more about soccer in the Middle East, and Qatar in particular, I read *When Friday Comes: Football, War and Revolution in the Middle East* by James Montague and *The Ugly Game: The Qatari Plot to Buy the World Cup* by Heidi Blake and Jonathan Calvert. For a deeper understanding of Qatar's unique history, I relied on the book *Qatar: Small State, Big Politics* by Mehran Kamrava, director of the Center for International and Regional Studies at Georgetown University's School of Foreign Service in Qatar. I also interviewed Dr. Kamrava and several other Qatar experts, including Dr. Steven Wright of Qatar University and Dr. David Roberts of King's College London. I relied on information and photos from "The Origins of Doha and Qatar Project" and U.S. diplomatic cables published by WikiLeaks as well.

For information about the world of soccer scouting, I found Michael Calvin's book, *The Nowhere Men: The Unknown Story of Football's True Talent Spotters,* to be revealing. I also learned a great deal from *Youth Development in Football: Lessons from the World's Best Academies* by Mark Nesti and Chris Sulley, a detailed look at best practices for producing the sport's next generation of stars. I visited Manchester City's academy, where the director at the time, Mark Allen, kindly walked me through their system for developing talent. I also spoke with coaches and scouts from other top clubs along the way, including Barcelona, Real Madrid, and AC Milan.

To learn what researchers and scientists have to say about the process of discovering and training elite athletes, I read *The Sports Gene: Inside the Science of Extraordinary Athletic Performances* by David Epstein and *The Gold Mine Effect: Crack the Secrets of High Performance* by Rasmus Ankersen. I also read *Thinking, Fast and Slow* by Daniel Kahneman to better understand how top athletes and other experts think. For a more soccer-specific focus, I relied heavily on the book *Science and Soccer: Developing Elite Performers,* which was edited by A. Mark Williams, the chair of the Department of Health, Kinesiology, and Recreation at the University of Utah. I also interviewed Dr. Williams, and he helped me to better under-stand what researchers currently believe are the most important fac-tors that determine whether or not a young player will be successful.

I conducted interviews with several other soccer researchers as well, including Dr. Daniel Memmert, head of the Institute of Cognitive and Team/Racket Sport Research at the German Sport University of Cologne, and Barbara Huijgen, a sports science lecturer at the University of Groningen.

To supplement these discussions, I read nearly 100 academic papers covering various aspects of soccer talent identification and development. The academic works referenced in the book include the following: "Football Academies and the Migration of African Football Labor to Europe" by P. Darby et al., published in the *Journal of Sport and Social Issues* in 2007; "Escape to Victory: Development, Youth Entrepreneurship and the Migration of Ghanaian Footballers" by J. Esson, published in *GeoForum* in 2015; "The Developmental Activities of Elite Soccer Players Aged Under-16 Years from Brazil, England, France, Ghana, Mexico, Portugal, and Sweden" by P. R. Ford et al., published in the *Journal of Sports Sciences* in 2012; "Determinants Analysis of Change-of-Direction Ability in Elite Soccer Players" by A. Chaouachi et al., published in the *Journal of Strength and Conditioning Research* in 2012; "Using Physiological Data to Predict Future Career Progression in 14- to 17-Year-Old Austrian Soccer Academy Players" by C. Gonaus and E. Müller, published in the *Journal of Sports Sciences* in 2012; "Talent Identification in Soccer: The Role of Maturity Status on Physical, Physiological, and Technical Characteristics" by C. Meylan et al., published in the *International Journal of Sports Science and Coaching* in 2010; "A Multidisciplinary Selection Model for Youth Soccer: The Ghent Youth Soccer Project" by R. Vaeyens et al., published in the *British Journal of Sports Medicine* in 2006; "No Relative Age Effects in the Birth Dates of Award-Winning Athletes in Male Professional Sports" by P. R. Ford and A. M. Williams, published in the *Research Quarterly for Exercise and Sport* in 2011; "Soccer Skill Development in Professionals" by B. C. H.

Huijgen et al., published in the *International Journal of Sports Medicine* in 2009; "Prognostic Relevance of Motor Talent Predictors in Early Adolescence: A Group- and Individual-Based Evaluation Considering Different Levels of Achievement in Youth Football" by O. Höner and A. Votteler, published in the *Journal of Sports Sciences* in 2016; "Skill Level and Eye Movement Patterns in a Sport Orientated Reaction Time Task" by D. A. Tyldesley et al., published in the *Proceedings of an International Symposium on Motor Behaviour: Contribution to Learning in Sport* in 1982; "Identifying the Processes Underpinning Anticipation and Decision-Making in a Dynamic Time-Constrained Task" by A. Roca et al., published in *Cognitive Processing* in 2011; "Perceptual-Cognitive Expertise, Practice History Profiles and Recall Performance in Soccer" by A. M. Williams et al., published in the *British Journal of Psychology* in 2012; "Developmental Activities and the Acquisition of Superior Anticipation and Decision Making in Soccer Players" by A. Roca et al., published in the *Journal of Sports Sciences* in 2012; "The Role of Deliberate Practice and Play in Career Progression in Sport: The Early Engagement Hypothesis" by P. R. Ford et al., published in *High Ability Studies* in 2009; "The Attention Window: A Narrative Review of Limitations and Opportunities Influencing the Focus of Attention" by S. Hüttermann and D. Memmert, published in *Research Quarterly for Exercise and Sport* in 2017; "Does Grit Influence Sport-Specific Engagement and Perceptual-Cognitive Expertise in Elite Youth Soccer?" by P. Larkin et al., published in the *Journal of Applied Sport Psychology* in 2016; "Psychological Talent Predictors in Early Adolescence and Their Empirical Relationship with Current and Future Performance in Soccer" by O. Höner and P. Feichtinger, published in *Psychology of Sport and Expertise* in 2016; "Increased Cortical Thickness in Sports Experts: A Comparison of Diving Players with the Controls" by G. Wei et al., published in *PLOS One* in 2011; and "The Hidden Foundation of Field of Vision in English Premier League (EPL) Soccer Players" by Geir Jordet et al., presented at the Seventh Annual MIT Sloan Sports Analytics Conference in 2013.

To understand how the soccer world is changing through an increasing reliance on the kind of data-driven analysis made famous by Michael Lewis's *Moneyball*, I read *Soccernomics: Why England Loses, Why Spain, Germany, and Brazil Win, and Why the U.S., Japan, Australia—and Even Iraq—Are Destined to Become the Kings of the World's Most Popular Sport* by Simon Kuper and Stefan Szymanski and *The Numbers Game: Why Everything You Know About Soccer Is Wrong* by Chris Anderson and David Sally. I subsequently interviewed Anderson, a behavioral scientist and former semiprofessional player who works with top clubs on the use of data analytics. I interviewed several others working in the field as well, including Daniel Altman, the founder of North Yard Analytics, and Paul Power, a lead data scientist at the company STATS. I also spoke with Ernst Tanner, the academy director at FC Red Bull Salzburg, which has been using data analytics in innovative ways at the youth level.

Finally, while I would have loved to have met some of the top stars mentioned in this book, like Messi and Neymar, I had to rely instead on books describing their rise into the soccer stratosphere. Particularly helpful were Guillem Balague's biography, *Messi,* and Luca Caioli's book, *Neymar: The Making of the World's Greatest New Number 10.* Graham Hunter's book, *Barca: The Making of the Greatest Team in the World,* was also illuminating in its description of the history and culture of Barcelona.

Photograph Credits

Index

Note: Page numbers in *italics* refer to illustrations.